STRIKING BACK:

THE SAUDI WAR AGAINST TERRORISM

What We Can Learn From It

DR. JOHN S. HABIB

Dedicated to former ministers of the interior

H.R.H. Prince Ahmed bin Abdel Aziz

H.R.H Prince Naif bin Abdel Aziz

H.R.H. Prince Mohammed bin Naif bin Abdel Aziz,

minister of the interior;

*and to all the faithful men and women who are actively
waging a relentless war against terrorism in their homeland.*

TABLE OF CONTENTS

PREFACE

This text is based on my formal university studies, on residence in various countries of the Middle East, North Africa, and Europe over a period of more than sixty years and on research in the Saudi kingdom during extended visits from 2008-2012.

I first developed my interest in the region as a student at the University of Michigan in 1952, forgoing a planned career in law. My interest broadened as a Fulbright scholar in Cairo, Egypt in 1954 where I studied Islamic philosophy with religious sheikh Sayyid Nowar from the Al-Azhar University. At that time, I also had the opportunity to explore Islamic issues during personal meetings with eminent French Islamic scholar Louis Massignon, renowned American Islamic scholar Dr. Edwin Calvery, and acclaimed Egyptian scholar of Islam, Dominican priest George Qanawati at the Dominican Institute for Islamic Studies in Cairo. Only a young college student at the time, I was treated by them with great kindness. I am indebted to them for encouraging my studies of Islam.

Subsequently, and for twenty-five years, I had the privilege of observing firsthand developments in the region from the advantageous perspective of an American diplomat with special responsibilities for national security matters. This experience was the result of regular tours of duty at American embassies and other official US installations in Cairo, Riyadh, Kuwait, Doha, Rabat, and Paris; and temporary assignments in Western Europe, the Middle East, and Southwest Asia. These provided me further insight on how

Middle Eastern issues were inextricably connected to international developments.

My experiences with the Middle East were broadened after I retired from government service and began private life as a management consultant in Geneva and Monte Carlo from 1982 to 1988. My association with Republicans Abroad, first as chairman in Monte Carlo and then as international treasurer, afforded me the opportunity to view the Middle East through the optic of domestic American political realities.

Subsequently I moved on to academe, first as an instructor and then as a full teaching professor for seventeen years from 1988 through 2005 at the University of Maryland University College, Europe, in Heidelberg, Germany. Most students were active-duty American military personnel assigned to bases throughout Europe, the Middle East, and North Africa. Since classes were held at the military bases this required travel to sites in Germany, Belgium, Italy, Egypt, Saudi Arabia, Kuwait, Spain, and France.

The opportunity to interact at the university level with members of the American military, officers, enlisted men and women, and civilians who were serving on the front lines of our national defense at various geographical locations was a unique experience. Whether the teaching subject matter was international terrorism, political problems of the Middle East, or generic courses on international relations and history, the academic environment was heightened from that of a typical university classroom to the actuality of relevance in real time and place.[1]

During these years, the University of Maryland allowed me to accept invitations to teach as visiting professor at the University of Washington, Seattle in 1995, at Al-Akhawayn University in

---

[1] The July 25, 1996, terrorist bombing of the Khobar Towers complex near Dhahran in Saudi Arabia killed nineteen American airmen and wounded hundreds more including many foreign nationals. The American airman sentry on the roof of the targeted building subsequently was a student in a seminar on terrorism that I was giving at an American air force base in Germany. He described to the class how he noticed a suspicious truck parked near the periphery of the complex and made a split-second decision to sound the alert. His fast thinking most certainly saved many more victims from death and serious injuries. Less than ten days prior to the bombing, I had stayed at the Khobar Complex after teaching a seminar on terrorism for American military stationed at Al-Kharj in Saudi Arabia.

Ifrane, Morocco in 2000, and at Mohammed V University in Sale-Rabat, Morocco in 2005 as Fulbright distinguished professor where I established a center for American Studies. These situations introduced completely new views of the Middle East.

Currently I am visiting scholar at Michigan State University, Muslim Studies Program, East Lansing, Michigan, where I had taught courses as diplomat-in-residence during the academic year 2005-2006.

The depth and range of these many years of involvement in the Middle East enabled me to broaden my view of regional issues beyond the limited perspectives of a government official, a businessman, and an academic.

Acknowledgments

This work would not have been possible without the encouragement and assistance of my many friends in the kingdom, among them senior government officials, men of religion, journalists, professors, business people, and ordinary folk. Most requested that they not be named in the text.

While all were not of one mind on what constituted solutions to the existential issues that confront the kingdom today, they all felt strongly that these differences must be resolved within the framework of time-tested, Saudi religious and cultural traditions.

Although I may have requested specific individuals to comment on certain parts of the text that particularly relate to their input for accuracy and fairness, none have demanded to see the final text as a condition of their assistance, and I have not shown it to any of them prior to publication.

Given the highly sensitive nature of the subject matter, it is understandable that some individuals most closely connected with monitoring and combating terrorists desired to remain anonymous, and I have respected their requests. All other sources are identified throughout the text or in footnotes.

I am also indebted to several West European counterterrorism officials who asked to remain unnamed. They spoke candidly to me about their countries' philosophies of combating terrorism; the difficulties they encounter in sharing information within security components of their own government; and the mutual challenges that confront them and their foreign- and native-born Muslim populations in the fight against Middle Eastern terrorism.

To each person who assisted me in this endeavor, in ways large and small and too many to count, I offer here my expression of recognition and appreciation. It can only be a small token of my larger indebtedness to each of them.

All of the above notwithstanding, the responsibility for this work, of course, is mine alone.

John S. Habib
Brussels, Belgium
Winter 2013

INTRODUCTION

Much has changed in the sixty years since the Middle East became the focus of my professional life, and much there has remained the same.

Large areas of the region that I first knew as desert and undeveloped land now house skyscrapers, luxury hotels, shopping malls, and private residences. Unimproved roads reserved for the few cars then in circulation are now freeways and multilane highways complete with snarled traffic jams. One only need mention present-day Cairo or Riyadh as examples.

At the human level, the people of the Middle East and North Africa are largely unchanged. For the most part, they are still effusive, generous, and welcoming to the stranger, but much of their previous spontaneity is gone. And some individuals whom I knew when we were junior diplomats just beginning our careers, or who were hunted revolutionaries living transient lives under assumed names, are now heads of state, ministers of foreign affairs, or senior officials of their national security establishments. It was surreal to watch them on television or reminisce with them privately about our past experiences when our lives were less dull and even less secure.

The changes at the political level are, perhaps, the most accented. The people are less emotional in their approaches to international problems that affect their lives than in the past. This does not mean they are less concerned about them only that they are more inclined to deal with them in different ways. One has only to consider their attitude toward the Palestine problem that had been driven by ultra-emotionalism yesterday but by pragmatism and legality today.

The people of the Middle East are also particularly resentful of the Western-based media and political campaigns' inclination to blame their indigenous cultures, particularly the religion of Islam, for almost all of their current woes—whether political, social, economic, or religious. They are more vocal in rejecting the West's refusal to acknowledge even a modicum of responsibility for current problems especially the rise of terrorism and violence there. While they are not uncritical of practices within their own culture that contribute to the problem, they want these issues to be considered within the relevant contexts of time, place, and circumstance.

Nowhere is such resentment felt more deeply than in Saudi Arabia which continues to collectively bear the brunt of frontal attacks on Arabs, Muslims, and Islam. And it should come as no surprise that the fiercest and deadliest battles against terrorism are taking place in that country between political and religious extremists, on the one hand, and the Saudi government and the overwhelming majority of the Saudi people on the other.

A scan of the literature on Saudi Arabia before 9/11 reveals that the anti-Saudi attitudes of most Americans were advanced by a few politicians with a deliberate anti-Arab, anti-Muslim bent and by human-rights activists critical of specific aspects of Saudi culture, especially those dealing with human and women's rights. But this criticism reached almost hysterical levels after the attacks on the World Trade Center and the Pentagon on 9/11, in which fifteen Saudi nationals of the nineteen participants in that crime were reportedly involved.[2] After 9/11 the print and electronic media joined the chorus, as did virtually every politician and numerous men of the cloth in cities and towns across America. The rare American voices that dared to plead for a modicum of balance were drowned out in the cacophony of condemnation of Saudis, Arabs, and Muslims. Consequently, non-Muslim men, including individuals from the Indian subcontinent and Hispanics, were murdered, their attackers

---

2   A. Cordesman and Nawaf Obaid." Al-Qaeda in Saudi Arabia, Al-Qaeda in Saudi Arabia: Asymmetric Threats and Extremists." (Washington, DC: Center for Strategic and International Studies), 19.

having assumed them to be Muslims or Arabs because of their complexions or dress.

This work, then, is intended to show how the Saudi Arabian Government views and treats terrorists and terrorism; how the kingdom became the target of terrorism due largely to anti-Islamic attitudes endemic in Western literature and Western colonial and imperialist policies, for which the kingdom bore little or no historic responsibility; how the dynamics of these past policies continue to fester and foster terrorist-related problems in the kingdom; and how they also inadvertently triggered dispositions to violence latent in Arab and Saudi culture that ultimately spawned homegrown terrorism. It seeks to enable the reader to view terrorism in Saudi Arabia from a perspective that many governments and much of the international print and electronic media frequently and deliberately withhold from the general public. Instead, the media is inclined to attribute terrorism to alleged violence inherent in the religion of Islam, itself. This study is meant to show that an understanding of history and the use of dialogue, reason, and common sense must be part of any sincere effort to combat terrorism anywhere, not only in the kingdom and in the Middle East.

The complexities of Middle East terrorism are too diverse and too profound to dismiss simply as the work of Muslim fanatics who seek to destroy our way of life. Terrorism must not be understood only in the context of individuals and groups who are wont to tack its sails to the winds of their own self-interests and virtually exculpate themselves from all responsibility. We cannot rid ourselves of terrorism in the Middle East by the use of force alone; it is fluid and ephemeral. Destroy it here, and it will reemerge there. But we can eradicate many of its sources that, ironically, are rooted in recurring foreign and economic policies of those very Western nations that today claim to be its victims.

The battle to defeat terrorism requires that we use more brains and less brawn. To win this battle we must accept and acknowledge our own responsibility for flawed policies that encouraged and laid the groundwork for terrorism against ourselves and allies even as we attack the malefactors.[3]

When the discussion in this work focuses on the Saudi government's specific antiterrorist strategy, I have used official Saudi documentary sources and the statements and writings of Saudi officials. When referring to personal expressions of Saudi writers and scholars, I have used and cited their published and unpublished writings. This particular battle is theirs, and they know it best.

In Chapter Nine, I have quoted extensively, at times verbatim, from Western and Arab researchers, particularly from former CBC journalist Nancy Durham and Carnegie Foundation researcher, Christopher Beam. They both interviewed senior Saudi officials directly involved with the Saudi antiterrorist program and were among the first Western reporters permitted to visit the new Saudi prisons and installations built exclusively for terrorist detainees. This method was, I believe, a more effective way to present their valuable experiences than by paraphrasing what they have written.

I have not, however, refrained from expressing my own analyses and voicing my personal opinions from time to time and have made it clear when I have done so.

All sources are fully documented in the footnotes and bibliography.

Quotes from senior American officials cited at the beginning of each chapter are from the Royal Embassy of Saudi Arabia undated Fact Sheet, Information Office Washington, D.C.

Not all of Saudi Arabia's terrorist experiences are applicable to other countries. Those that involve radical changes in international frontiers, the unilateral usurpation and annexation of territory, and the expulsion and transfer of indigenous peoples from their homes and property are virtually irreversible in the foreseeable future. They require almost unbearable compromises to bring closure to these issues, such as Kashmir and Palestine. But others are reversible. They require that a psychological and humane approach be used in dealing with terrorists as individuals, not just collectively as members of extremist organizations and groups.

---

3   John S. Habib, Unpublished op-ed. "New York and Washington: September 11." *International Herald Tribune*, September 2001.See Appendix A for full text.

Retribution, prevention, and rehabilitation are among the methods we can learn from the Saudis.

The terms terrorism and terrorist, as used in this study, are the official definitions of the country whose nationals are victims of the acts or the country and organization that take responsibility for them.[4] Given the absence of a universally accepted definition, this approach is fair and balanced, because even close allies differ over what specific group or activity may properly be called terrorist.[5] For example, the United States and Israel consider Hamas to be a terrorist organization and officially eschew all contact with it; some European and Arab nations, on the other hand, recognize Hamas as a valid expression of the Palestinian people's will that derives its legitimacy from winning free and democratic elections.[6] These

---

4   Various agencies of the United States government have separate definitions of terrorism.

According to Wikipedia (July 10, 2013), in Title 22, Chapter 38, of the United States Code (C), the Department of State defines terrorism as "premeditated, politically motivated violence perpetrated against noncombatant targets by subnational groups or clandestine agents." Whereas Title 18 of the same code defines international terrorism as "activities that...involve violent acts or acts dangerous to human life that are a violation of the criminal laws of the United States or of any State, or that would be a criminal violation if committed within the jurisdiction of the United States or of any State; [and] appear to be intended...to intimidate or coerce a civilian population... to influence the policy of a government by intimidation or coercion; or...to affect the conduct of a government by mass destruction, assassination, or kidnapping; and [which] occur primarily outside the territorial jurisdiction of the United States or transcend national boundaries in terms of the means by which they are accomplished, the persons they appear intended to intimidate or coerce, or the locale in which their perpetrators operate or seek asylum."

5   "There is neither an academic nor an international legal consensus regarding the definition of the term 'terrorism.' Various legal systems and government agencies use different definitions of 'terrorism.' Moreover, the international community has been slow to formulate a universally agreed upon, legally binding definition of this crime. These difficulties arise from the fact that the term "terrorism" is politically and emotionally charged." From Wikipedia, (July 10, 2013).

6   For Saudi Arabia, terrorism is a crime aiming at destabilizing security and constitutes a grave offense against innocent lives, as well as against properties, whether public or private. Such as, blowing up dwellings, schools, hospitals, factories, bridges, airplanes (including hijacking), oil and pipelines, or any similar acts of destruction or subversion outlawed by the Islamic Shariah law. It also regards the financing of such terrorist acts as a form of complicity to these acts that leads only to bring accessory to them and to bring a conduit for sustaining and spreading of such evil acts. See Appendix C, Council of Senior Ulema Fatwa on terror financing, May 7, 2010.

countries conduct overt contact with Hamas. Arab countries have consistently excluded armed struggle against foreign occupiers of their land from the definition of terrorism, and Turkey has made an exception for the use of armed force to combat Kurdish groups that use violence to advance their fight for independence.

Arabic personal or proper names, except when cited as part of a direct quote, are spelled uniformly but without transliterating the Arabic letters that have no equivalents in English.

"There were Saudis, as well as Americans and others, killed in that bombing in Riyadh, just as at the World Trade Center there were people from all over the world killed in the World Trade Center. What we're really seeing with terrorism is it doesn't matter where the attack takes place; this is an attack on civilization. This is an attack on the international system. This is an attack on civilization as we know it. And that's why we're getting great cooperation from everybody involved."

Dr. Condoleezza Rice,
National Security Advisor
to the White House, May 28, 2003:

PROLOGUE

The Arab revolutions and uprisings that began in February 2011 and the deaths of Al-Qaeda chief Osama bin Laden and Libyan leader Muammar Kaddafi in May and October, respectively, of that same year may have recast the perimeters in which the war on terrorism have been fought to date. They have not, however, changed the fundamental issues that launched the war. They may create an environment where democratic governments can take root and flourish, or they may create situations where terrorism and reaction spread and engulf the region in turmoil and chaos. Algeria and Mali are two examples. It is too early to know.

But it is not too early to know that the majority of these people have spoken; they clearly want to install democratic forms of government and live and prosper in a free society. The responsibility for this rests, for the most part, on their shoulders. To succeed in this endeavor, they must be given the time and space to extricate themselves from the problems that festered over many decades of misrule and oppression. This will not be an easy task, as the situations in Egypt, Tunisia, Syria, and Yemen have demonstrated. The international community can help by being patient and understanding as these countries work their way toward representative government. These countries cannot create this reality if Western powers, Russia, and China exploit these problems as just another opportunity to mold the circumstances to serve their own political and economic interests.

Already it appears that the vultures of opportunism are circling over devastated Libya and seeking to gain advantage for ready access to its vast oil resources, lucrative markets, and billions in hard currency.

In Egypt, other vested interests—foreign and domestic—are busy derailing what political progress has already been achieved there.

The popular uprisings in Tunisia and Egypt that caused the flight of President Zayn Al-Abidin to exile in Saudi Arabia and the formal house arrest and conviction of President Hosni Mubarak in Egypt are the logical results of Western colonialism and imperialism that characterized the history of independence in those countries.[7] The same is true of the similar upheavals that have overthrown the forty-four despotic years of Muammar Kaddafi's regime in Libya and that seriously threaten the stability of regimes in Yemen, Bahrain, Syria, and even Morocco.

President Zayn Al-Abidin created an environment in Tunisia that favored Western political and economic policies—most notably those of France, the mother colonial power, and its successor, the United States of America. Such was the repression in Tunisia that a well-educated citizen had turned to street vending from a cart because he could not find other employment. The police confiscated his cart and beat him without mercy in the process. When he attempted to lodge a complaint at the local commissariat, he was rebuffed. Out of sheer desperation, he immolated himself.

President Husni Mubarak created a similar environment in Egypt for Great Britain, the mother colonial power, and its successor, the United States of America. He rose to power after Anwar Al-Sadat was assassinated. He acquitted himself well for his first decade as president of a country that was plagued with difficult problems, domestic and foreign.

Both presidents began their careers as reasonable men. However, they were encouraged to expand their power by leaders of the international community who sought advantageous positions for themselves and their countries at the expense of the Tunisian and Egyptian people.

Both the Tunisian and Egyptian regimes, superficially democratic and progressive, were fundamentally repressive and regressive. Both were given favored nation status by the democratic powers of Europe and the United States.

The rule of Colonel Muammar Al-Kaddafi in Libya and the several Al-Assad regimes in Syria, all overtly repressive, were hostile

---

7 See Mohamed Ayoob. *The Many Faces of Political Islam: Religion and Politics in the Muslim World* for a compelling presentation of colonialism and imperialism's impact on the contemporary Arab-Muslim world.

to the West due to the legacy of Western policies that were still entrenched in both countries long after they formally became independent. The very rise to power of these leaders evolved from that historical legacy.

The regimes in Bahrain and in Yemen, both favorable to the West, were fundamentally flawed: Bahrain because its majority Shiite population is ruled by a minority Sunni royal dynasty that has been traditionally insensitive to Shia sectarian needs; Yemen because its various religious, regional, and political constituencies are virtually irreconcilable. For example, the Zaidi Shi'ite tribes, notably the Hashid and Bakil, in the north, have been in a state of endemic conflict with the Shafai Sunni populations in the south for centuries. The annexation of the former British Crown Colony of Aden and the British-ruled Sultanates in the south by the Republic of Yemen further complicated the governance of that country as a unified political entity. The Sultanate of Lahaj, for example, one of the autonomous political units under direct British rule, and the British Crown Colony at Aden, were relatively more progressive than the regions of northern Yemen, which had little or no experience with modernity.

There is no evidence on record that Britain or France, the two most powerful, democratic Western countries, made any credible effort to establish the basis for genuine democratic rule in any country they ruled or controlled for many years. To the contrary, national resistance forced both countries to abandon their colonies. Unfortunately, after the failure of President Wilson's tireless efforts to lay the groundwork for democracy in these colonies during the Versailles Peace Conference at the conclusion of World War I and immediately thereafter, the United States gradually but systematically adopted policies similar to those of the two colonial countries.

Over many years, our foreign policy makers systematically turned their backs on young revolutionaries before they became hostile to America, only to embrace them after they had won their wars of liberation.[8] The instances are too many and too brutal to write off as misjudgments. One example is the government's commitment to France to forbid American diplomats to meet publicly or privately

---

8   An exception, junior senator John F. Kennedy denounced French colonialism in Algeria on the senate floor on 2 July 1957. Algeria won its independence in 1962.

with Algerian revolutionaries as they began their struggle for independence from France in the late 1950s.[9] Another is Secretary of State Henry Kissinger's guarantee of absolute American support for Israel's anti-Arab terrorist attacks over many years. In addition he gave American commitment not to punish Israel for these terrorist attacks, and provided a guarantee for virtually unlimited military and financial support for that country.[10]

Ultimately both of these commitments backfired. Algerians won their revolution without any material or moral support from the US, and France secretly negotiated Algeria independence with the revolutionaries without informing the American government. Subsequently, after it achieved independence in 1962, Algeria became a haven for terrorism, where hijacked Western passenger aircraft were welcomed, and indigenous Algerian terrorist movements developed that almost tore the country apart.

Nevertheless, it was Algeria that assisted with the release of the fifty-two Americans hostages, in January 1981, held by Iran for 444 days.

Despite Kissinger's guarantees, Israel also subsequently suffered decades of murderous Palestinian terrorist attacks that caused it to retaliate brutally and disproportionately and thereby lose much of its credibility and respect in the world. Arguably, its national security is more precarious today than ever before.

As dangerous as he was, Osama bin Laden did not create the environment in which his brand of terrorism flourished. He was born into it and only later exploited it. It may be said that he was as much a victim of his own terrorism as were the thousands who paid the price of his murderous activities. Neither his demise nor the uprisings that are sweeping the Middle East and North Africa today are likely to change the resentment that continues to foment the violence and terrorism in that part of the world. Instead these developments are only likely to change the framework in which the future of international terrorism and its practitioners are measured, defined, and debated.

The contemporary environment of terrorism in the Middle East can be said to be the legacy of the West, which was hostile

9   As an officer assigned to the American Embassy, Cairo, from 1958–1962, I was subject to this agreement.

10   Milton Viorst, "The Kissinger Covenant and Other Reasons Israel is in Trouble," *Washington Monthly*, June 1, 1987.

to the Arab and Islamic civilizations for centuries. This attitude is evident from the writings of prominent, highly respected Western-European democrats, among them Alexis de Tocqueville, the famed, French author of *On Democracy in America*, first published in 1835. In a separate work that appeared in 1841, he wrote:

> On the one hand, I have reported from Africa the painful idea that at this very moment we are waging war in a manner more barbaric than the Arabs themselves. From their standpoint, they are now meeting civilization. This manner of waging war appears to me to be as unintelligent as it is cruel.
>
> On the other hand, I have often heard men in France, whom I respect but with whom I disagree, find it wrong to burn crops and sack silos and to seize unarmed men, women, and children.
>
> As far as I am concerned, these are distressful necessities that every people that wish to wage war on the Arabs are obliged to submit. And, if it be necessary to be frank, these acts do not revolt me any more than many others that the right of war confers and which have taken place in all of the wars of Europe. Why is it more objectionable to burn harvests and to imprison women and their children than it is to bombard innocent populations of a besieged city or to seize merchants' vessels belonging to an enemy power?[11]

Given that this type of anti-Arab-anti-Islamic animosity was later nurtured and continues to serve contemporary Western neo-imperialist and neocolonialist interests, it may well be that only mutual acknowledgement and a move toward full reconciliation of the differences that were born of this environment will curb the pent up anger and alleviate the resentment that still permeates the Arab and Muslim world. This, because the fact remains that wherever Western imperialism and colonialism thrived, their legacies of

---

11   Alexis de Tocqueville, Travail sur Algerie, vol. 1. La Pléiade rd. Paris: Gallimard, 1841, 704–705. For a critical discussion of De Tocqueville's attitude toward the war in Algeria see Olivier Le Cour Grandmaison, Le Monde Diplomatique, June 2001.

political corruption and sectarian and economic exploitation continue to lie heavy on the backs of formerly colonized peoples.

There is no better example than that of sub-Saharan Africa, a region rich in human and natural resources that even today is ruled in large measure by indigenous politicians working in tandem with the neocolonialists and imperialists. If proof of this is still necessary, one need only remember that all parties to the destructive civil war that has raged in Libya or that are now involved in the bloody antigovernment civil war in Syria and violence in Yemen unanimously eschew any formal Western intervention that would introduce troops into their country, despite their fundamental disagreements on many other substantive issues.

For several decades now, the current wisdom has been that the Arabs were tired of and unconcerned with the Palestine problem, a ploy propagated in part by pro-Israeli international media. What the current Arab Spring has actually proven, however, is that Palestine continues to be the heart that pumps the emotional and political distress in the Arab-Muslim world today and even terrorism itself to some extent.

There are several reasons for this. First, almost all indigenous Palestinians are Arab and the majority is Muslim. Second, the Palestine problem is the epitome of imperialism and colonialism at its worst. All oppressed people, regardless of national origin or religious persuasion, can identify with a part of their agony. Third, Palestine reveals the absolute hopelessness of an entire nation that is confronted with the conspiracies of international power brokers. In the United Nations, many of these international power brokers conspired to expropriate a historic land that was already populated by an ancient indigenous people and to turn most of the land over to an alien people. It armed and supported, economically and politically the new arrivals and dressed their own deeds in the garments of international legality. It then looked the other way as the new Zionist arrivals systematically expelled or made the indigenes irrelevant.

All the great powers, democratic and undemocratic, were complicit in the perpetration and perpetuation of this Palestinian tragedy, and their decision has come back to bite each of them in the form of terrorism.

How Arab regimes treat this problem in the future will continue to be the measure of how their own people assess and acquiesce in their leadership.

Saudi Arabia, never a direct victim of imperialism or colonialism, nevertheless inherited many of the problems created by the West in other parts of the region, especially the resentment and violence over the displacement of the Palestinian people.

Saudi Arabia's founder, Abdel Aziz bin Abdel Rahman Al Saud (Ibn Saud), was confronted with comparable anger and resentment of his own people and of some of his most trusted advisors with regard to the imperialistic and colonial policies of the West—most notably the United States and Great Britain—over the creation of Israel. He rejected their counsel to break with the West, but he never acquiesced in these Western policies; he went out of his way to publicly oppose them. What distinguished him from other nationalist leaders was that he never acted rashly. He did not succumb to the temptation of turning to violence, as did Osama bin Laden, or resort to provocative, non-redemptive foreign-policy initiatives, as did several Arab nationalist leaders in Egypt and Iraq in the mid-1950s and thereafter. Had he done so, it is not likely that Saudi Arabia would be the strong and prosperous nation that it is today.

Today the kingdom is wealthy, a regional political force and an economic world power. It reached that status because its founder, Ibn Saud, never lost sight of the fact that the best thing he could do for his people and his country was not to involve them directly in the problems of its neighbors and to use, instead, his influence discreetly and through diplomacy. By mediating the Lebanese civil war at the Taif Conference in 1973 his successors enhanced the country's reputation for fairness and common sense.

In permitting the stationing of American troops in the country during the first Gulf War in 1993 against the advice and guidance of prominent religious Saudi leaders and several influential members of the Al-Saud family, the Saudi government unleashed a storm of public opposition and debate that is still raging beneath the surface. Its recent, direct intervention to quell the public unrest and to prop up the regime in Bahrain raise serious questions about the current Saudi regime's capability to navigate the troubled waters of support for a legitimate regime without suppressing popular dissent.

Can Saudi Arabia maintain its extraordinary survival and development in a region torn incessantly by wars, revolutions, and foreign interventionism and now confronted with international terrorism?

If he were living today, Ibn Saud's reply could well be, "We have given you a nation, if you can keep it."

"What happened is you have great information sharing from the Saudis. We were immediately able to work across the globe to get these packages segregated."

Janet Napolitano,
Secretary of Homeland Security, CNN,
October 31, 2010:

CHAPTER 1

GEOPOLITICAL INTRODUCTION TO CONTEMPORARY SAUDI ARABIA

On the west, Arabia shares more than1,000 miles of the Red Sea with East Africa, and on the east more than 650 miles with Iran on the Persian Gulf. Today it has land borders with Iraq, Jordan, Kuwait, Oman, Qatar, the United Arab Emirates, Yemen, and is now connected with the island nation of Bahrain by a causeway.

The Arabian Peninsula's strategic geographic location in Southwestern Asia made it inevitable that it would be the target of Western interest in direct proportion to the weakening of the Ottoman Empire, which still had a tenuous hold on its Arab territories as late as the outbreak of World War I in 1914 and after more than four hundred years of continuous occupation.

As early as 1656, Oliver Cromwell noted the necessity of securing a permanent base at the end of the Mediterranean Sea. By 1713 Britain achieved this objective when Spain ceded Gibraltar under the Treaty of Utrecht and thereby controlled egress and exit into the western Mediterranean. In 1800 it seized Malta, and then Aden in 1839. By agreement with the Ottoman Empire, it took control of Cyprus in 1878. In 1881, the Convention of Constantinople gave it responsibility for the Suez Canal, thus ensuring British control of the Red Sea from the north and south and entry and exit into the eastern Mediterranean. In 1820 Britain signed a treaty with Bahrain and became its protectorate in 1861. Treaties with the Trucial States in 1892 granted Britain primacy in those territories and responsibility for their foreign affairs. Treaties signed in 1899 with Sheikh Mubarak of Kuwait and in 1916 with Abdullah Al Thani of Qatar made Britain the unchallenged master of the Mediterranean, the Red Sea, and the Persian Gulf.

And thus, Great Britain dominated the seas surrounding the Arabian Peninsula, as well as some of its territories for almost three hundred years, until 1973 when financial and other problems obliged Great Britain to formally pass the baton to the United States which then became the dominant power in those areas.

During this period, more fundamental developments were occurring in the Arabian hinterland struggle between Ottoman hegemony, British imperialism, and Saudi nationalism. Within 150 years these three forces would clash head on.

The centuries old Ottoman presence in what now constitutes Saudi Arabia was limited to coastal regions. Its influence and control was tenuous at best. Beyond that, the Ottomans were Sunni Muslims, and the inhabitants of Arabia accepted the Ottoman Caliphs-Sultans as the legal and moral leaders of the Islamic community.

At that time, the Ottomans looked north to Europe for territorial aggrandizement and economic expansion. The Arab territories that today include Saudi Arabia had virtually no commercial or economic value to the empire, and even less political interest beyond ensuring that they did not fall under the control of foreign powers. The Ottomans allowed the northern Arab territories to become a backwater of underdevelopment and neglect and the Arabian Peninsula to degenerate into a lawless place where indigenous Bedouin tribes fought internecine battles among themselves to achieve temporary hegemony over small stretches of land where victories were fleeting and defeats never long lasting.

In 1745 Sheikh Muhammad bin Abdel Wahhab, a conservative religious reformer and itinerant preacher from central Arabia, preached religious revival popularly known today as Wahhabism in territories that now constitute Saudi Arabia. It was a call to return to the fundamental teachings of Islam and the elimination of all traces of religious innovations that had permeated much of its practice in Arabia at that time. The objective was to restore pure Islam to the superstition-ridden Arabian society.

That same year, Muhammad bin Saud, a minor ruler of Al-Diriya, a small town in the region of Najd in central Arabia responded to that call. He championed the Islamic revivalist cause of Muhammad bin Abdel Wahhab, and together they forged an alliance that was simple and irrevocable. Muhammad bin Saud pledged himself and his family to uphold the faith of Islam as taught by Abdel Wahhab. In return Abdel Wahhab promised Ibn Saud dominion. The sword and the political authority attached to it would be the domain of the Al-Saud family and the Islamic scriptures and the religious, moral and educational authority that went with it would be the domain of the Al Al-Shaikh as the reformer's family came to be known. Each family would be supreme but not absolute in its respective sphere since each shared a check on the authority of the other. Nevertheless, the lines of responsibility and authority were clear and unambiguous, and each family respected them.

This alliance of these two families remains the backbone of power sharing in the kingdom to this very day.

The successful wars for national unification of Arabian territories that began in the eighteenth century under the aegis of the Al-Saud family and their Wahhabi allies were revolutionary beyond a doubt. They radically changed the traditional governance of the territory from one of endemic anarchy to one of strong central government. The new alliance replaced unorthodox practices of Islam with a strict interpretation that became known as Wahhabism and, through the force of arms, actively sought to diffuse all of these changes beyond its borders. It was precisely this dynamism in the political and religious condition of Arabia that caused consternation in Western Europe and in the Sublime Porte, itself.

United the Al-Saud and the Wahabbis imposed their rule over much of the Arabian Peninsula, the former with their swords and the latter with their religious doctrine. At the height of their power, the Al-Saud and the Wahabbis threatened to bring down the very pillars that supported the Ottoman regime in Istanbul. This caused the sultan to order his viceroy in Egypt, Muhammad Ali, to crush the movement. Muhammad Ali charged his son, Ibrahim Pasha, with the task, and the latter succeeded in driving the Al-Saud–led Wahhabis back to their capital, Al-Diriya, which was totally destroyed in 1818. The ruins still stand as mute testimony to the extent of the destruction. Even in victory, however, the Egyptian armies that defeated the Wahhabis and their Saudi champions did not linger long in that hostile desert and returned to Egypt.

For more than two centuries, the fortunes of the two families waxed and waned between the apogee of power when they dominated much of the peninsula and the nadir of influence when they lost it. In 1891, after years of internecine combat between rival Al-Saud factions, the last of the Saudi territories reverted to the control of the Ottomans and their allies, the well-respected Al-Rashid family, whose reputation for bravery and hospitality was legendary. In that year, Abdel Rahman bin Faisal Al-Saud, the last of the ruling Saudi leaders, and his twelve-year-old son, Abdel Aziz, went into self-imposed exile to Kuwait. With that, it seemed that the sun had set irrevocably on Saudi-Wahhabi power.

By the early 1900s Britain had established itself on the eastern Arabian littoral, most notably in Kuwait, and made discreet contact with Hussein bin Ali, the Sharif of Mecca, the Ottoman sultan's appointed viceroy in Arabia. British officials made rudimentary contact with influential political sheikhs and emirs in the Arabian heartland, Nejd, with the intention of bringing all of Arabia under British hegemony.

Abdel Aziz bin Abdel Rahman Al Saud, a young Saudi prince popularly known as Ibn Saud, harbored a program of hegemony of his own, namely to unite the territories under the political control of the Al-Saud family and the religious authority of Wahhabism.

On the night of January 15, 1902, Ibn Saud, a young man of twenty-one years, slipped out Kuwait accompanied by a small band of family members and friends. He headed for Riyadh, the traditional Saudi capital, conquered it and changed forever the course of history in the Arabian Peninsula. With that conquest, he began the task of restoring his family's lost territories in the peninsula.

By the approach of World War I, Ibn Saud and the British were working simultaneously toward the objective of divesting the Ottoman Turks of their Arabian holdings while working at cross purposes to impose their own hegemony over the entire peninsula.

The British government in London overriding the recommendations of the British government in India, which had closer ties with and a keener understanding of the existing situation in the peninsula, designated Sharif Hussein as their point man in Arabia. The British intended to make him king of the Arabs. This was a major geopolitical mistake that haunts Britain to this very day because the United States won the coveted prize of ultimately establishing a special relationship with the Kingdom of Saudi Arabia.

After World War I broke out, Sharif Hussein declared for the British and led an Arab revolt against his legitimate Islamic leader, the Ottoman sultan. The majority of the Muslim world considered this as an act of treachery. Ibn Saud maintained his independence of the British but continued working discretely with them to defeat the Turks. The British provided both leaders with money, weapons, and political support, with the intention that Hussein would become king of the Arabs and Ibn Saud would rule a principality in Arabia under the aegis of the Sharif.

The British won the war in Europe but failed to impose their hegemony over the Arabian Peninsula. Hussein, no match for Ibn Saud in political acuity or in military capability, was routed from his territory in the Hedjaz and fled into exile with his sons. Ibn Saud imposed the rule of the Al-Saud family over vast territories in the peninsula including the Hedjaz, the former domain of the

5

Hashemites, Al-Asir, Najd, and the Eastern Province and with it the dominance of the Wahhabi persuasion of Islam.

As a result, the territories that now constitute Saudi Arabia were never subject to European imperialist or colonialist occupation. Therefore, the struggle for national liberation or irredentism was never a factor in Saudi Arabia's self-determination, as was the case in other Arab countries under imperial or colonial rule, such as in Egypt under the British or in Syria and Lebanon under the French.

Consequently, Saudi Arabia was never the arena of struggles that gave rise to native resistance groups or terrorism against foreign occupation. To the contrary, the wars for territory in Arabia that determined the political fate of the peninsula at the beginning of the twentieth century involved opposing indigenous groups in open and primitive warfare on camel-back and on horseback and wielding spears, swords, and outdated muskets.

Each time the Saudis came to power, they did so on the basis of their own military victories and on their Wahhabi credentials in sharp contrast to the sons of Hussein bin Ali, Faisal and Abdullah, whom the British ultimately installed on thrones in Iraq and Jordan, respectively. Of all the British handpicked rulers in the region, only Abdullah II, the great grandson of the Sharif Hussein bin Ali, still reigns in Jordan. The other well-known great grandson, Faisal, was killed in the coup d'état that overthrew his Iraqi regime in 1958.

THE CONTEMPORARY SAUDI POLITICAL SYSTEM

Saudi Arabia is a constitutional monarchy, but certainly not in the Western sense. It is ruled by the nonelected Al Saud dynasty. Its constitution is the Quran and the Sunna of the Prophet Muhammad. Its legal code is the Islamic Sharia that derives its legitimacy from both.

According to the wishes of the founder of the kingdom, Abdel Aziz bin Abdel Rahman Al Saud, succession to the throne passes from his sons, brother to brother, and not from father to son. The current monarch is Abdullah bin Abdel-Aziz Al Saud. He is the fifth son to directly succeed the founder. The other rulers were Saud,

Faisal, Khalid, and Fahd, in that order. All successions occurred without violence, although that of Saud to Faisal was not without its intra-family problems.

The ruler is authoritarian but not autocratic. Limitations on his rule are virtually nonexistent as long as he rules in accordance with the Quran, the Sunna, and the Sharia and with a modicum of common sense. He may not impose arbitrary changes, even if he is so inclined, and must respect public opinion which is powerful in the kingdom, although expressed in ways quite different than in Western democracies. There are only limited local elections in the country and women today are still not fully emancipated politically in the Western sense.

It is important to make these points here to overcome the idea prevalent in different parts of the world, even in the Middle East, that the Saudi king is above the law and that he can ignore the rights of the people with impunity as if he were a European dictator or president of an Arab country with pseudo -democratic Western parliamentary institutions, such as those that existed in Tunisia and Egypt before the popular revolts there in 2011.

Saudi Islamic scholars acknowledge that there is no human-legislated Bill of Rights or Bill of Human Rights or written constitutional guarantees for the individual in the kingdom. They insist, however, that the divinely-inspired Qur'an and the Sunna and the Sharia law that has evolved from them embody these rights more efficaciously than the guarantees conceived and written by Western politicians and their philosopher-theorists.[12]

Accountability of the Saudi king to the people and their representative is real, not theoretical. On November 2, 1964, after he refused to abdicate in favor of his younger half-brother Faisal bin Abdel Aziz, King Saud, the eldest living son and first successor of founder, Ibn Saud, was formally and peacefully deposed. Senior Al-Saud princes armed with a formal religious decree (fatwa) issued by the highest ranking religious scholars (ulema') and in consultation (shura) with different leaders of the Saudi people,[13] charged him

---

12   Suleiman Al-Hageel Abdul Rahman, *Human Rights in Islam and Refutation of the Misconceived Allegations Associated with These Rights*, 2nd ed. , 1420 (Islamic year) 1959 (Georgian calendar)..

13   John S. Habib, *Saudi Arabia and the American National Interest*.169.

with gross misgovernment and of misappropriation of its wealth that was detrimental to the nation and that threatened the common good.

The Saudi ruler has one exceptional power guaranteed by the Qur'an that most rulers could only dream of, namely, that no legal challenge to his legitimacy as ruler may be made or enforced however oppressive his rule, because anarchy (fitnah) is more dangerous to the common good than oppression and unjust rule. Clearly, even with this caveat, there are exceptions when the common good is grossly undermined by misrule, as the deposition of King Saud demonstrated.[14]

Ibn Saud attributed his rise and hold on power first to God and then to his own sword. At the outset of his mission to unite the territories, he was a penniless young prince living in exile. He began his venture to restore the lands of his ancestors and was supported in this endeavor by his brothers, sons, cousins, and a small group of friends who believed in him. Subsequently he transformed these followers into a broad coalition that included tribal and sedentary emirs, religious leaders, townspeople, and Bedouin. As a result, Saudi Arabia is the only country in the Arab Middle East and North Africa that determined its own destiny without the interference of foreign powers. It negotiated and demarcated its own borders and created its own system of government, legal systems, and national identity based on indigenous Arab and traditional Islamic values.

At the turn of the twentieth century, in its first decades of existence after unification, the Kingdom of Saudi Arabia was virtually unknown and irrelevant on the stage of world politics. By the end of the century, it had become a regional political actor, a key international economic power, and an influential global religious force. These successes also made the kingdom a prime target of Western political and religious fringe groups and neoconservative advocacy groups that used the outbreak of

---

14 "Prudence, indeed, will dictate that Governments long established should not be changed for light and transient cases; and accordingly all experience hath shewn that mankind are more disposed to suffer, while evils are sufferable, than to right themselves by abolishing the forms to which they are acctomed." Preamble, US Declaration. of Independence.

terrorism in the kingdom as a pretext to promote allegations that Saudi Arabia itself was a perpetrator of terrorism. Despite the great disparity and incompatibility in their political and religious views, the common objective of these several diverse groups was to destabilize the kingdom and ultimately achieve regime change there.[15]

Today Saudi Arabia is in the vanguard of the international war against terrorism. Its success in combating it at home has caused other countries to turn to it for help in combating violence on their own territories, even though the root causes in each country are substantively different.

Saudi scholars, Arab political analysts, and western scholars attribute much of the terrorism that afflicts the kingdom today, including the home-grown variety, to past and present British and French colonial policies that redrew the political map of the region, exacerbated sectarian differences, and set up alien, Western systems of government that were designed to serve Western, colonial interests.[16] These same scholars and analysts also attribute some of the terrorism to subsequent American foreign policies that were inscrutable or incoherent and interspersed with an occasional flash of brilliance.

The Organization of the Islamic Conference, established in 1969, has boldly rejected the efforts to equate Islam with terrorism. As demanded by different Arab and Muslim organizations, it has consistently and successfully resisted UN efforts to define "resistance" to foreign occupation as terrorism. This refers largely to the Israeli occupation of Palestinian territories but could also be related to the India-Pakistan dispute over Kashmir, as well as similar cases.[17]

---

15 "Stability is an unworthy American mission, and a misleading concept to boot. We do not want stability in Iran, Iraq, Syria, Lebanon, and even Saudi Arabia; we want things to change. The real issue is not whether but how to destabilize." Michael Ledeen, *Wall Street Journal*, September 4, 2002.

16 Mohammed Al-Bishr, ed., *Saudi Arabia and Terror: Cross-Cultural Views*. See the different articles in this text. .See Hans Kohn, *Nationalism and Imperialism in the Hither East* for an excellent treatment of the sharp differences in the British and French approach to colonialism and imperialsm.

17 Patrick Goodenough, "Almost Ten Years after 9/11, UN Still Grappling to Define Terrorism", April 21, 2011.

Threats from terrorists may be the most obvious but are not the only challenge to the kingdom's internal stability. As a sovereign nation, it controls its national territory and has demonstrated that it has the will and capability to impose effective public security measures. More troubling are the allegations, some subtle and others less so, that emanate from foreign sources that accuse the Saudi government of officially engaging in and funding terrorism.[18] Although none of the accusations has ever been substantiated, they have been widely disseminated internationally and consequently play a significant role in turning international public opinion against the kingdom.

For example, the Saudi political and religious establishments are faced with blatant accusations that the kingdom is an intolerant, autocratic state that officially funds and directs international terrorist operations and that Wahhabism, the kingdom's official expression of Islam, justifies, condones, and blesses acts of terrorism against the West and its allies.[19] These charges, featured in major print and electronic media and spread by prominent publishing houses throughout the world, stimulate and contribute to anti-Saudi sentiment worldwide, to resentment in the kingdom, and provide fodder for terrorists to justify their violence against the kingdom.

Even before the terrorist assault of 9/11, the Kingdom of Saudi Arabia had been singled out as the target of systematic misinformation, especially in the high-profile Western print and electronic media and by well-known publishing houses. This kind of reporting adversely influences international public opinion against the kingdom and encourages the Western public to support policies that it would otherwise be likely to reject. Deliberate unfairness against any country does not serve the American national interest. To the contrary, it incites contempt and rage against the countries where the misinformation originate, much as we Americans are angered by

---

18   Dore Gold, *Hatred's Kingdom: How Saudi Arabia Supports the New Global Terrorism*.

19   Philip Seib, "News Coverage of Saudi Arabia's Response to Terrorism", page 350. See also   Richard Curtis and Delina Hanley,"Israel-Firsters Wage Negative Media Campaign Against the Kingdom." 362.in Mohammed Al-Bishr, *Saudis and Terror, cross-Cultural Views.s*

deliberate, unfair reporting from abroad that turns others against us through the dissemination of lies and deliberate untruths.

Biased reporting about Saudi Arabia is particularly harmful to American interests because it damages our existential relationship with the kingdom that encompasses our regional and international cooperation in the common fight against international terrorism, our favorable trade balance, and the reliable and uninterrupted oil supplies at reasonable market prices for us and for our allies. These factors do not exempt the kingdom from appropriate scrutiny. They do, however, mandate that the kingdom not be deliberately brutalized by contrived and unfair reporting for the sake of special, vested interests that are harmful to our own.

One such example is *Hatred's Kingdom: How Saudi Arabia Supports the New Global Terrorism,* by Dore Gold, an American who immigrated to Israel and subsequently became an Israeli ambassador to the United Nations. He is an influential molder of American public opinion. If Mr. Gold's thesis is true one would have to conclude that the most powerful Western nations, the United States, Great Britain, and France, also support the new global terrorism because of their close military, political, economic, and commercial ties with the kingdom.

Several other books also deliberately target the Government of Saudi Arabia and the religion of Islam as intrepid supporters of terrorist activities against the West. These include Charles Allen's *God's Terrorists, The Wahhabi Cult, and the Hidden Roots of Modern Jihad*; Andrew McCarthy's *Willful Blindness: A Memoir of the Jihad*; and Stephen Schwartz's *The Two Faces of Islam: The House of Sa'ud, from Tradition to Terror.* None of these efforts provide convincing evidence to document their allegations.

The ill-concealed, anti-Saudi attitudes of American and European politicians, fostered in part by these so-called eminent experts at the local and national levels, tend to legitimize these anti-Saudi, anti-Islamic allegations. As a result, the kingdom is assailed by Islamic extremists for cavorting with the Christian West that they deem hostile to Islam and is simultaneously demonized by Western critics for consorting with militant Islam. The calls by Western neoconservatives to overthrow the Saudi regime, simply because they do not like it and ostensibly to spread Western-style democracy, also serve the objectives of terrorists.[20]

Not all sources of violence originate beyond the kingdom's frontiers. Provocations from abroad can and have transformed indigenous attitudes that were once benign into hatred and even violence. For centuries and well into the last half of the twentieth century, the kingdom and its people lived in isolation from the outside world, partly because the peninsula had little commercial attraction and partly due to their own latent distrust of strangers and, to some extent, each other. Contact between the populations of its vast and disparate regions was either nonexistent or infrequent at best. The lack of roads and other systems of communications ensured that. In any event, the people were not disposed to social change and rejected religious innovation. Their deep religious fervor bordered on zealotry at times, and their adherence to the core Islamic pillar for charity motivated them to contribute to the poor and the needy. Their disposition toward religious struggle, jihad, whether practiced in their efforts to overcome the vicissitudes of their daily lives or to sacrifice their lives in the legitimate defense of Islam, was sacred.

As long as these convictions were limited to the confines of the traditional, passive life in the kingdom, they were self-confining and benign. When exposed, however, to the systematic violence that the West was inflicting on their Muslim brethren beyond their own frontiers, these convictions often encouraged militancy and demands for strong responses.

Saudis, like most Arabs and Muslims today, no longer depend solely on local print or electronic media for international or even local news. In addition to social media, such as Facebook and Twitter, and virtually unlimited blogs of every stripe and slant, they have access to wide selections of European, American, and other foreign TV channels through satellite dishes, to foreign radio broadcasts, and to internet connections that are not always effectively monitored by official, rigid scrutiny or control. The live talk shows and animated debates and interviews that are diffused on TV channels, such as

---

20 Michael Ledeen," Neoconservative Michael Ledeen Advocates Overthrow of Iraqi, Iranian, Syrian, and Saudi Arabian Governments'" *Wall Street Journal*, September 4, 2002.

Al-Jazeera and Al-Arabiya, all sharpen popular Saudi knowledge of current events and whet their appetite for more. Unlike most Westerners, especially Americans, who accept, as a matter of course, that their electronic and print media will stress local events, Arabs and Muslims are consummate consumers of international news because they are keenly aware that the foreign policies of powerful nations deeply affect their own destinies.

The Saudis have always had an affinity with their Arab and Muslim brethren. This is true even more today as international TV programs deliver the faces of people who look like them, dress like them, bear identical and similar names, and who are their virtual alter-egos in language, culture, and religion directly into their home. This has reinforced Saudi natural empathy for Muslims and Arabs and transformed them into alter egos of themselves. Little wonder that scenes of Arab and Muslim cities under bombardment by Western warplanes, Palestinian homes being razed in real time by Western-manufactured bulldozers, and terrified women and children fleeing in panic that flash on Saudi television sets traumatize the Saudi public, inflame the passions of the rich and the poor, the educated and the unlettered, the religious devout and the backsliders and even the indifferent among them.

We in the West understandably recoil from the singular horror of 9/11 that was played and replayed on television sets, yet we often ignore the cumulative effect of smaller but no less destructive 9/11s that systematically target Arabs and Muslims and that are transmitted around the world. Repercussions of the daily violence perpetrated against Arabs and Muslims in Iraq, Afghanistan, Pakistan, and Chechnya at the hands of Westerners resonate in the kingdom and create an environment of anger and resentment among its people.

In mosques, coffeehouses, private homes, and public meetings, cries arise not only from the usual religious hotheads and political extremists but also from the ordinary citizenry demanding strong responses to halt this violence. The anti-Western sentiment of some Saudis is not likely to dissipate as long as Western policies continue to contribute to the tragic scenes that appear daily on their television screens.

The Saudi government has consistently refrained from reacting in a way that would provide its public with short-term satisfaction but that would ultimately result in long-term damage to the collective national interest. Saudi officials have paid heavily for this with accusations levied by some of their own citizens that accuse them of not doing enough to protect their coreligionists, a theme that Al-Qaeda was swift to exploit.

In the past, the Saudi leadership has opted for preserving the country's own existential relations with the United States in the hope that new elections there would bring to power bold leaders who would modify foreign policies enough to accommodate a modicum of Arab legitimate interests. It now appears that they have little hope whatsoever that this will occur given President Barack Obama's speech in May 2011 outlining his administration's new Middle East policy. His speech later that month to the American Israel Political Action Committee also totally supported, however faintly masked, the Israeli plan for a final Palestine settlement. The president flatly stated to Palestinian president, Mahmoud Abbas, that he would veto any Palestinian request to seek the admission of Palestine as a full member of the United Nations in September 2011.

The Saudi people are dismayed by the West's firm and unequivocal condemnation of the violence that is perpetrated by individual Arabs and Muslims and by silence and lack of outrage when worse cases of violence are perpetrated against Arabs and Muslims by the West's own governments and their Israeli ally.

The Saudi Government, as part of the international community, can be counted on to act reasonably within these constraints, but it cannot control the outrage aroused in its own people and fellow Arabs and Muslims in other countries by provocative Western policies.

The Saudi public today is virtually unanimous in holding Britain and France's imperial and colonial policies and the United States' virtual absolute support for all things Israeli largely responsible for the genesis of terrorism in the region [21] Saudis are increasingly

---

21 Ledeen. Op.cit. Also see articles by Ismat Abul Maguid, Combating Terror in the World.152, and John Duke Anthony, "Western Capriciousness and Terrorism, A

angry that Western powers attribute terrorism to alleged flaws in Arab culture and in Islamic religion.

Partial Tally of the Toll." 163 in Mohammed Al-Bishr, ed. *Saudis and Terror Cross Cultural Views*.

"The Saudis are a key ally in the global war on terror".

Ambassador Cofer Black,
Coordinator for Counterterrorism, House Committee
on International Relations, Subcommittee on the
Middle East and Central Asia May 24, 2004:

CHAPTER 2

PUNITION: THE MASK OF ANTI-SAUDI TERRORISM

According to Dr. Abdullah Al-Mutlaq "terror is the use of violence in the pursuit of political objectives." [22]

Terror is not unique to any one culture, religion, or political form of government. The most democratic and ruthless of governments all engage in one form of terrorism or another, as do individuals and organizations.

Acts of terrorism evoke fear and demands for retaliation among governments but not from the masses of the people. Israelis resumed their rhythm of life even as rabbis collected bits and pieces of human flesh after a bomb explosion in a marketplace.

---

22   Dr. Abdullah Al-Mutlaq. Lecture. "Terrorists Are neither Heroes nor Martyrs but Criminals and Deserve the *Hirabah* Punishment." King Faisal Hall Riyadh, Saudi Arabia. January 29, 2002."

Palestinians buried their dead and then went on with their lives in the aftermath of massive, destructive air attacks on their homes and villages. After the assaults on America on 9/11, we Americans did not panic; we went on with our lives, outraged at what had been done to but not cowered.

The general public is terrorized by the serial killers or rapists in their midst, not by the anecdotal terrorists. Not only are the former common criminals closer to home, but the risks of the average citizen being one of their victims are considerably greater than that of being the victim of a terrorist attack.[23] Today Americans are increasingly vocal in their opposition to giving up any more of their privacy and dignity to the exigencies of government antiterrorist measures, especially invasive body searches by individual security employees and electronic devices, even as their government insists that these measures are necessary for their own protection and security.

There is no generally accepted definition of the term "terrorism." There is, however, universal agreement that its *methodology* is violence, its *product* death, destruction, and devastation, and its *objective* political change. And since virtually every country is a potential practitioner or a potential victim of terrorism, members of the international community may do well to discard their own definition and replace it with one that accurately reflects the circumstances that it is meant to describe. A start in this direction could be to use motivation as a key consideration, because while the methodology and the product of terrorism are always static in every terrorist act, the motivation is dynamic. Antiterrorist slogans, like the Axis of Evil, may be clever statements for political consumption at home, but they are otherwise meaningless and ineffective.

Antiterrorist strategists must broaden their mind-sets about what motivates the individuals who perpetrate terrorism in order to devise methods of containing and eliminating these incentives.

---

23 The reign of terror waged in February 2013 by Dorner, a former Los Angeles police officer and veteran of the war in Afghanistan, resulted in the murder of at least three police officers, several others seriously wounded, and the tragic death of two young innocent civilians before it played itself out in a dramatic shoot-out and his fiery death in mid-February.

This is what Saudi Arabia has done and continues to do in its multifaceted battle against terrorism.

Terror, wherever practiced, has one face but wears many different masks. In some cases it wears the mask of irredentism, revolution, or punition. In others, its activities are conducted through overt or covert means while wearing the guise of self-defense. The remedies and solutions that are most efficacious in dealing with each case are as radically different as are their ultimate objectives. Irredentists seek to acquire lost territory or rights; revolutionaries are bent on liberation at home and spreading their ideology abroad; and practitioners of punition militate to make adversaries pay a heavy price for their policies, even as they know that the prospects of winning the fight are virtually nonexistent.

All practitioners of terrorism, individuals, non-governmental organizations, or sovereign governments, justify their terrorism by using the guise of self-righteousness. Now and then one among them may admit that a particular violent act was a horrific miscalculation,[24] but none eschew their right to wreak violence upon human beings, individually or collectively, for reasons that they claim are justified usually keyed to the concept of national security. In this respect, some nations describe certain operations as terrorist when perpetrated by their adversaries, yet justify similar activities as covert action or legitimate self-defense when carried out by themselves or their allies.

Covert action is a euphemism for terrorism: both are conducted clandestinely in order to achieve political objectives, and both are, by definition, non-attributable to the perpetrator whether it is a state or an organization or an individual.

The key to dealing with terrorists in Saudi Arabia or any other country, for that matter, whether the objective is to combat, accommodate, or negotiate with them, is the capacity to understand the motivation that each different mask represents.

Terrorism in Saudi Arabia today is not sui generis, that is, the causes are not rooted in indigenous Saudi issues but rather in the

---

24 The Real Irish Republican Army apologized for the August 18, 1998, bomb blast that killed twenty-eight civilians in County Tyrone, North Ireland, calling it a mistake and unintentional.

collective Western colonial policies in the Middle East, and in the historic anti-Islamic polemics long before the kingdom became an independent nation.

It is punitive.

We know that because the perpetrators themselves acknowledge this. After each attack, the terrorists openly justify the operation by asserting, for example, that it was undertaken to punish the Saudi leadership and its regime for allowing Christian soldiers to be based in the Islamic holy land during the Iraq war, or to punish the Saudi royals for their alleged hypocrisy in adherence to Islamic practices, or to penalize the Saudi people for its complicity with the regime and for not rising up against its leadership, to mention a few.

Punition is possibly the most difficult and dangerous form of terrorism to suppress because it has no realizable end objective in itself.

The Saudi government has centered its approach to combat terrorism on punition because Saudi terrorists do not use irredentism, revolution, and national liberation from foreign occupation as pretexts to justify their violence.

In recruiting, training, and funding a highly motivated cadre of professionals, intellectuals, technicians, and administrators to lead the fight and in housing them in state-of-the-art facilities, the Saudi government realized that fighting terrorism cannot be left to individuals or groups that have a private agenda or that seek to promote their own special interests or those of others. It concluded that the fight had to encompass all the principles that Saudis were taught and embraced from an early age: (1) respect for the law and acceptance of corresponding punishment if found guilty of violating it, (2) compassion, (3) family solidarity, and (4) opportunity to rebuild one's life and to be reintegrated into society. [25]

---

25 In creating this program, HRH Prince Mohamed bin Naif bin Abdel Aziz, the assistant minister of iinterior for security affairs at that time undoubtedly was influenced by his grandfather, Ibn Saud. The latter forgave Faisal Duwaish, one of his most trusted Ikhwan lieutentants, who led the revolt against him at the Battle of Sybella, twice before punishing him severely after a third betrayal. Ibn Saud also forgave Majid bin Khuthaila, another of his rebellious Ikhwan lieutentants at Sybella. Majid reconciled with Ibn Saud. Today Majid's children and grandchildren

The Saudis understand that fighting terrorism is not the moral equivalent of an election result that can be reversed after two or four years or merely the crafting of new policy to replace a flawed one. Flawed antiterrorist policy, as they have learned from their own past experiences and from that of other countries, is often more counterproductive than the violence it was intended to combat and to prevent. The invasions of Afghanistan and Iraq are two examples of this. After more than ten years of wars that have resulted in massive death and destruction, terrorism continues unabated in both countries, and there is no end in sight.

Even when special interest groups promote their own agenda, they run the risk of becoming a casualty of their own distorted ambitions, if not in their own time then in the generations that follow. The Israeli-Palestinian conflict is an example. After almost one hundred years of conflict, their differences are more accented today and the potential for them getting completely out of control tomorrow is growing.

Combating terrorism is not just a tough job for the relatively few who are entrusted with the task of formulating policies and shouldering responsibility for eliminating it. It is a grueling task that requires the mobilization and participation of the entire nation, not just security agencies. The Saudi program does that effectively. The program enlists the expertise of various secular ministries as well as the religious establishment and actively promotes national vigilance programs among the citizenry.

The Saudis realized that punitive terrorism is a very personal act. To combat it effectively, they recognized that they had to identify terrorist groups. More importantly, they learned that the elimination of punitive terrorism had to be done at the personal level. Thus, their programs are keyed to dealing with the terrorist as an individual with his own particular motivation and needs.

---

are lawyers, university professors, doctors, military officers and pilots. All presently contribute to the development and dynamism of the kingdom.

From their own experience and from that of other countries, they realized that every terrorist operation is unique; and that each terrorist attack is no less and no more than the sum total of its individual perpetrator's beliefs, even in operations orchestrated by a powerful organization.[26]

Each individual who participates in a terrorist attack has his or her own specific reason for so doing. The mastermind of a terrorist operation—no matter how charismatic, cunning, clever, or experienced—may not really know the particular, personal, and deep motivation that inspires each individual to participate in a destructive terrorist mission, much less volunteer for a suicide mission. And the mastermind probably does not really care as long as the dedication and motivation are present, sincere, and consistent with the specific terrorist mission.

The combat soldier who risks his life in defense of his country out of loyalty and love for it is not likely to bear a personal grudge or entertain a personal vendetta with the adversary. He lays down his arms after his country makes peace. Full American-German and American-Japanese reconciliation after World War II are cases in point. Private individuals may have continued to harbor anger at Germans and Japanese, but none were known to advocate the subsequent destruction of either nation.

In contrast, the terrorist carries a personal grudge, and he will not divest himself of his anger or the determination to fight, even if his current terrorist leadership does. He will seek other options or act alone. The numerous splinter factions of various "terrorist" organizations—whether European, Palestinian, Irish, or South American, for example—are mute testimony to this reality. The core membership of these splinter groups is composed of individuals

---

26 In sharp contrast, President George Bush's reaction to 9/11 was to strike at the Taliban and Al-Qaeda on the other side of the globe with massive force and threats, and we are still there battling the two groups. An antiterrorism specialist from the Rand Corporation that Secretary of Defense Donald Rumsfeld invited to brief a special committee at the department recommended that the United States effect regime change in the kingdom and, if necessary, occupy the oil wells and the holy shrines at Mecca and Medina, the two most sacred sites of Islam. Far from expressing any regrets after his briefing was exposed and debunked, he published a book to justify his recommendations: Laurent Murawiec, *Princes of Darkness: The Saudi Assault on the West.*

22

who believe that the mother organization had become soft and had betrayed or abandoned many of the original objectives.

This very personal element in terrorist mentality is the one key factor that is often overlooked by American and European antiterrorist strategists. Even when terrorists are induced to change sides, as in the so-called surge in Iraq, the fundamental motivation is usually for monetary gain or for other personal, political considerations and not because of a change in their convictions or ideology. And when they cooperate with the foreign soldiers, they are not loathe to turn their guns on them when on joint missions, as has happened in Iraq and in Afghanistan on more than one occasion, and even here at home.

Terrorist organizations can provide the impetus and the religious or political justification for violence and facilitate access to networks of money and logistical support. They can nurture existing grudges and turn them in the direction of terrorism, but it is unlikely that they can motivate an individual to become a terrorist out of whole cloth.

Organizations can and have stimulated and encouraged a predisposition to terrorism in an individual who may already harbor a grievance and a sense of injustice. These individuals are usually normal people and not from the criminally-disposed class. Their disposition to use violence in the pursuit of justice is always stronger than their loathing to carry out the violence necessary to achieve it. This is not much different from normal Americans who eschew violence in their daily life but take up their weapon with a vengeance in defense of our homeland and perhaps even commit war crimes in the process.

Viewing terrorists as individuals rather than as members of organizations and trying to meet them on their own rational level as the Saudis do appears to be a more effective and successful method of preempting them than simply hunting them down and annihilating them as irreversible evils.

Terrorism, then, except those acts involving only one person in a specific operation, is a union of individually motivated acts performed collectively.

A further problem with combating terrorism is that the success of the operation is almost always limited in time and place and does not benefit another cause. For example, in regular warfare, the defeat or weakening of a common enemy may benefit one side of the embattled participants. Defeating an enemy or pinning him down on one front may measurably help your ally fighting on another. This is not the case with a successful terrorist operation. The benefits gained by one organization's successful operation rarely enhance the objectives of another, although it may contribute to supporting the overall significance of terrorism as an effective medium to destabilize governments through violence.

The attacks on the World Trade Center in New York and the bombing of trains in Spain were anecdotal in the sense that neither one nor the other advanced the terrorist objectives in the other country.

It is one thing to disrupt terrorist activity; it is something else altogether to analyze and understand its fundamental causes and meet them head on.[27] This practice is at the heart of the Saudi methodology.

The Saudi antiterrorist program concentrates on the individual; by convincing a person to renounce terrorism, the terrorist organization is weakened.

---

27   At the conclion of a lecture on the evil of terrorism and Islam's injunction against engaging in it by Dr. Abdullah al-Mutlaq, a member of the Senior Scholars Council of Saudi Arabia, a member of the audience expressed his appreciation but then asked the question, "What about the terrorism that Jews and Americans carry out against Muslims all over the Islamic World? What is the Islamic response to it?

"We've gotten terrific cooperation in Saudi Arabia...over the years. And it's not just law enforcement; it's also from the intelligence side of the house."

Robert Mueller,
director of the FBI, Council on Foreign
Relations, February 23, 2009:

CHAPTER 3

THE ROOTS OF TERRORISM IN SAUDI ARABIA

Contemporary terrorism in the Kingdom of Saudi Arabia is rooted in post–World War I policies that Britain and France devised and implemented to divide the former Ottoman Arab territories between themselves. Although originally intended to ensure their political and economic interests in the Levant long before the kingdom had become an independent state, these policies negatively impacted Saudi Arabia, as the Levantine territories became enmeshed in wars, revolutions, and dictatorships as direct consequences of these policies.[28]

Nevertheless, policy makers who have enhanced their reputations by associating the kingdom with terrorism lost no time in pointing out that fifteen of the nineteen terrorists who engineered the assault on America in September 2001 were Saudi nationals. They deliberately failed to mention that a modicum of responsibility could possibly be attributed to cumulative Western policies (most notably those inflicted on Palestine) that were imposed on the countries and peoples of the region prior to that devastating terror attack. To that extent, those policy makers shared responsibility for that crime. One could not help but be struck by the parade of senior American officials, both past and present and from almost every Western government, that condemned the attacks on television or in the print media without alluding to a possible connection between that violence and the exploitive Western foreign policy in the region over the centuries.

Contemporary terrorism in the Middle East and in Saudi Arabia is also rooted in the penetration of alien Western ideologies. Among them are socialism, communism, Zionism, and ethnic nationalism. These ideologies all challenged the traditional Islamic and Arab values by encouraging revolution, violence, and disruption of the existing social order. On the other hand, capitalism based on free trade and commerce had been the touchstone of the economic life in the Middle East since time immemorial. Islam not only preserved and encouraged it as an economic theory but also raised it to a revered station in Islamic doctrine and daily life. And it outlawed violence as a means of political change.

During the rule of the Arab territories, Ottomans deliberately allowed the Arab lands to become a backwater of underdevelopment because they looked north to Europe for territorial aggrandizement and economic growth. But they encouraged free trade and

---

28 "Eighty-five years later, in a 2002 interview with John Kampfner, The *New Statesman*, British foreign secretary Jack Straw observed, "A lot of the problems we are having to deal with now, I have to deal with now, are a consequence of our colonial past...The Balfour Declaration and the contradictory assurances which were being given to Palestinians in private at the same time as they were being given to the Israelis—again, an interesting history for , but not an entirely honourable one."

free economies and protected the Arab territories from the encroachment of the dangerous isms noted above, which eventually came to plague the region after the Western powers took control of these territories at the end of World War I.

Today the explosive situation raging in Syria, Bahrain, Yemen, Iraq, Lebanon, and Palestine can be attributed to Britain and France's foreign policies of yesterday in those beleaguered countries. That should come as no surprise to the politicians of today, who deliberately ignore the lessons of the recent past and continue to craft policies that are fraught with disaster in order to serve their vested interests and those of their current allies. These politicians manipulated the destinies of the people of that region and those of the international community by tailoring the facts on the ground to suit their preconceived policies, thereby postponing the day of reckoning in doing so. They created far worse problems for themselves by not objectively addressing the basic problems cogently in the first place.

In virtually every case where the great powers decided to craft their military policies to mesh with their preconceived political objectives rather than with realities on the ground, they caused tremendous losses in human and material resources for their citizens, as well as their own reputation for credibility. And they have passed on the horrendous consequences of these policies to future generations. Iraq and Afghanistan are cases in point.

Efforts to destroy Hezbollah in Lebanon only resulted in making it stronger there. The same occurred after the West's failed effort to dislodge Hamas from power in Gaza through a clumsy putsch. That effort ended up solidifying Hamas's control and creating a breach in Palestinian unity, which prevails to this day. If past experience is any guide to the future, these Western tacticians will continue their efforts to destroy both Hezbollah and Hamas until they finally succeed. But again, if the past is any guide to the future, they will have created conditions for an even greater dichotomy between what they intend and what they end up with.

Iran is a classic example. After Mohammed Mossadegh was elected Prime Minister in 1951 the great powers could not wait to get rid of the demon. In 1953 the CIA succeeded in fomenting a coup against him and then reinstalled the Shah, who did their bidding for a generation. But his corrupt rule ultimately brought the fundamentalist Mullahs to power in 1979 led by Imam Khomeini. Today the great powers are now conspiring to dislodge his Mullah successors and have declared Iran to be a terrorist state, and the heart of the Axis of Evil.

The capacity for duplicity in dealing with the peoples of the Middle East, especially the Arabs and including the Kurds, is seemingly endless. The current Western campaign to get rid of the inconvenient Mullahs appears, to some analysts, as a dangerous and recklessly transparent plan to rid the region of four troublesome players simultaneously: Iran, Syria, Lebanese Hezbollah, and Palestinian Hamas. Although encouraging Kurdish separatism during the Iraq war, the West insists that the territorial integrity of Iraq be maintained now that the war is over.

AMERICAN FOREIGN POLICY, PALESTINE, AND TERROR

Without exaggeration the religious extremism that produced terrorism was first introduced into the Middle East by the European Zionists.

What is more extreme than an alien people's claim to the land of Palestine based on a biblical promise and a religious affinity with a different people who had lived there more than two thousand years ago? Many of the people who today claim a right to live in Israel are converts to Judaism from other religions or no religion at all; many others claim to be secular Jews who have abandoned the practice of Judaism; others profess to be atheists even as they justify their claim to Palestine on the bible. Some of Israel's most acclaimed Zionists were atheists by their own admission, including its first prime minister, David Ben Gurion.[29]

The problem arises not in the Zionist claim to the land but in the international community's elevating that claim to the point of denying the rights of the indigenous people still living on that

29 Wikipedia, List of Atheists in Politics and Law. Asia/Middle East.

land. The latter people have unbroken continuity of living and cultivating that land and may themselves be the progeny of the original people of Palestine who adopted different religions that arose there over the course of history. Palestinians who today are Muslims and Christians may have been Jews who embraced Christianity during the Christian era and then Islam during the Islamic era. The problem was also exacerbated by the political, economic, and financial support of the Zionist claim by Britain and France and then by the United States for religious, political reasons or out of a feeling of guilt for not opposing forcefully Hitler's systematic attempt to exterminate the Jewish people during World War II.

The Muslim-Arab state in Spain existed from 711 to 1492, more than seven hundred years. It was finally dismantled about five hundred years ago, after the Christian reconquest. Andalusia, the Arabic name for Spain, is a province of contemporary Spain and the last territory that the Muslims held in Iberia. It currently retains much of its original Arab-Islamic character in language, music, monuments, architecture, physical traits, and even in family names of some of its inhabitants.

No contemporary nation would seriously entertain the thought of reconstituting Andalusia as an Arab-Muslim state in support of an irredentist Arab-Muslim movement that claimed the right to return there based on previous residence or proprietorship of more than seven hundred years.

There are political reasons that underline the Western powers insistence on expediting the immigration of foreign Jews to Palestine to create an independent Jewish state. One objective was to create conditions in the region that would guarantee the West continued political and economic control through destabilization. How else to explain Britain and France's divisive policies that went in the face of the unanimous political opposition of the entire Arab and Muslim world and many countries of the third world. Both countries had centuries of experience in diplomacy, wars, and governance of foreign peoples. Both had democratic forms of government. Both persisted in these policies even as violence erupted between the Arab-Muslim and Jewish communities.

Later they were joined by the United States that disregarded clear warnings of what was likely to result if an alien Jewish state were created in Arab Palestine.

In a series of letters exchanged with President Franklin D. Roosevelt between the years 1944 and 1945, King Ibn Saud outlined the general Arab opposition to the creation of a Jewish state in Arab Palestine. Some letters were based on the Arab interpretation of history: the Arabs had made their homes in Palestine without interruption since time immemorial in various stages of their historical development, and their forefathers had built Jerusalem long before the Israelites had invaded and conquered Palestine and later abandoned it. The Arabs, therefore, were currently the rightful inhabitants of the land. [30]

Another Ibn Saud's letter appealed to human conscience: to displace the indigenous Palestinian Arabs in order to make room for foreign European Jews who had been horribly persecuted by the Nazis was undoubtedly a travesty of justice. The Palestinians had not harmed the European Jews. The allies were the victors; they had defeated the Nazis. Therefore, he argued, the European Jews should be repatriated to their original European lands and their homes and their wealth and properties fully restored to them.

Still other letters appealed to the question of practicality. The small territory of Palestine, the king wrote, could provide refuge for only an insignificant number of Jews relative to their larger number worldwide. What was the point of changing Palestine's Arab character and disrupting the tranquility of the region for this?

And then on a more somber note, Ibn Saud cautioned the president that, unless the American government changed its policy toward Palestine and ceased to support the creation of an independent state for Jews in Arab Palestine, the entire region would be destabilized and American national interests there would be threatened.

Almost the entire turbulent history of Arab-American relations has revolved around Palestine in one way or another.

---

30 Mohyiddin Al-Qabesi, *The Holy Quran and the Sword*. Letter No 1, November 29, 1938.

All of the above arguments made little or no impression on President Roosevelt. He was determined to promote British Prime Minister Winston Churchill's and World Zionist Movement head Chaim Weizmann's scheme to bribe Ibn Saud with two hundred millions of British sterling as payment for his efforts to support the forced departure from Palestine of its entire Arab population thereby making all of Palestine available to Jewish immigrants.[31] This would require a face-to-face meeting with the king and Weizmann. This amount was the current dollar equivalent of $635,600.000.00, an astronomical sum even today for any nation, much less an impoverished desert kingdom like Saudi Arabia. The offer was made through a retired American colonel. Ibn Saud rebuffed the offer and prohibited anyone in his entourage or government from ever meeting with Weizmann or anybody from his organization. Nevertheless, FDR decided to personally present the offer to the king. With this in mind, he rerouted his return to the United States from the famed Yalta Conference and travelled to Egypt to meet the king.

The meeting occurred on February 14, 1945, aboard the *USS Quincy* anchored in the Bitter Lakes in Egypt. Ibn Saud was transported to the meeting on a US navy ship. He was allowed to bring a small number of live sheep to be slaughtered aboard for his meals and those of his entourage as a special concession for him in contravention of naval regulations

The two unlikely heads of state, one a university-educated scion of a wealthy American east-coast family who, armed with the latest weaponry in existence, had just led the Allied Forces to victory over the Nazis; the other was a formally uneducated scion of an Arab tribe who had united much of the Arabian peninsula on horseback and camelback armed only with swords, spears, and antiquated muskets. They got on well together and ended up as friends. Between exchanging gifts and stories, they engaged in serious talks on bilateral relations. However, each time the president steered the conversation to how the king could help advance the Anglo-American project to create a state for the Jews in Palestine by supporting the transfer plan, Ibn Saud deftly changed the subject.

---

31 John S. Habib. *The Transferred Plan Rebuffed.* (Riyadh, Saudi Arabia: Al-Dara, 2000).

Unfortunately, the president of the United States came to the meeting laboring under the disillusion about Palestine shared by most Americans and Europeans. Namely, that Palestine had been a desert that the enterprising Jews caused to bloom and that the Palestinian Arabs were nomadic Bedouins who, if removed from Palestine to another desert land, would be just as happy and would probably never know the difference anyway. In any case, there were too few of them to worry about. Transporting them outside of Palestine would not be a difficult undertaking, he had been told. It would only require packing up a few tents on camels and pitching them in another desert safely out of Palestine. The president was ready to support any such project.

When the king finally did respond in his own time, he drew a completely different picture of Palestinian life and culture. He recounted to Roosevelt that the Palestinian people were members of an ancient culture, that they were an integral part of the rich Arab-Muslim civilization, and that they continued to thrive in cities, towns, and villages and were very skilled farmers and agriculturalists. If the land was backward and undeveloped, it was the result of Ottoman occupation and neglect for hundreds of years. That said, he unequivocally repeated and reemphasized what he had previously written: the Arabs in general, and the Palestinians in particular, would not accept that a Jewish state of any size be forced on them in any part of Arab Palestine and that the Jewish refugees of Nazi aggression should be resettled in their original homelands and their stolen property returned to them. The alternative to this would be to create an enduring, endemic state of hostility where none previously existed between the United States and Europe on the one hand and the Arab and the Muslim worlds on the other.

After that, the president never raised the issue of a Jewish state in Palestine or the Churchill-Weizmann transfer plan with the king again. He promised that as president he would take no action on this matter that could adversely affect the Arabs without first consulting Ibn Saud. The president emphasized that in making this commitment, he was speaking only for himself as president and not for the entire US government. He subsequently put this promise in writing in the form of a letter to Ibn Saud.

Upon his return home and while reporting to a joint session of Congress on March 1, 1945, on the results of the Yalta Conference, the president made this observation about his meeting with Ibn Saud: "I learned more [about Palestine and the Near East] by talking with Ibn Saud for five minutes than I could have learned in an exchange of two or three dozen letters."[32]

Roosevelt died on April 12, 1945, almost two months to the day of his meeting with Ibn Saud. His death was a godsend to the Zionists who supported the partition of Palestine, because it removed a powerful American president who was likely to advance a policy on partition that was quite different than what his successor, Harry S. Truman, did. Daniel Greenfield explained Truman's motivation in the *Sultan Knish* blog in June 2012:

> But FDR's death put Truman in the driver's seat. And while, privately, Truman was a bigot, in public he needed to build up a different image going into a tough election. While FDR could do anything and still count on the Jewish vote, Truman was not nearly so confident. He lacked FDR's New York background, his casual elitism, and the halo of liberalism that went with it. And while Truman did not like Jews, he did not have much sympathy for the British desire to drag the US into an extended occupation either. And so he cut the knot, by allowing Israel to be created, but imposing an embargo on any military shipments to Israel, and even imprisoning pilots who volunteered to fly for Israel.[33]

The policy of the special relationship with and unconditional support for Israel developed from Truman's decision. It ultimately grew into an unintended absolute American commitment to the viability and security of Israel at incalculable costs to American national security, the lives of its citizens, and its reputation for fairness and justice in the international community.

---

32 William A. Eddy. *FDR Meets Ibn Saud*. America-Mideast Educational and & Training Services, Inc. 2005). 41, Selwa Press, Vista, California.

33 Daniel Greenfield. Sultan Knish blog. "A Special Relationship-Jews, America and Israel." June 2012.

This absolute American support of Israel is not the only reason for Arab-Muslim hostility, but it is without doubt the bedrock on which all other hostility and violence are based. In the *Guardian* on January 6, 2010, Seumas Milne wrote:

> From the wider international perspective, it is precisely this Western embrace of repressive and unrepresentative regimes, such as Egypt's, along with unwavering backing for Israel's occupation and colonization of Palestinian land that is at the heart of the crisis in the Middle East and Muslim world.[34]

During Ottoman rule, the Arab territories remained intact, and there had been no international terrorism. There was no Hamas, no Hezbollah, no PLO in all its deviant forms; there was no Al-Qaeda, no Islamic fundamentalism reflecting anger and resentment at Western policies. Most importantly of all, the Ottoman sultans were firm in rejecting Zionist claims to Palestine and consistently rebuffed Zionist offers to buy their way into Palestine by paying off the tremendous Ottoman debt. Under the Ottomans, there was no Arab-Israeli problem or Israel-Palestine violence. Islam prevailed as the official religion of the empire. The post-Ottoman, endemic violence and hatred and the plague of terrorism are fruits of these Western policies that followed in the wake of British and French imperialism and colonialism after the fall of the Ottoman Empire. Ultimately they found their way to the Kingdom of Saudi Arabia

The terrorist attacks against Western countries were often triggered by their own self-serving terrorist-like policies that are virtually unknown to the average Western citizen and that are deliberately withheld from the general public by governments and local and international media with an anti-Arab bias.

Even after having been the victim of devastating and murderous attacks—civilian and military, at home and abroad—the US government still refuses to acknowledge that its commitment to support Israel bears any relationship to anti-Arab-anti-Muslim

---

34 Seumas Milne, "Terrorism Is the Price of Support for Despots and Dictators," *Guardian*, January 6, 2010.

animosity. Rather, it continues to support Israel militarily, politically, and economically and to share its latest scientific and military technology and provide it with the financial and diplomatic wherewithal to continue its occupation of Arab territory.

The Palestine problem and all the other regional problems that it has generated have found their way to Saudi Arabia. The kingdom was among the countries that fought partition long before it occurred. When war broke out in 1948, it was a belligerent. In the 1956 war that Israel launched against Egypt in tandem with Britain and France, the kingdom supported Egypt. In 1967, when Israel invaded Egypt, Syria and Jordan, King Faisal took the lead in providing political and financial aid to Egypt, although relations between the two countries were at an all-time low. The king wisely distinguished between the hostile policies of individual Arab regimes and existential issues that threatened Arab and Islamic national security. In the 1973 war, King Faisal also supported the Egyptian-Syrian coalition as it attempted to regain the territories lost in the 1967 war. He embargoed oil sales to the United States and the Netherlands in the first overtly unfriendly act toward the United States by the kingdom.

The King Fahd plan presented in November 1981 was adopted by the Arab Summit at its meeting in Fez. It was rejected by Israel. At the 2002 Arab Summit in Beirut, Crown Prince Abdullah's Arab Peace Initiative was adopted and then reaffirmed at the Riyadh Summit in 2007. It provided for the full recognition of Israel by every Arab state in exchange for Israel's withdrawal from all occupied territory, including Jerusalem, and the right of return of Palestinian refugees or their compensation. Prime Minister Ariel Sharon and his successor Prime Minister Benjamin Netanyahu rejected it outright.

Al-Qaeda and other terrorist groups in the kingdom and in the region have consistently condemned the kingdom for its continued strong ties to the United States despite its absolute unequivocal support and protection of Israel and a persistent anti-Arab, anti-Islamic bent.

The Israeli-Palestinian problem remains the core of terrorism in the Middle East and will remain so in the foreseeable future. Before it is all over, it may well drag Saudi Arabia into a destructive, regional war that could destroy the kingdom's entire modern infrastructure.

American governments and foreign policies that ignore Palestinian rights and international norms of conduct are in flagrant conflict with its fundamental principles of justice and fairness. These policies will continue to sustain and nourish the opposition of the Arab, Muslim, and Palestinian people and be an impediment to fighting the American war on terrorism in the region.

CHAPTER 4

ISLAM, SAUDI ARABIA, AND TERRORISM

Prior to 9/11, Saudi Arabia was often demonized in the West, especially in the United States, by certain special-interest organizations and human rights or democracy advocacy groups because of these groups' opposition to some of the kingdom's social, political, and cultural policies, for example, the banning of women from driving on public roads, its system of nonelected government, and the separation of the sexes at public and private functions. Suffice it to say that seldom was one ever likely to stumble on an article in a newspaper or in a periodical that contained a modicum of sympathetic understanding toward the kingdom. Even when the kingdom went out of its way to guarantee oil shipments to the US and its allies and to stabilize oil prices in times of economic stress and political crises, the media ignored the gestures or simply characterized them as self-serving.

There appears to be an unwarranted, ingrained prejudice among most Americans or Westerners and even among some Arabs, against Saudi Arabia and its citizens. Most know very little about the country and its people and care even less.

After 9/11, this anti-Saudi–anti-Islam attitude engulfed the entire world and transformed the kingdom into the alleged perpetrator of terrorism because fifteen of the nineteen 9/11 terrorists were Saudis and because the belief was promoted far and wide that Islam and Wahhabism were both inherently terrorist.

Islam and Wahhabism are both unjustifiably linked to international terror based in Saudi Arabia. It is essential, therefore, to understand what Wahhabi Islam actually teaches and discredit what others unfairly impugn to it.[35]

The Wahhabi expression of Islam evolved concurrently with and is an integral part of the first Saudi state.[36] Wahhabism, then, is neither a new school of Islam nor a new sect. Rather, it is a rigid application of the most conservative of the four recognized schools of Sunni Islam, namely the Hanbali School. To understand what Wahhabis believe, one must examine the core beliefs of the other four Sunni schools of Islam, the Maliki, the Shafai, the Hanbali and the Hanafi. The differences between them are not substantive; rather they are in the nuancial interpretation of orthodox doctrine. Although some of its adherents are known to have advocated intolerance toward non-Muslims, Wahhabism doctrine does not teach that. It is true that some Wahhabi extremists have accorded themselves wide berth to preach their intolerance from the pulpit and to spread it in school textbooks. After 9/11, the Saudi government recognized this lapse and moved swiftly to counter and combat these activities by vetting elementary school texts, by removing offensive, inflammatory material and by suspending and then reeducating the offenders who were on the public payroll.

---

35 Natana J. Delong-Bas. *Wahhhabi Islam, from Revival and Reform to Global Jihad.* provides a sympathetic, scholarly review of Wahhabism.

36 John S. Habib, "Wahhabi Origins of the Contemporary Saudi State," in *Religion and Politics in Saudi Arabia: Wahhabism and the State,* ed. Mohammed Ayoob and Hosan Kosebalaban.

Those who remained defiant were permanently removed from the workforce.

A word here on the term fatwa is appropriate because it is often used in relation to terrorism and Saudi terrorists and because Bin Laden and his associates issued them to justify their ill deeds. A fatwa is a formal religious legal opinion that is publicly issued by a qualified Islamic scholar. Since there is no religious hierarchy in Islam, any Muslim scholar that has developed a following and a reputation for expertise in Islamic learning can issue a fatwa. Consequently, scholars with different views may issue a conflicting fatwa on an identical or similar question. To render a measure of unanimity to this irregular situation, different accredited associations of learned Islamic scholars deliberately avoid issuing fatwas that are inconsistent with generally accepted Islamic practices and principles while respecting each other's right to differ.

The word jihad is also used promiscuously. It literally means to struggle, no more no less. Its meaning changes substantially within the context in which it is used. It can refer to one's personal struggle in daily life or in battle, as in defense of Islam. The perimeters of jihad are strictly defined in the teachings of the four orthodox schools of Islam. The word jihad has also been deliberately used by Osama bin Laden and some of his followers to justify their violent acts, and also by Western anti-Muslims to deliberately distort the meaning of the word and thereby demean Islam.

As Muslim scholars have pointed out, Islam is a peaceful but not pacifist religion. While it does not promote violence, neither does it recoil from the use of force in self-defense. Islam's proverbial tolerance of other religions is one of its great virtues. In my chapter *Lack of Knowledge of Others*, I wrote:

> Tolerance was revolutionary in concept and universal in application. It came into a world where religious tolerance and persecution reigned.
>
> Islam required its adherents to tolerate Jews and Christians, pure and simple. Not to love them, not even to socialize with them. They were obliged, to use the

vernacular, "to put up with them; to leave them to their own doings."

Given that some doctrines were so abhorrent to them, it is a wonder that they had the self-discipline to put up with them.[37]

Proof of Islamic tolerance is prevalent in the modern Middle East today. After 1,400 years of Islam, millions of indigenous Christians still inhabit Islamic countries. Lebanon's Christians represent at least 33 percent of that country's population. Egypt alone counts more than ten million indigenous Egyptian Coptic Christians. And pockets of Jews still live in Arab countries, although the hundreds of thousands that previously lived and thrived in Morocco and Tunis for hundreds of years (thousands of years in Iraq and Egypt) left voluntarily or were encouraged or forced to leave in the wake of Israel's creation, the ensuing war of 1948, and the subsequent wars between Israel and Arab states. Others were deliberately encouraged or forced to immigrate to the new Jewish state by Zionist recruitment programs. Such Zionist campaigns operated publicly in pre-Nasir Egypt as late as 1952. [38] In the case of Yemen, Israel actually negotiated the mass exodus of the ancient Jewish presence there[39] with then ruler Imam Ahmed. In contrast, after 700 years of Muslim rule in Spain, the entire population of Muslims and Jews were annihilated, either through brutal force or expulsion or by forced conversion within fifty years of the Christian re-conquest of Spain.

Much of today's prejudice against Muslims and Islam can be traced back hundreds of years before 9/11 to the deliberate demonization of the prophet Muhammad and Islam by early Christian polemicists and religious thinkers. Their distorted ideas and writings became standard fare in the Christian world for the understanding of Islam. They were transmitted so thoroughly throughout the ages that they were accepted as factual. These

37 John S. Habib, Lack of Knowledge of Others." 121-122, in Muhammad Al-Bishr, ed. *Interfaith Dialogue: Cross Cultural Views.*

38 Gudrin Kramer, *The Jews in Modern Egypt, 1914–1952.*

39 *Operation Magic Carpet,* Jewish Virtual Library, Nisam Mishal, "Those were the Years, Israel's 50th".133. Israel Foreign Ministry.

distortions may well account for the latent anti-Muslim bias that exploded in the United States after 9/11.

These deliberate distortions continue to this day. For example, during Pope Benedict XVI's lecture at the University of Regensburg in Munich, Germany, September 12, 2006, on "Faith, Reason and the University, Memories and Reflections" he wove into his lecture thoughts reminiscent of his days as a professor there with an intellectual discussion of faith and reason.

In 2006 deliberate media distortions of his lecture caused extensive riots and anti-Western and anti-Christian outbursts in some Islamic countries by reporting Pope Benedict's repetition of Byzantine emperor Manuel II Paleolog's statement on Islam expressed around the year 1391:

"Show me just what Muhammad brought that was new, and there you will find things only evil and inhuman, such as his command to spread by the sword the faith he preached."

The media deliberately reported the pope's reference to the emperor's statement out of context, as the pope himself was obliged to point out immediately after the media's reporting, but it was too late. The reaction of outrage in the Muslim world and elsewhere had already erupted. The media also omitted to mention the pope's own description of the emperor's statement as "unacceptable" because the emperor knew better than to have said that Islam was deliberately spread by the sword. The media also deliberately failed to mention that this statement was made in long, on-going friendly, intellectual exchanges between the emperor and a Muslim expert on Christianity in Ankara. Here is the text of what the pope actually said:

> In the seventh conversation (διάλεξις - controversy) edited by Professor Khoury, the emperor touches on the theme of the holy war. The emperor must have known that surah 2, 256 reads: "There is no compulsion in religion". According to some of the experts, this is probably one of the suras of the early period, when Mohammed was still powerless and under threat. But naturally the emperor also knew the instructions,

developed later and recorded in the Qur'an, concerning holy war. Without descending to details, such as the difference in treatment accorded to those who have the "Book" and the "infidels", he addresses his interlocutor with a startling brusqueness that we find unacceptable, on the central question about the relationship between religion and violence in general, saying: "Show me just what Mohammed brought that was new, and there you will find things only evil and inhuman, such as his command to spread by the sword the faith he preached.[40]

I found this deliberate manipulation of the pope's lecture particularly offensive because many people, including myself, were deliberately misled by the unfair way it was reported on radio, TV, the printed and the electronic media, and by the way it was replayed by critics of Islam. [41]

The nuances of these theories may be different but their theme was unchanged, namely that the prophet Muhammad was a fraud, an imposter bent on gaining power and wealth and that his religion, Islam, was wicked, sensual, and fanatic. These ideas were spread in relatively modern times in English, French and German: in works as Dr. Prideaux's, "The True Nature of Imposture, Fully displayed in the Life of Mahomet", first published in 1696-1697; in the Brampton Lectures, delivered by Joseph White in 1784 at Oxford University; and spread in 1785 by Voltaire in his tragedy "Le Fanatisme, ou Mahomet le Prophete." One theory advanced by Keller in "Der Geisteskampf des Christentums gegen den Islam", published in 1896, even claimed that Islam was God's instrument of punishment for heresy or schism.[42] Some Christian scholars, such as Dr. Henry Preserved Smith, challenged these arguments. In 1897, he tried to expose misconceptions about Islam:

---

40 "Pope's Speech at University of Regensburg (full test) on September 20, 2006. Catholic Culture. Org.

41 Daniel Pipes, "Pope Bendict Criticzes Islam", New York Sun, September 19, 2006.

42 Henry Preserved Smith, *The Bible and Islam.* 11-13

It is evident, therefore, that Mohammed's starting point was the fundamental position of revealed religion...that God speaks through chosen men to make His will known to the world.

This position is the key to his activity.

There are thinkers, however, to whom it is incomprehensible that a man should, in all honesty, put forward a claim to speak as the messenger of God. They are compelled to seek some ulterior motive for his activity. The whole medieval world was incapable of understanding the Prophet of Islam.

The only thing which these centuries would see was that Mohammed was the deadly enemy of their civilization. They could explain his impulse only as the direct act of Satan.[43]

Their efforts had virtually no success in changing Western attitudes toward Muslims and Islam.

After 9/11, Americans and Westerners were heard to say, "Why do they hate us?" This reflected the consistent failures of Western educational institutions to inform their own citizens of the extent to which their own countries had colonized, exploited, alienated, and antagonized Muslim peoples long before 9/11 and the extent to which some educators, historians, and intellectuals had deliberately distorted the religion of Islam.

For centuries, Muslims have felt exploited economically and ridiculed culturally long before 9/11. It is worth noting what Jamal Al-Din Al-Afghani, was thought to have taught. He was one of a prominent group of Muslim intellectuals that included Muhammad Abduh. They were confronting European imperialism and colonialism in the Middle East at the end of the nineteenth century.

The Christian world, despite its internal differences of race and nationality, is, as against the East and especially against Islam, united for the destruction of all Mohammedan states.

---

43   Smith, op.cit, p.10

The Crusades still subsist, as well as the fanatical spirit of Peter the Hermit. At heart, Christendom still regards Islam with fanatical hatred and contempt. This is shown in many ways, as in international law, before which Moslem nations are not treated as the equals of Christian nations.

Christian governments excuse the attacks and humiliations inflicted upon Moslem states by citing the latter's backward and barbarous condition; yet these same governments stifle by a thousand means, even by war, every attempted effort of reform and revival in Moslem lands.

Hatred of Islam is common to all Christian peoples, not merely to some of them, and the result of this spirit is a tacit, persistent effort for Islam's destruction.

Every Moslem feeling and aspiration is caricatured and calumniated by Christendom. The Europeans call in the Orient "fanaticism" what at home they call "nationalism"and "patriotism." And what in the West they call "self-respect", "pride", "national honor" in the East they call "chauvinism," What in the West they esteem as national sentiment in the East they consider xenophobia.[44]

Islam had and continues to have its share of fanatics, some of whom have perverted the message of tolerance that characterized Islam since its earliest years. Osama bin Laden and Al-Zawahiri are the contemporary representatives of this genre. These two used the religious writings of earlier nineteenth-century Muslim writers to exploit their political grievances against the West. The following, written by a Young Turk in August 1912, expresses the intensity of this feeling:

We say: the man whose judgment is so perverted as to deny the evidence of the One God and to fabricate gods of different kinds cannot be other than the most ignoble

---

44 Stoddard op. cit. p.64-65.

expression of human stupidity...Among Misbelievers, the most odious and criminal are those who, while recognizing God, create Him of earthly parents, give Him a son, a mother; so monstrous an aberration surpasses, in our eyes, all bounds of iniquity; the presence of such miscreants among us is the bane of our existence; their doctrine is a direct insult to the purity of our faith; their contact a pollution for our bodies; and relation with them is a torture for our souls.[45]

There is plenty of invective in the writings of Jews, Christians, and Muslim fanatics that can be used to turn one group against the other. The history of the Middle East proves that neither the majority of people nor their leaders collectively allowed these fanatics to encroach on their peaceful coexistence during the first decades of Islam or to disrupt their mutual intellectual discourse during the golden years of Muslim rule in Spain. At the court of the Umayyad Caliphs in Damascus, scholars, philosophers, and theologians of the three monotheistic religions freely disputed and challenged each other's Holy Scriptures. That has changed dramatically in the twenty-first century, and increasingly so after 1948. Demonization of Islam has become almost a noble pastime among some groups and a profession among others despite Islam's overall excellent record throughout history before and most notably after the Crusades.

The European Crusades that were formed, ostensibly to liberate the holy places of Christendom from the hands of the Muslims still weigh heavy on Muslim minds. Muslims are sensitive to the very mention of the word "crusades" or "crusaders", as President George Bush Jr. discovered when his speechwriter referred to the American response to 9/11 as a "crusade." The ruthless behavior of European Christian soldiers against Muslims, Orthodox Eastern Christians, and especially toward the Jews who were murdered and the survivors among them expelled from Jerusalem, is beyond

---

45 Ibid. Attributed to Sheikh Abd-ul-Haak. This intolerant attitude only underscores the fundamental principle in Islam of tolerance that allowed Christians and Jews unfettered freedom in matters of religion as "people of the book", despite their controversial doctrines.

dispute. It was the European Christian military rulers who expelled the Jews, but it was Saladin, the Muslim leader, who reconquered Jerusalem, and ransomed them with his own money, allowed them to return, to rebuild their homes, and to reside in the Holy City.

That is forgotten in the current media onslaught to portray Islam and Muslims as fanatical and ruthless people.

Twenty-first century Muslim radicals and terrorists use these historical precedents in tandem with the suffering and disruption caused by the colonialist and imperialist policies of the last centuries to radicalize the youth and to recruit them to commit violence in the name of Islamic jihad.

The methodology of these radicals was to distort the concepts of the relationship between the governed and their governments. These include the following duties: to hear and obey (al-sam wa al-taa) the pledge of allegiance (al-bayah); loyalty to Muslims and non-allegiance to non-Muslims who are regarded as enemies (al-wala wa-al-bara); the promotion of virtue and the prevention of vice (al-amr bi al-maruf wal nahy en al munkur); the concept of judgment (al-hakimiyyah) and the obligation of applying Divine Law (the Sharia) and jihad in Islam.[46]

By adopting extremist interpretations of these concepts, radicals used the Holy Qur'an and the prophet's traditions (Hadith) to justify violence against governments and civilians in the name of Islam. And they targeted the youth, especially the most vulnerable, for recruitment and to accept the doctrine of takfir, namely that certain individuals or groups that were previously considered Muslims had now become unbelievers (kuffar) and, therefore, were legitimate targets for violence, including murder.

Over the centuries since its revelation, Islam has experienced a constant renaissance of Islamic thought, usually in response to some outside foreign threat. For example, in the nineteenth century, Jamal Al-Din Al-Afghani, Muhammad Abduh, and later, Taha Hussein and others were concerned with the influence of the Western penetration of the Islamic countries. They were all nonviolent and peaceful. However, some revivalist groups,

---

46 Abdullah F. Ansary, "Combating Extremism: A Brief Overview of Saudi Arabia's Approach,"112.

including some members of the Muslim Brotherhood,[47] preached and engaged in limited violence in direct proportion to the new threat of Israeli usurpation of Palestinian territory and against Arab regimes that were suspected of being soft on Israel and of introducing creeping Western ways into Islamic domains.

For some contemporary scholars, the development of religious extremism in Saudi Arabia goes back about fifty years. At first, it started out as benign and apolitical in the form of the movements that emulated those created by Mohammed Abduh and his followers. Then, some religious figures started giving public lectures and making and distributing tapes. Extremist religious and political thinking imported by non-Saudi religious movements influenced them. Some of these individuals who were persecuted in their own countries found refuge in Saudi Arabia in the 1980s and started to spread their ideology throughout the Saudi population, which was vulnerable because the people accepted as correct what was presented to them in the name of Islam.

These individuals gradually took the lead in Islamic studies in the Saudi public schools and universities, where they created groups of followers and students who, in turn, spread these views to others.

Extremism had been spreading in Saudi Arabia long before it turned to terrorism, largely among the youth through secret meetings, camps and trips. Most of them had been living in circumstances that were conducive to being isolated from mainstream society, reading selected books, listening to selected tapes, and listening to certain individuals who indoctrinated them with radical ideology.

The war to oust the Soviets from Afghanistan provided a crucial breeding ground for the development of extremism among these young men, and when they returned home, they found a suitable target. Namely, the hundreds of thousands of Western troops, men and women, stationed in the Holy Land of Islam and poised for the invasion of Iraq. The writings and tapes of several prominent Saudi religious scholars that opposed the stationing of troops in the kingdom further radicalized these young Saudis, even though

---

47 A quasi-political-religious-social organization founded in Ismaliya, Egypt, by Hassan Al-Banna in 1928. It survived severe Egyptian government crackdowns in 1948, 1954, and 1965. Once formally outlawed, it was legalized after the 2011 Egyptian revolution, and reorganized as the Freedom and Justice Party.

the Council of Senior Ulama' in Saudi Arabia had issued a fatwa permitting the stationing of non-Muslim troops in the kingdom

During the war in Afghanistan and the war in Iraq, there was no lack of reasons to target the American presence in the Middle East and their ally, the Saudi government itself. The atrocities committed against Iraqi civilians by American soldiers and the humiliation of others in Iraqi prisons, such as the notorious Abu Ghraib prison incidents in Baghdad, exacerbated tensions. These excesses, however limited, were flashed around the world in graphic photos depicting nude Iraqi Arabs and Muslims threatened by attack dogs or being dragged on a leash like dogs. Or their nude bodies piled one on top of the other in contorted forms. These depictions not only revolted the world audience in general but caused dismay and consternation in the Arab-Muslim world in particular.

The roots of terrorism planted during centuries of colonization and exploitation were amply nourished by the international community's creation, arming, and funding of the State of Israel and further exacerbated by the West's subsequent creation and financing of Israel's war machine. The systematic humiliation by successive military defeats in the 1948, 1956, 1967, and 1973 wars created an atmosphere of virtual helplessness in the Arab world.

The rise of national liberation movements that advocated violence to combat the foreigner occupiers glorified the use of terrorism, and gave birth to different movements, including the Palestine Liberation Organization and its several splinter groups, including Hamas, and the Lebanese Hezbollah Each brought a new dimension to the struggle. Each would find its way to Saudi Arabia sooner or later in one form or another.

THE IKHWAN OF NAJD: TERRORISTS OR SAUDI ISLAMIC WARRIORS?

In the aftermath of the involvement of the Saudi nationals in the 9/11 attacks, speculation arose as to whether Ibn Saud's Ikhwan was the forerunner and possibly the prototype of contemporary Islamic terrorism in the kingdom. I was invited to participate in one such discussion with the history department professors at King Saud University in Riyadh in 2009.

I took the position that there was no real connection between Ikhwan and the modern terrorists and that such a thesis was untenable.

Early in his campaign to regain his ancestral territory, Ibn Saud transformed the nomads, the Bedouins of Arabia, as his principal instrument of warfare by converting them to Wahhabi Islam. They became his special warriors, known collectively as the Ikhwan Brotherhood of Nejd.[48] He obliged them to sell their flocks of animals and resettle in villages called hujjar that he had built specially for them. As sedentary and no longer nomadic they were rapidly available to be mobilized for war. Imbued with a burning faith and loyalty to Ibn Saud, they became a virtually invincible military force. As recent converts to the Wahhabi expression of Islam, their dedication and loyalty to him were second only to their zeal to fight and die as martyrs in the way of God (fi sabil Allah). The Ikhwan were, for the most part, self-disciplined and a source of pride for Ibn Saud. Some of them, however, were not and he warned the recalcitrant among them not to "encroach upon the rights of others" unless they were prepared to face his retribution.[49] While Hussein bin Ali, the Sharif of Mecca, depended on British largesse and arms, he had neither a fighting force that was dedicated and loyal only to him that could match the zeal of the Ikhwan nor the personal military leadership and political acuity of Ibn Saud. Thus, after Ibn Saud unleashed his Ikhwan warriors against the Hejaz, the Sharif was ultimately forced into exile with his two sons, Abdullah, for whom the British created the independent territory of Trans-Jordan, and Faisal, whom they made king of Iraq after the French unceremoniously ended his brief reign as king of Syria.

As early as 1919, one British captain alleged that the "Bedouin are systematically terrorized into "conversion,"[50] but there is no viable evidence to support this contention. Two other occasions caused them

---

48   Not to be confed with the the Muslim Brotherhood of Egypt.

49   Ameen Rihani, *Ibn Sa'oud and His People*. 191.

50   Note by Captain Garland of the Arab Bureau, June 11, 1919, Public Record Office, MSS, Foreign Office, vol. no. 4146, document no. E 91521.

to be directly associated with this term also. The first was their brutal conquest of Taif that spread fear and horror among the population of the Hejaz and created conditions that enabled the fall of Mecca, Medina, and Jidda with the minimum of bloodshed. [51] The second was after a rebellious contingent of Ikhwan set upon and slaughtered a group of innocent nomadic Saudi shepherds and stole their livestock.

Subsequently, after several of Ibn Saud's senior lieutenants challenged his legitimacy as ruler on religious grounds, he and contingents of loyal Ikhwan confronted and defeated these Ikhwan warriors, led by Faisal Al-Duwaish, at the Battle of Sibylla in 1932 after which he disbanded the movement altogether. Some members joined the newly formed government militia; others found jobs in the new Saudi Government administration, and others retired to their native villages.

And on the jacket of the first edition of my book on the Ikhwan, *Ibn Sa'ud's Warriors of Islam*, I also indirectly associated them with terrorism. [52]

Without a doubt, the Ikhwan caused fear and apprehension among the populace of the Western Province during their heyday of power. During my residence in the kingdom from 1966—1970 I learned this from conversations with individual Saudis who witnessed these developments firsthand. This information was verified from my own direct conversations with individual Ikhwan in their own settlements (hujjar), including the two most notorious known for their fanaticism, Al-Artawiya and Al Ghut Ghut. What distinguishes them from the modern terrorist is that they acted as part of an organized army in battle and under the direct command of their leaders. While this may not mitigate the ruthless acts they may have perpetrated individually or collectively, it does put them within the same standards that sovereign nations claim today for the excesses of the own armies, some of which they describe as collateral damage.

There is no evidence that Ibn Saud ever countenanced, encouraged, or knew in advance of the ravages that some Ikhwan would perpetrate in Taif. To the contrary, all evidence indicates that

---

51   John S. Habib, *Ibn Sa'ud's Warriors of Islam*.114–115.

52   Ibid, "If they struck terror into the hearts of their adversaries, they also brought peace and security to a troubled land."

he was anguished and moved to tears when he received the news. The attack on the innocent nomadic shepherds also motivated him to confront the rebellious Ikhwan and settle accounts with them.

Beyond that, it is not tenable to associate Ikhwan excesses with the Wahhabi expression of Islam. The Ikhwan had only recently been transformed from ascetic nomads, individualistic and accountable only to themselves and to their own leadership. Most deported themselves, as did the overwhelming majority of the Wahhabi population, with civility, dignity, and self-control, even as they made every effort to avoid contact with individuals and groups that did not conform to their religious beliefs.

It was not the Wahhabi expression of Islam that inspired some of the Ikhwan's disreputable acts but rather their deviation and aberration from adhering to its tenets. Some of the onus for their misdeeds must be attributed to several of their most powerful tribal leaders, who encouraged these excesses for their own personal gratification. Other responsibility must be laid at the feet of unscrupulous religious Wahhabi leaders fired by their own zealotry.

That does not mean that there are no similarities between the tactics of contemporary Saudi terrorists that target the current Saudi regime and those who perpetrated dishonorable acts in the name of religion in the past. Indeed, there are some. The terrorists of today emulate the rebels at Sibylla when they accuse the current Saudi leadership of consorting with Christians, corrupting Islamic society by introducing Western ways that were alien to Islam into the country, and dealing with the Christian West to the detriment of Muslims. They also make similar allegations of un-Islamic behavior as justification to challenge Saudi authority.

In fact, the leaders of the rebellion at Sibylla had ulterior motives; they clearly intended to carve out separate emirates where their word would be law. The transparency of these accusations was obvious in the case of their most powerful rebellious leader, Faisal al-Duwaish. In defeat, he fled to Kuwait. There, he placed himself at the mercy of the very British that he had previously condemned as unbelievers (kuffar) and after having denounced Ibn Saud for having dealt with them. Similarly today's terrorists also harbor personal political ambitions, including the revival of an Islamic caliphate ruled by one of them.

"We work as well with partners in the Middle East. While they may disagree with some of our policies in their region, they agree that policies like diversion can make their own nations safer, and they are doing a great job. I would cite the Saudis, especially in their work on diversion and on this pernicious ideology. CIA Director Michael Hayden has said that we are doing well in the war against al-Qaida, and he cites near strategic defeat of al-Qaida in Iraq, near strategic defeat of al-Qaida in Saudi Arabia, significant setbacks for al-Qaida globally as a lot of the Islamic world pushes back on their form of Islam.

James Glassman,
Undersecretary of State for Public Affairs, Washington
Foreign Press Center, July 15, 2008:

CHAPTER 5

EARLY TERRORIST INCIDENTS IN SAUDI ARABIA: FORERUNNERS OF AL-QAEDA AND AL-QAEDA IN THE ARABIAN PENINSULA[53]

The first terror incident in Saudi Arabia, in the sense that the term "terrorism" is used today, occurred in 1968. It was not the work of Islamic terrorists but rather that of pro-Nasir Yemeni army officers who had infiltrated the kingdom with the express mission of destabilizing the country by spreading confusion and disarray. With this in mind, they detonated bombs in Riyadh that damaged the private residences of several high-ranking Saudi princes, the

___

53   See Appendix E.

residence of the Mufti, the offices of the United States Military Training Mission located in the Ministry of Defense, and the living quarters of members of the same American military mission located in the Zahrat al-Sharq Hotel and my government office, which was also located there. Had the explosions at the Ministry of Defense occurred just a few minutes later than they actually did, it is almost certain that a number of military advisors would have been killed and seriously injured.

On the same day, the American Embassy, located in Jidda at that time, and several Saudi government buildings were also attacked. Some Palestinians extremists allegedly abetted these terrorists. In those days, there were no guards or security at personal residences in Riyadh and none at the Zahrat Al-Sharq Hotel. At the Ministry of Defense, only an unarmed concierge checked the comings and goings there. Even after the bombings, there were still no security guards assigned to these buildings. Those bombings were simply written off collectively by the Saudi government as aberrations because of the virtual absolute security prevailing in the kingdom at that time.

Even as the causes of the Riyadh bombings were still being investigated, a huge blast rocked the home of the senior Saudi officer who was heading the investigation. It also rattled my home. I raced to his home and reached it minutes after the explosion. He was still sitting on the bed covered with the fallen debris. He had miraculously escaped death and serious injury.

Eventually all of the culprits were identified and arrested. They were active military members of the new Egyptian-backed Yemeni Republic. They had infiltrated into the kingdom and had been living and working in Riyadh as menial laborers and domestics. Many of those implicated in the bombings were employed as cleaning staff and as kitchen help at the Zahrat Al-Sharq Hotel that housed the American advisors of the Military Training Mission in Riyadh. These terrorists had daily, unlimited access to the living quarters of the American military personnel residing there and to the entire complex of the hotel.

After I reported the attack in detail to the American ambassador in Jidda, he instructed me to fly there in order to report to him personally. This travel was necessary because of the lack of secure online communications between my office in Riyadh and the embassy in Jidda.[54] The distance between the two cities is approximately 600 miles (1,000) kilometers. Given the absence of a continuous paved road between Riyadh and Jidda in the 1960s, the travel time was at least two days overland by four-wheel jeep and four to five bumpy hours by military aircraft depending on the make and model.

The meeting in Jidda was chaired by the ambassador and attended by his senior counselors as well as the CIA chief of station, Jidda. All expressed their deep concern that the public execution of these terrorists might violate specific caveats of US-Saudi agreements under which we supplied the Saudis with training and equipment for its public security agencies. They were particularly concerned that these executions would arouse the ire of Congress which was adamant that these American-supplied resources not be used to suppress popular dissent in the kingdom.

The ambassador suggested in the strongest terms that I raise the issue of executions with my high-level contacts in the ministry of interior in order to persuade the Saudi government to commute the death sentence of these terrorists.

I countered with the thought that we not interfere with the Saudi system of justice. I mentioned that I not only had followed the investigations closely but that I participated in some of them. I was completely satisfied that they had been conducted fairly.

---

54   My assignment to Riyadh was highly unusual given that I was then only a middle-grade officer. The entire Saudi government was located in Riyadh at that time including the king, his ministers, and all of the ministries.except the Ministry of Foreign Affairs and the Ministry of Commerce. They were deliberately located in Jidda to obviate the visits of diplomatic personnel to Riyadh, which was not encouraged. All diplomatic representations, including the American Embassy, were located in Jidda, more than one thousand kilometers to the west. There were no paved roads between the two cities, and air travel was unreliable I was assigned to Riyadh at this time because I already had diplomatic experience at the American embassy in Egypt, knew Arabic, and because of my extensive historical knowledge of Islam and the Arab world. In this position I had direct access on a daily basis to the most senior officials of the realm, with many of whom I was acquainted on a first-name basis. I could make immediate contact with them, depending on the urgency of the matter. All this, of course, took place under the personal supervision of Herman F. Eilts, the American ambassador, and with the approval of the highest levels of the Saudi government.

Also, I was acquainted with several of the perpetrators because they worked as domestic help at the Zahrat Al-Sharq Hotel. Their trial was fair, and their punishment was no more severe than that meted out to common criminals and these culprits were terrorists not common criminals.

I made the point that I was convinced that the Saudis would go ahead with the executions regardless of American reservations given that they were formal punishments dictated explicitly by Islamic law. Beyond that, I was certain that no Saudi king would even contemplate embroiling himself in a controversy with the religious authorities over a matter of religious principle where even the king had no compelling authority. And certainly not the reigning king, Faisal bin Abdel Aziz, who himself was a scholar trained in Islamic law and the direct descendant of the legendary Sheikh Muhammad Abd Al-Wahhab, on his mother's side.

By the time the meeting had concluded, the ambassador left the decision up to me but not before making it indisputably clear to all present that if there was an adverse reaction in Washington over these executions, I would bear much of the blame.

I mention the above details because this affair occurred in the 1960s. The American response to executing terrorists was subsequently far different after we were attacked on 9/11 at the World Trade Center, the Pentagon, and the foiled attack on the White House or Capitol Building that may have been aborted due to the heroism of the passengers on the hijacked airplane that appeared to be aimed at one of these two symbols of American national democracy.

After I learned the exact date and the time that the perpetrators were scheduled to be executed in Justice Square immediately following Friday morning prayers, I asked the colonel in command of the Riyadh mission to order all personnel, civilian and military, American and foreign that reported to him to remain indoors. I was concerned for their personal safety in the event that hostile crowds converged on and threatened the mission. I then went to Justice Square (Sahat Al-'Adel) alone where a large crowd had gathered to witness the executions.

There I witnessed the personal executioner of the then governor of Riyadh, HRH Prince Salman bin Abdel Aziz, currently the crown prince, dispatch the 21 condemned terrorists single-handedly, one by one. The crowd watched without emotion and clapped softly with a sense of relief that the miscreants had been caught and duly punished. Afterwards, there were no public hostile reactions to the executions.

The bodies of the executed were suspended by their waist for public viewing and taken down at sunset. Those of us who lived in the kingdom at that time were accustomed to a virtually crimeless society when the theft of a purse was a cause célèbre. Nevertheless, after the Riyadh bombing there still were no meaningful increases in security at private residences, ministries, or public buildings and none at the Zahrat Al-Shark hotel. The government did not consider that the bombings and executions posed a recurring threat to public security.

But things began to change after November 20, 1979, when the Grand Mosque in Mecca was invested by religious radicals led by Juhayman Al-Otaibi, a member of a prominent Nejdi family whose father in his day had also opposed the then reigning Saudi monarch, Ibn Saud. Juhayman proclaimed his brother-in-law, Muhammad Abdullah Al-Qahtani, to be the Mahdi, an Islamic version of the messiah concept. The takeover was put down decisively after two weeks by Saudi forces assisted by French and Pakistani swat teams.[55] As one newsman reported:

> At dawn on January 9, 1980, in the public squares of eight Saudi cities, including Mecca, sixty-three Grand Mosque militants were beheaded by sword on orders of the king. Among the condemned, forty-one were Saudis, ten from Egypt, seven from Yemen (six of them from what was then South Yemen), three from Kuwait, one from Iraq, and one from the Sudan. Saudi authorities reported that 117 militants died as a result of the siege, 87 during the fighting, 27 in hospitals. Authorities also noted that

---

55   In a written comment on this unpublished mancript, Saudi officials denied that French and Pakistani forces participated in the liberation of the Grand Mosque.

nineteen militants received death sentences that were later commuted to life in prison. Saudi security forces suffered 127 dead and 451 wounded.[56]

After this incident, overall public security still had not been visibly increased not even around public buildings. Again, the Mecca takeover was considered, like the terrorist bombings in Riyadh and in Jidda, to be another aberration that involved Islamic fanatics who had more nerve than capability.

Since the incident in Riyadh in 1968, Saudi Arabia has been the target of more than ninety-eight terrorist incidents that caused the deaths of more than eighty innocent civilians and the injury of approximately 609 others. More than sixty-five members of the Saudi Security Forces were killed during counterterrorism and around 390 were injured. More than 160 terrorist plots that targeted domestic and foreign interests and the lives of Saudi nationals and expatriates living in the kingdom were foiled.[57]

Of the terrorists captured, 80% were Saudis, and 20% percent of different nationalities. They came from all different classes, high, middle, and low. Not all were religiously devout. Some were motivated by money and others by the quest for political power.

The leaders wore suicide belts during the operations and preferred to end their own lives rather than be captured. The terrorists that were captured were fully debriefed on their ideological persuasions, funding, and logistical support. This information helped the security forces foil other plots, seize accomplices, and track down other radicals still on the lam. As a result, many of the terrorists still at large fled the kingdom for Yemen where they regrouped and began to conduct operations.[58]

---

56 Pierre Tristam, "1979 Seizure of the Grand Mosque in Mecca." About.com. Middle East issues.

57 Al-Ansary, Abdullah F. and Al-Zahrani, Omar S, *"Combating Money Laundering & Terrorism Financing"*, p. 2.

58 Interview with Dr. Abdel Rahman Hadlaq, Riyadh, May 2009. These figures are based on this interview and have changed since that date. They give the reader an idea of the rate of casualties inflicted by terrorists.

THE EMERGENCE OF AL-QAEDA IN SAUDI ARABIA

Osama bin Laden had developed a scheme to destabilize the kingdom and drive a wedge between the Saudi government and the Saudi people and its allies, most notably the United States. In this, he vastly overestimated the extent of the Saudi people's support for him and underestimated the capability of the Saudi government and its friends to deal effectively with him and his organization.

Al-Qaeda was founded by Osama bin Laden, a Saudi of Yemeni origin, whose father, a formally uneducated day laborer, had through uncanny native intelligence, skills, and hard work founded one of the largest and well known construction companies in the kingdom. In the process, he became a multi-billionaire and a friend of the Al-Saud royal family. His son Osama inherited part of the fortune after his father died in a plane crash.

In the 1980s, the American Government was confronted with the task of devising a plan to end the Soviet Union's military occupation of Afghanistan and its support of the puppet government.

Part of this strategy was to exploit the zeal of individual Muslims of all nationalities to defend their religion against atheistic communism. The project included identifying, engaging, training, and equipping these Muslims, and if some of them were zealots and maybe even fanatics, so much the better.[59] Many Saudis volunteered to join the battle, and did so with the lavish approval of their government. At this time, these Muslim recruits were called mujahidin ("fighters on behalf of religion") from the Arabic trilateral root jihad ("to struggle"), the same root from which the term "jihad" is formed. [60] Osama voluntarily joined the American effort and used much of his personal funds to finance his activities developing a large personal following in the process.

According to one report,[61] Al-Qaeda evolved from a group called MAK (Maktab al Khadimat), which the authors translate

---

59   I learned of this plan during my assignment to the American Embassy in Paris from 1980–1982.

60   After Western targets were hit, the term the term mujahidiin was replaced with the word terrorist.

61   Cordesman and Obaid, *Al-Qaeda in Saudi Arabia,*2.

as the "Office of Order" but which may also be translated as the "Office of Services." It was formed by Osama bin Laden and a Palestinian militant named Abdullah Yusif Azzam between the years of 1982 and 1984. The major objective of MAK was to collect funds from charities. According to the same report, the funds were used to channel money from the Middle East and North America to train Islamic militants, many of whom were senior operatives in Afghanistan. Later these funds were used to finance Islamic-related causes in Bosnia, Kosovo, Chechnya, the Philippines, and Indonesia.

One may be forgiven for harboring a hint of suspicion that a connection of sorts may have existed between the MAK and the American project mentioned above.

Together with American logistical and political assistance, the mujahidin effort was successful in defeating the Soviets, and the last Soviet troops left Afghanistan by February 15, 1989. During the withdrawal, 523 Soviets paid with their lives.

Beyond a doubt, Osama bin Laden and his cohorts honed their terrorist skills during this struggle.

In anticipation of the Soviet withdrawal, some of the mujahidin leaders were planning to redirect their efforts to other regions and proceeded to create new organizations. Azzam wanted the MAK to be devoted exclusively to carrying out operations against military targets; bin Laden, on the other hand, wanted to extend terrorist activities to civilian targets as well. Accordingly, Osama bin Laden organized Al-Qaeda in 1988 to include terrorist activities against nonmilitary targets. In 1989, Azzam was killed in a bomb attack, after which many of the MAK personnel joined forces with bin Laden. In 1989, Osama returned to Saudi Arabia but fled to the Sudan in 1991 after his detention in Jidda for arms smuggling, for which he was banned from traveling. At that time, his passport may have also been revoked. In the Sudan, he fleshed out the organization he created in Afghanistan to include membership rosters and committees to oversee terrorist training, target selection, and financing activities.

Although Bin Laden had always intended to overthrow the monarchy in Saudi Arabia, he did not act on that impulse immediately. Instead, he embarked on terrorist activities at home and abroad.

In 1994, the Saudi government froze his assets. On April 09, 1994, it revoked his citizenship. After the assassination attempt against Egyptian president Husni Mubarak, he was expelled from the Sudan. In 1995, he returned to Afghanistan, where the Taliban had come back to power. Among his most spectacular operations were the simultaneous assaults on the World Trade Center in New York and the Pentagon building in Washington, DC, on 9/11/01.

Osama Bin Laden was killed in a CIA operation mounted by Navy seals against his hideout in Abbottabad, Pakistan, on May 2, 2011. After the raid, his body was brought to Afghanistan for identification and then buried at sea in an undisclosed location within twenty-four hours of his death.

THE EMERGENCE OF AL-QAEDA IN THE ARABIAN PENINSULA (AQAP)

AQAP's predecessor, al-Qaeda in Yemen (AQY), came into existence after the escape of twenty-three al-Qaeda members from prison in the Yemeni capital, Sanaa, in February 2006. Several escapees helped establish the group and later identified fellow escapee Nasir al-Wahishi as the group's new amir. The deputy amir was Sa'id al-Shahri, and the military commander was Qasim al-Rimi, all veteran extremist leaders.

AQAP emerged in January 2009, following an announcement that unified Yemeni and Saudi operatives under a common banner. It signaled the group's intention to serve as a hub for regional operations targeting local government and Western interests, both in Yemen and Saudi Arabia. The group is now pursuing a global strategy.

AQAP is based primarily in the tribal areas outside of Sanaa, which, for the most part, remain outside the control of the government.[62] Since 2009 Yemen-based al-Qaeda in

---

62 *"Al-Qa'ida in the Arabian Peninsula,"* The National Counterterrorism Center, Counterterrorism Calendar 2011.

the Arabian Peninsula has orchestrated high-profile attacks and expanded its activities outside of Yemen most notably by sending Nigerian-born Umar Farouk Abdulmutallab to detonate an explosive device aboard a Northwest Airlines flight as it flew over Detroit, Michigan, on December 25, 2009. Had it succeeded it would have been the first attack on the homeland by an al-Qaeda affiliate since September 11. Anwar al-Aulaqi was also a known leader of AQAP. Named a specially designated global terrorist by the United States Government, he was killed in 2011 in an American drone attack.

On December 14, 2009, Secretary of State Hillary Clinton designated Al-Qaeda in the Arabian Peninsula, aka Al-Qaeda in Yemen, as a terrorist organization. Two AQAP leaders, Nasir al-Wahishi and Said Ali al-Shihri, were designated as terrorists.[63]

Nasir al-Wahishi was reportedly killed in a drone attack in northwestern Pakistan on December 28, 2010 when two missiles were fired on a militant camp at the Ghulam Khan sub district of North Waziristan.

Said Al-Shihri was reported killed in an explosion in Yemen, although there has been no confirmation of this.[64]

Al-Qaeda Yemen (AQY) operatives conducted near-simultaneous suicide attacks in September 2006 against separate oil facilities in Yemen, the first large-scale attack by the group. AQY later claimed responsibility for the attack and, in its first Internet statement in November 2006, vowed to conduct further attacks. Al-Qaeda's second-in-command, Ayman Al-Zawahiri, congratulated AQY and encouraged additional attacks in a statement in December 2006.

In early 2008, AQY dramatically increased its operations, carrying out small-arms attacks on foreign tourists and a series of mortar attacks against the Italian embassies in Sana'a, the Presidential Compound, and Yemeni military complexes. In September 2008, the group conducted its largest attack to date, targeting the

---

63   "The Anwar Aulaqi Timeline." http://awlaki.sethhettena.com.

64   Bill Roggio, "AQAP Deputy Emir Said al Shihri Alive." The Long War Journal, February 16, 2011.

embassy in Sana'a, using two vehicle bombs that detonated outside the compound, killing nineteen people, including six terrorists.

"The world cannot succeed in defeating global terrorism without Saudi Arabia's victory over terrorism and extremism on its own soil. We stand with the Saudis in that fight, and this conference is a testament to their commitment- to their dedication to combating terrorism."

Frances Townsend,
White Hoe Homeland Security Advisor,
Counter-Terrorism International Conference, February 7, 2005

**HRH Prince Muhammad bin Naif bin Abdel Aziz,
Minister of Interior**

**HRH Prince Naif bin Abdel Aziz, former
Minister of Interior**

**HRH Prince Ahmed bin Abdel Aziz, former
Minister of Interior**

CHAPTER 6

THE SAUDI ANTITERRORIST PROGRAM[65]

In crafting its counterterrorist policies, the Saudi political and religious establishments cannot escape the reality that many Saudis and other Arabs and Muslims sympathize with some of the anti-Western rhetoric of extremists even as they abhor and eschew their violent methods. The people may understand the need for forbearance and patience in combating terrorism, but they also need concrete actions in response to Western provocations that can be deemed terrorism, for example, the continued building of Israeli settlements on land recognized by the international community to be indisputably Palestinian.

---

65 See Appendix B.

The Saudi leadership has built its counterterrorist strategy so that it meets the most fundamental of Arab-Islamic values in order to gain the trust and support of the masses. Foremost among these are forgiveness and rehabilitation for the penitent and severe punishment for the recalcitrant. It is built on three premises: retribution, the forcible dismantling of terrorist cells, prevention, the elimination of conditions that allow terrorism to flourish, and rehabilitation, the reintegration of former terrorists into society as law-abiding citizens. All of these require consultation (shura) and dialogue between the differing parties with an eye to reconciliation. During his lifetime Ibn Saud practiced shura and consistently exhorted the Saudi and Arab people to engage in it to resolve disputes great and small. He quoted profusely from the Qur'an which encouraged this practice. Saudi Arabia is doing this while simultaneously working with certain members of the international community to resolve regional problems of terrorism, some of which were generated by the West's own policies. [66]

With regard to retribution, the government has mobilized its public security capabilities to arrest, capture, and kill the terrorists locally while working with its foreign counterparts to do the same internationally through the mutual extradition of captured terrorists.

To this end, the Saudi ministry of interior has routinely published several lists of names of Saudi nationals and non-Saudi nationals wanted in the kingdom for terrorist offenses, distributing these lists publicly at home and abroad.

Use of armed force and state of the art technology play essential roles in combating terrorism. Force is used as a first response to quell an ongoing terrorist attack, to dismantle terrorist plots in preemptive operations, and to arrest suspected terrorists. Technology helps to identify and track and capture individual terrorists, to uncover their modus operandi, to thwart plots, and to confiscate money and weapons.

Technology has significantly contributed to the success of rolling up terrorist groups and to the larger goals of the program, namely removing the causes of nefarious behavior and the rehabilitation of its perpetrators. This contrasts sharply with counterterrorist objectives

---

66 Mohyiddin Al-Qabesi, *The Holy Quran & The Sword.* Quoting Ibn Saud, "I also recommend that our people to exchange advice for faith is Advice..." We want shura to combine Sunna with Allah's command in the Quranic Verse.s

of other countries where force and technology are used almost exclusively to capture and execute them or to incarcerate and punish them indefinitely leaving the perpetrators little or no hope that one day they may rebuild their lives by eschewing their violent ways.

With regard to prevention, the Saudi government has enacted new legislation that closely monitors and regulates the collection and distribution of charity-based contributions; governs bank transfers; and limits the amount of money that may be transferred or taken out of the country personally. All these are intended to ensure that these funds are not used to finance terrorist activities. It has used the influence of religion and education to deter the young from embracing violent attitudes and has revised its school curricula to eliminate provocative, anti-Western material.

The third, rehabilitation emphasizes reform rather than retaliation and retribution. It measures success in the numbers of terrorists captured and persuaded to renounce their evil and un-Islamic ways and ultimately released to the custody of their families and re-integrated into Saudi society rather than on a head count of those killed or imprisoned indefinitely.

The strategy of reconciliation and rehabilitation is an integral part of the Saudi counterterrorist policy because compassion and mercy are inherent in Islamic culture and constitute an integral part of Islamic jurisprudence. Because of the concerted, deliberate, and unfortunately successful efforts of several influential anti-Muslim individuals and groups, this statement may come as a surprise. They have convinced the unsuspecting public to associate Islam and Muslims with violence.

The fact of the matter is that the God of Islam is the Compassionate (Al-Rahman). He is the Merciful (Al-Rahim).[67] Saudis, as do Muslims throughout the world, invoke the words "In the name of God, the Merciful and the Compassionate" daily to

---

67 King Fahad's announcement of a month long amnesty: "It also had a practical effect. Al-Qaeda had long accused the Saudi regime of being un-Islamic for cooperating with the US and for not fully implementing Shar'ia law. In the speech announcing the amnesty, King Fahd included a verse from the Qur'an that highlighted the importance of forgiveness in Islam. By demonstrating that the kingdom was governed by the law of God, the government reasserted its religious authority. This maneuver had the effect of undermining the legitimacy of al-Qaeda, which has long used Islam to justify its actions." Cordesman, Al-Qaeda in Saudi Arabia, p.14.

begin a meal, address a public gathering, ward off evil, or even for something as banal as lifting a heavy object. It is with these words that Muslims begin their five daily obligatory prayers.

The rehabilitation programs include re-education in social responsibility, instruction in religion, and re-education in obligations to the nuclear and extended family and to society as a whole. The prospects of economic opportunity and material inducements are held out to them, as well as conjugal visits and visits by other family members. These visits provide comfort and encouragement during their re-education while incarcerated. In brief, a large measure of Saudi counterterrorist policy is based on a delicate balance of compassion that offers the possibility to the repentant of a normal life rather than indefinite incarceration or execution for the incorrigible.

The Saudi government has also endorsed a private initiative of its citizens to engage the terrorists in dialogue and debate. It is called the Al-Sakinah[68] or the Tranquility program; it is manned and operated by native-born Saudi volunteers who are adept in the use of the Internet. They include religious scholars who are experts in the various nuances of Islam and in the art of persuasion and argument, as well as ordinary individuals who are committed to fighting terrorism.

Saudi officials with whom I spoke dismissed the notion that torture is officially condoned and practiced. They pointed out that the high rate of success achieved by other methods obviates the necessity for such extreme measures. Nonetheless, former detainees and human-rights advocates continue to make these allegations.

Instances of torture and abuse have previously been documented in the Saudi prison system.[69] A recent mobile-phone video showing a guard beating a prisoner at al-Ha'ir raised further concerns. As a result, the government has a high desire to portray positive conditions for cooperating suspects. Previous examples of this have

---

68   This word appears in the Qur'an at least three times in its Arabic and Aramaic forms.
See Hannah Kasis. *A New Concordance of the Qur'an.*

69   (State Department Country Reports on Human Rights Practices, 2006. (Al-Sharq al-Awsat, December 15, 2004; Al-Youm, January 5, 2005. See also Boceuk, *"Jailing Jihadis: Saudi Arabia's Special Terrorist Prisons,"* Terrorism Monitor 6, no. 2, January 25, 2008..

included government-sponsored testimonies of suspected terrorists jailed at al-Ha'ir praising the conditions of their incarceration and statements, encouraging others to cooperate with authorities. These measures sought to combat the perceptions of mistreatment and to promote participation in periodic amnesties.

Judging the merits of these mutual recriminations and denials about the use of torture in Saudi Arabia is as difficult to evaluate as are similar charges levied against counterterrorist programs in Western democracies and in non-democratic countries. On the one hand, sovereign nations can conceal their excesses behind their own interpretation of what legally constitutes torture and select from a large menu of plausible denials; on the other hand, the suspected terrorist may embellish or exaggerate his treatment during the period of incarceration in order to demonstrate his courage and dedication to the higher cause or to seek the sympathy of the world or even be awarded financial compensation.

I am inclined to consider all such mutual allegations and denials with a generous dose of skepticism and common sense unless they are fully documented.

Finally, the deliberate, spurious allegations that the Government of Saudi Arabia funds and orchestrates international terrorism as a matter of official policy, that it assisted and abetted the attacks on 9//11, and that its Wahhabi expression of Islam advocates and condones it, are all unsubstantiated.[70] No credible evidence has surfaced to justify these charges, which, if true, would make the United States, Britain, and France and other Western democracies deliberate coconspirators because of their long and close, special relationships and extensive cooperation with the kingdom. The recent announcement that the United States has agreed to sell the Saudis a large number of F-15 aircraft over a period of years at a staggering cost of thirty billion dollars should further dispel this notion.[71]

---

70 Anthony H. Cordesman and Nawaf Obaid. *"Al-Qaeda in Saudi Arabia Asymmetric Threats and Islamist Extremists."* rev. ed. Center for Strategic and International Studies, 2005, 19. "Despite allegations in the media and elsewhere that the Kingdom furnished material support to al-Qaeda, the independent and bipartisan 9/11 Commission formed to investigate the attacks of September 11 concluded that no such support existed."

71 "To Sell Jets to Saudis."Bullfax.com, Market news and Analysis.08/08/2010.

The Saudi success in combating terrorism at home is based on the adherence to the fundamental principle that the family is the backbone of society and that it, not the state, has the primary obligation to ensure the good behavior of the citizenry.

King Abdullah bin Abdel Aziz is the driving force in the kingdom behind the domestic and international antiterrorist campaigns. He is committed to eliminating terrorism there and in the international community. In October 2007 President George Bush authorized Secretary of State Condoleeza Rice to officially designate the kingdom as a reliable ally in the war against terrorism.

At the domestic level, the king has caused laws to be enacted, allocated enormous funds, created the necessary governmental infrastructure and administrative agencies, and appointed strong, capable leaders to ensure that the antiterrorist program has every tool to be effective.

On April 7, 2003 the King Abdul-Aziz Center for National Dialogue was founded. Its objective is to combat extremism and promote moderate culture among all sections of society and consolidate national unity. A national dialogue conference with all sectors of society participating has been held every six months since 2003.

At the international level, the king has personally taken the lead in organizing world meetings to combat terrorism by visiting heads of state in their countries and receiving world leaders in the kingdom to promote international antiterrorist cooperation. These include two visits by President George W. Bush to Saudi Arabia in 2008.

In February 2007, the president of the Russian Federation, Vladimir Putin, made an official visit to Saudi Arabia. At meetings with King Abdullah and other high-ranking Saudi officials, including Crown Prince Sultan bin Abdel Aziz, they discussed a range of issues. During the visit, the king awarded Putin the Order of Abdel Aziz.

In October 2007, the king made a state visit to England where he met with Queen Elizabeth who was quoted as saying, "Britain and Saudi Arabia must work together to fight terrorism that seeks to destroy the way of life of our citizens."

On November 6, 2007, the king visited Pope Benedict at the Vatican. This visit was significant coming as it did after the Pope had earlier quoted a fourteenth century Byzantine emperor who called Islam "evil and inhuman." The pope apologized, saying that the remark was mistakenly interpreted but not before several serious violent outbreaks had occurred against Christians in different parts of the Islamic world.

In November 2009, French president Nicholas Sarkozy had his third meeting with the king in two years during which they discussed Middle East developments at length.

In 2008, the king sponsored a conference at the United Nations, attended by eighty heads of state or a representative to discuss ways of increasing and improving dialogue and cooperation between all the various faiths of the world not just the three Abrahamic religions.

Most recently, the king sponsored the international conference on the "Phenomenon of Takfir" on June 22, 2011 under his royal patronage.[72] This conference was more than a scholarly exercise because, under the Takfir doctrine, extremist-terrorist Islamic leaders justify the killing of Muslims whom they claim have abandoned Islam. It was meant to be the formal refutation by acknowledged world authorities on Islam of arguments used by radical or extremist Islamic scholars to justify their terrorist acts directed against Muslims and non-Muslims alike.

The five objectives of the conference were to: (1) clarify the provisions toward Takfir, (2) explore intellectual and historical roots of the phenomenon of Takfir, (3) state the reasons for the phenomenon of Takfir, ((4) highlight the dangers of the phenomenon of Takfir and its effects, and (5) propose appropriate solutions for the treatment of the phenomenon of Takfir.

This conference underscored the Saudi conviction that combating terrorism is more than just the arrest, imprisonment, and punishment of apprehended terrorists; it is a humanitarian effort as well.

Domestically, King Abdullah has made substantial changes to critical and strategic personnel positions. These include the

---

72 Rafiq Tschannen, "Naif Opens Takfir Conference In Madina", The Muslim Times, September 21, 2011

appointment of his reform-minded son-in-law Prince Faisal bin Abdullah to the influential post of minister of education, replacing the highly conservative former minister Abdallah bin Humaid who had been minister since 2005.[73] Bin Humaid previously occupied the post of secretary general of the Muslim World League, the multi-billion-dollar Saudi operation designed to spread Wahhabism throughout the world. Another critical personnel change was the naming of a reputed moderate, Abdul Aziz bin Humain, to head the omnipresent religious police (Al-Mutawa). That government agency enforces the rigid Wahhabi codes of public dress and morality. Al-Humain replaced Sheikh Ibrahim Al-Ghaith. Saleh bin Humaid, the former head of the Consultative Council, was named to head the country's Supreme Judicial Council, replacing Sheikh Salih Ibn al-Luhaydan, The latter allegedly publicly approved of jihadists killing owners of satellite-television channels in late 2008. In 2004 he allegedly sanctioned the Saudi jihadists to kill Americans in Iraq.

The Grand Ulema' Commission is being re-established with diverse Sunni leaders that will dilute the influence of the hard-core Wahhabis. The king also replaced the cultural minister with Abdel Aziz Khoja, the open-mindel former ambassador to Lebanon, reshuffled the human-rights commission leadership, and created a new position of deputy minister of education for female affairs. He appointed a woman, Nora bint Abdullah al-Fayez, a US-educated former teacher to the post, making her the most senior woman in the Saudi government.[74]

King Abdullah has designated the ministry of interior as the responsible agency for formulating and executing policies of antiterrorism in the kingdom. That ministry is the single most powerful agency in the country. Its influence permeates all sections of the government in one way or another. For example, the Provincial Governments, the Special Investigations for Internal Security,

---

73 According to Saudi human-rights expert Ali Al-Ahmed, president of the Washington-based Institute for Gulf Affairs, "This could be a watershed for Saudi education,". "Prince Faisal is known to be effective and have the king's trust. He is someone capable of overhauling the curriculum." Nina Shea, "New Hope for Reform in Saudi Arabia," *National Review Online*, February 16, 2009.

74 Shea Nina, "New Hope for Reform in Saudi Arabia." February 16, National Review On Line.

the Coast Guard, the Border Police, the General Investigation Department, the Civil Defense, the fire departments, Public Security Sections, Special Investigations, the Passport Department, and the Criminal Investigations all fall directly within its jurisdiction. It also carries out sentences handed down by the courts and is responsible for coordinating with the religious enforcement agency, The Organization for doing Good and Avoiding Evil (Hy'at Al Amr bil Ma'arouf wal Nahi en Al Munkir) and with the religious police (Al-Mutawa).

The overall success of the ministry's multifaceted antiterrorist strategy has commanded the admiration of many nations of the international community. That success is due in large measure to the bold and imaginative efforts of the current and former ministers, their deputies, and the entire professional cadre that staff and administer the multi-faceted program. It is a tribute to them that, having learned from their own past mistakes and from the mistakes of other countries, they crafted an antiterrorist strategy based on retribution, prevention, and rehabilitation that has succeeded in containing terrorism and all but eliminating it in the kingdom, setting examples for other countries to develop similar programs of their own.

The Saudi princes who head this antiterrorist program and the entire cadre of professional colleagues are highly dedicated and skilled. They are strong-willed and firm in their convictions. They are as flexible in dealing with captured terrorists as they were rough and tough in tracking them down. These attributes are characteristic of ministry officials of high and lower ranks involved in public security in general and responsible for implementing the antiterrorist project in particular, an observation based on my contacts with a number of them over many years, well before the outbreak of the terrorist threat. To ensure that they remain up to date on the latest techniques in combating terrorism, most officers are periodically enrolled in advanced programs that are designed to hone their knowledge of and experience in dealing with terrorism.

HRH Prince Naif bin Abdel Aziz Al Saud held the portfolio of this ministry since 1975, until his death in 2012. As Chair of several key national oversight committees, in addition to his ministerial responsibilities, Prince Naif's power and influence extended far beyond the tasks of that particular ministry. His authority and power was further expanded in March 2009, when HRH King Abdullah appointed him Second Deputy prime minister. In October 2011 following the death of his brother, HRH Prince Sultan bin Abdel Aziz, Minister of Defense and Crown Prince, he was named crown prince and retained his position as minister of interior. He was committed to protecting the Saudi system of government and to maintaining its inextricable links to the Wahhabi expression of Islam, for which he made no apologies.

Like powerful officials in other countries that are charged with the heavy burden of safeguarding the public and national security of their nations, Prince Naif had his admirers and detractors.[75] The admirers described him as open-minded and as less ultra-conservative than he was made out to be; his detractors asserted that he was inflexible and unprogressive.[76] What is not disputable is that he worked effectively with and won the respect of his counterparts from other nations in their common fight against terrorism. As guardian of the kingdom's security, he acquitted himself superbly under the most trying domestic and international circumstances.

During his time as minister, he delegated much of the day-to-day responsibilities for running the ministry to his full brother, HRH Prince Ahmed bin Abdel Aziz, who has been the deputy minister since 1975. "His commendable performance in managing the logistics of the kingdom's internal security apparatus is an achievement that has brought kudos from the international community, appeasement from the religious scholar *(Ulema')* and has been applauded by the general populace While he maintained a low profile during his long tenure as deputy, Prince Ahmed enjoyed the respect and confidence of the overriding majority of the Saudi people as much for his reputation as a devout Muslim as for maintaining a low profile and staying out of the public eye".

Upon the death of Prince Naif, King Abdullah appointed Prince Ahmed as Minister of Interior, but after only a few months in office,

---

75   http://en.wikipedia.org/wiki/Naif bin Abdul-Aziz Al Saud.
76   Bill Tierney, "Who is Prince Nayef," the *Weekly Standard* 8, no. 15 (December 23, 2003..

he asked the king to relieve him of this position for personal reasons. The king accepted his request and appointed his nephew, Prince Muhammad, the son of deceased Prince Naif, to replace him.

Prior to his death, Prince Naif had confided overall responsibility for the Saudi antiterrorist program to his son, Prince Muhammad who created the rehabilitation-of-terrorists program.

As Minister of Interior, Prince Muhammad can be expected to meet the exigencies of this sensitive office. Already he is highly respected by Western intelligence agencies for his imaginative techniques in undermining Al-Qaeda's operations to recruit and train radicals to carry out bombing attacks in the kingdom and elsewhere. His magnanimity toward terrorists and his willingness to meet them personally to help them reform their lives can only further his ability to win them over, although his generosity has not always been reciprocated. In August 2009, he narrowly escaped death and serious injury from a suicide attack on his person as he was receiving well-wishers during a reception at his home during the holy month of Ramadan. He had instructed his security detail not to search the guests. Nevertheless, he has not allowed this attempt on his life to derail his commitment to the program of rehabilitation. Rather, it has only strengthened his resolve to pursue these efforts. [77]

The above named officials represent only three of the hundreds of competent and dedicated officials, many of them holding PhDs from Saudi, North American, and West European universities and professional certificates and technical credentials from higher educational institutions elsewhere. They include specialists in law, diplomacy, finance, religion, psychology, sociology, and medicine, among others. I have had the opportunity to speak with many of them over the course of several years and came away with the impression that they are dedicated officials eager to develop and implement an effective anti-terrorist mission.

---

[77] Jonathan Wright, "The End of Saudi Rule." Reuters Dispatch, October 2001. One analyst at the Institute for Advance Strategic and Political studies in Washington, predicted that "only Crown Prince Abdullah would put up a fight if it came to a civil war between the House of Saud and the country's religious fundamentalists. The others have packed their suitcases for Geneva."

The kingdom's antiterrorist program[78] consists of two parts, a Security Strategy and an innovative Advocacy and Advisory Strategy.

The Security Strategy is the intra-agency effort that coordinates the capabilities of all Saudi security forces to track, arrest, capture, disrupt, and otherwise obviate all ongoing and potential terrorist activity. It is a first response effort. Its objective is the immediate protection of public safety. As part of this hard strategy, Saudi Arabia has already arrested thousands of suspects, seized large caches of arms, and extradited suspects from other countries. In this regard, it is not much different than the strategy that most other countries employ domestically. This includes liaison and exchange of information with the security agencies of friendly countries, especially Britain and the United States, and even un-friendly countries with which it shares common enemies. It periodically publishes and distributes internationally several lists of most-wanted Saudi terrorists.[79] It has allowed dozens of former inmates of Guantanamo to return to the kingdom. Some were prosecuted; others were entered in rehabilitation programs.

The Advocacy and Advisory Strategy is the innovative element of the Saudi antiterrorist program. It consists of comprehensive soft measures that are not based on force.[80] This is a two-pronged approach: prevention and treatment. They include (a) a counseling program, (b) a tranquility campaign, (c) a religious-authority campaign, (d) a media campaign, (e) a national solidarity campaign against terrorism, (f) the development of public education, (g) the monitoring of preaching, (h) the review of sponsored publication, (i) national dialogue conventions, (j) control of charities, (k) internet filtering, (l) antiterrorism legislation, and (m) increased international cooperation.

---

78 Unless otherwise indicated, much of the information in this chapter is based on my personal meetings with Dr. Hadlaq, Dr. Abdullah F. Al-Ansary, and with other Saudi officials in Riyadh in May 2009 and on Dr. Al-Ansary's paper, "Combating Extremism," Middle East Policy 15, no. 2 (2008). I have rephrased or quoted verbatim without specific attribution from this paper with his personal permission given on July 14, 2010.

79 See appendix D for names on several lists.

80 See appendix B for official Saudi Ministry of Interior programs.

The Counseling Program (Al-Munasahah) founded by HRH Prince Muhammad bin Naif is intended to wean prisoners already under detention away from their radical ideology through psychological and sociological counseling by engaging them in religious dialogue. It is available mainly to prisoners that have not been directly involved in terrorist acts.

These prisoners, of whom 10 percent are estimated to be hardcore militants and 90 percent to be followers and sympathizers, fall into three categories:

1. Individuals who had actively participated in or abetted terrorist acts.
2. Sympathizers who publicly defended them but did not perpetrate terrorist acts.
3. Persons who passively supported terrorists through noncooperation with the authorities.

Prisoners who have committed terrorist acts or who are under investigation for involvement in terrorist attacks may take part in the counseling program in order to benefit from religious rehabilitation. They may not be released after completing it because they are still subject to the criminal justice system and constitute a threat to national security.

The Counseling Program is administered by the Advisory Committee in the ministry of interior and is composed of four subcommittees: psychosocial, religious, security, and media.

The Psychosocial and Social Subcommittee consists of more than thirty psychologists. They evaluate the prisoner's psychosocial condition in order to determine whether he is mentally fit to engage in dialogue.

The religious committee is composed of more than 160 Muslim clerics, scholars, and university professors who engage the detainees in discussions on a whole range of topics, from the legitimacy of aiding non-Muslims and obeying man-made (as opposed to divine) law to suicide operations, to expelling the foreigners from the Arabian Peninsula, and rights of the People of the Book (Ahl al Kitab).[81]

---

81 Christians and Jews because they share similar revealed scriptures with Muslims.

The Security Subcommittee is tasked with risk assessments (recidivism), making recommendations to release detainees, and monitoring procedures to be followed after their release.

There is a keen awareness of the necessity to measure the extent to which detainees that claim to have renounced their ways may not be truthful. But the general estimation is that the program has been very successful. On April 8, 2007, for example, Muhammad Al-Njimi, a member of the Counseling Program, announced that of 700 detainees released, only nine returned to their previous evil ways and that 1,500 of the 3,200 prisoners in the program have been released. The others have not completed the program.

The Media Subcommittee: Saudi Public TV supports the antiterrorism campaign by broadcasting programs that feature the confessions of terrorist and their repentant testimonies as well as interviews with well-known Saudi scholars who recanted their earlier fatwas and urged terrorist suspects to surrender.

The Tranquility Campaign: The ministry of interior has endorsed an independent internet project called the Tranquility (Al-Sakinah) Campaign. The Ministry of Religious Endowments and Islamic Affairs monitors and defines the policy and activity of this campaign in an advisory role.

.The psycho-social section is composed of psychiatrists and sociologists who study the psychological and social dimensions of the extremist groups.

The monitoring section keeps track of all internet forums, websites, chat rooms, and other venues that circulate information.

The publishing section disseminates fatwas, opinions, advice, and tapes in various electronic news groups.

The Religious Authority Campaign: This committee allows the religious establishment to exercise its legal authority to oversee matters related to religion, morals, and education.

Other efforts promoted by the kingdom include:

The Care Program administered at the Muhammad bin Naif Counseling and Care Center. The persons participating in this program are termed "beneficiaries." The objective is to help them gain self-confidence so that they can find employment and become productive citizens.

The Training Program: This is a confidence-building course to facilitate the beneficiary's social reintegration.

The Health Program: Provides full health care at the center under the supervision of medical specialists.

The Sports Program: Provides organized sports activities that promote closer relations between the beneficiaries and supervisors, who are better able to assess the detainees' behavior and willingness to integrate in society.

The Art Program: Provides beneficiaries with lessons in the art of drawing and painting. A Saudi expert holding a doctorate in this field supervises it.

A National Solidarity Campaign makes the public aware that extremism is contrary to the true values of Islam and the need for toleration and moderation.

A Shielding Campaign: Launched by the Ministry of Religious Endowments and Islamic Affairs, it is preventive in nature; it is intended to safeguard the youth against radical ideology and deviance through sermons, mosque activities, and general education. Its public relations department has issued its first book in its Shielding Series, which included the transcripts of meetings between the then Minister of Interior Naïf bin Abdel Aziz and Saudi imams and preachers.

The Saudis are helping in the war against terror. They have cooperated with us by exchanging information and intelligence with regard to security measures...We should remind the people (Americans) that Saudi Arabia had stripped Osama bin Laden of his citizenship because of his activities...There are several things Saudi Arabia has been doing and we constantly explore with the Saudi leadership new areas of cooperation in the antiterror campaign and other issues.

Colin Powell,
Secretary of State, Asharq Al-Awsat, August 29, 2002.

CHAPTER 7

RETRIBUTION[82]

According to ministry of interior spokesman, Major General Mansour al-Turki, 11,527 Saudis and non-Saudis have been arrested since September 11, 2001. Of this number, 583 individuals, including a number of foreigners, were found not guilty or had served their time. In all, 1,612 have been convicted of terrorism changes; 616 suspects are currently being investigated; and 603 are currently on trial. In addition, the ministry of interior has completed its investigation of hundreds of others whose cases have been passed to prosecutors for retrial procedures. Charges are in preparation against an additional 934 people, and an investigation of 1,931 other suspects is currently in process.[83] The Arabic name

---

82 See Appendix D.

83 Ghaznfar Ali Khan, "Hundreds of Foreigners Behind Bars for Terrorism." *Arab News,* Sunday, Riyadh Daily, vol. XXXVI, no. 144.

for the program is Al-Munasahah. It includes separate programs to combat terrorism (retribution), to treat terrorists (prevention), and to re-integrate them into the larger Saudi society (rehabilitation).

The above figures[84] reflect the tireless efforts of the Saudi Ministry of Interior that formulates, implements, evaluates, and administers the nation's antiterrorist strategy programs and policies.

Public security in the kingdom is still excellent today, although it began to diminish gradually long before the onset of current terrorist activity because of the increase in the number of foreign workers, modernization, expansion of communications and roads and freeways, and the gradual liberalization of Saudi society from what it had been more than a generation ago.

THE COURT OF DIVERGENCE

The Kingdom of Saudi Arabia has established a specialized court linked to the Supreme Court within its judicial system. It operates under the administrative supervision of the supreme council of the judiciary in order to maintain judicial independence. This court began its hearings in December 2008 and has handed down judgments against a large number of defendants convicted of involvement in terrorist activities, including money laundering and the financing of terrorism.

The court adheres to the kingdom's judicial regulations in all cases brought before it; it conducts trials in accordance with the Code of Criminal Procedure. A committee whose members include the minister of justice and the president of the Supreme Council of the Judiciary select the judges from a group specially trained and qualified to deal with terrorist crimes. They do not have exceptional powers. They must adhere to the kingdom's various regulations and procedures, including the Code of Criminal Procedure, in letter and in spirit that are meant to safeguard the rights of defendants and to ensure that they obtain a fair trial.

This court tries its cases in special premises to avoid the mixing of defendants accused of terrorist crimes with those who are

---

84 These figures are necessarily dated because antiterrorists operations are still going on, but they give an idea of the numbers of individuals involved.

involved in commercial or labor-related cases, for example. The separate premises were also necessitated by the security measures needed to guarantee the safety of judges, defendants, witnesses, and other persons involved in these terrorist cases and to ensure that these proceedings unfold smoothly.

These judges have participated in training programs that cover terrorist crimes of money laundering and economic crimes, as well as means of combating them. The main objective was to improve their skills and capabilities and to familiarize themselves with domestic and international programs that are involved in combating these crimes.

The judges are seated in special premises at the general court in Riyadh. They are provided with closed-circuit computer networks linked directly to the criminal departments responsible for the prosecution of terrorist cases at the general court in Riyadh in order to maintain the confidentiality of the defendants' files. Similar trial courts will be located in other main regions of the kingdom, namely Mecca and Jidda, and in the Eastern Province.

In order to ensure transparency and civil control over the conduct of these trials, local human-rights organizations are permitted to attend trials in these specialized courts. The Human Rights Commission has assigned a team consisting of six members of its board to attend these hearings in order to verify that the statutory procedures are observed and that the defendants' rights are protected.

From December 2008 through July 2010, the court indicted at least 1,314 individuals, convicted 323, and sentenced them up to thirty years in prison for money laundering and for terror financing.

SAFEGUARDS FOR DUE PROCESS AND PROTECTION OF CIVIL LIBERTIES[85]

In combating the terrorist threat, the kingdom has taken all measures to protect the rights of the people by maintaining a

85 Abdullah F. Ansary, "Law and Practice of the Kingdom of Saudi Arabia Concerning the Detention and Rehabilitation of Individuals in Terrorism Cases." Paper presented to the Twelfth United Nations Congress on Crime Prevention and Criminal Justice, Salvador, Brazil, April 12–19, 2010.

balance between freedom and the requirements of security. This safeguard not only defers to the law in this respect but also to common sense, given that the people are more inclined to cooperate with authorities if they are convinced that their own rights are protected. A prime element is the concern by the authorities for the welfare of detainees' families that are usually innocent of their family member's misdeeds but who nonetheless may be considered his first victims.

The family of a person detained in a case involving terrorism is informed immediately of his arrest including the reasons for his detention and the location where he is being detained. This is in conformity with Royal Decree No. M/39 of 2001, Article 2, that conforms with international standards that balance the state's need to protect its national security obligations with the human and civil rights of detainees and to ensure transparency, safeguards, and mechanisms of accountability.

Other legal safeguards require that penal punishment may be imposed, whether under Sharia principles or under statutory laws only after the determination of a final verdict when a trial has been conducted in accordance with Sharia principles.

Article 4 also provides for any accused person to have the assistance of a lawyer or representative to defend him during the investigation and trial stages, and for the accused to have his counsel with him during all questioning. On January 11, 2010, the kingdom's Consultative Council approved an amendment to the Law of Criminal Procedure, obliging the court to appoint legal counsel for a defendant without the financial means to hire one.

Article 28 of the Detention and Prison Law (Royal Decree No. M/33) of 1978 prohibits the practice of all forms of torture and any assault on prisoners or detainees in any way; it also outlaws the practice of cruelty, ill-treatment or coercion, seizure of property, violation of personal freedoms, and unlawful imprisonment, banishment, or compulsory residence in a specific location or dwelling. It prescribes penalties for perpetrators that do so. Article 8 of the Statute of the Board of Grievances (Diwan Al-Mazalem), the administrative judiciary system of Saudi Arabia, provides for compensation in the case of abuse of authority.

The Bureau of Investigation and Public Prosecution is responsible for enforcing the above article under the provisions of the Law of Criminal Procedure.

The Kingdom of Saudi Arabia emphasizes that its judicial system, which is rooted in the Islamic Sharia, is consistent with all principal standards for a fair trial, including:

a) Presumption of innocence is maintained until final judgment is handed down.
b) The adjudication of all disputes in accordance with the Islamic Sharia as stipulated in articles 7, 8, and 45 of the Basic Law of Government (1992) and article 26 of the Statutes of the Judiciary (2007).
c) The independence of the judiciary which is subject only to the authority of the Islamic Sharia.
d) Equality before the law as stipulated in Article 47 of the Statute of the Judiciary.
e) Public trials with live testimony.
f) Freedom of defense and the right to be assisted by legal counsel.
g) Conduct of proceedings in an adversarial manner.
h) Presentation of statements of non-Arabic speaking persons through interpreters.
i) Public announcement of the trial verdict.
j) Prompt adjudication of the cases.
k) Confinement of the proceedings to the charges brought in the case.
l) The right to file appeals and objections against judgments.

The defendant must be given access to the file of charges against him in order to view the evidence and a copy of the indictment specifying the charges against him. At the first hearing, the court arraigns the defendant, reads out and explains the charge and requires him to respond to them.

In accordance with the provisions of the Islamic Sharia, the courts will take no account of any confessions obtained through coercion, torture, or cruel, inhumane or degrading treatment.

All hearings or trial must be conducted in public unless the court determines that it would be in the best interests of all parties to conduct the hearings in camera in order to safeguard morality, protect family privacy, or preserve public order on condition that in all cases judgment is pronounced at a public hearing.

TREATMENT OF DETAINEES AND THEIR FAMILIES

The Saudi authorities have severely limited the efforts of terrorist organizations to exploit the economic conditions of detainees' families by providing them with material assistance on an as-needed basis. The authorities have found that this was an effective way to limit the capabilities of recruiting new members.

The steps that the kingdom has taken include:

Weekly meetings with HRH Muhammad bin Naif, the Minister of the Interior, or his representative with families of persons who have been detained or released in terrorism cases. He allocates sufficient time to answer their questions, listen to their problems, and respond to their requests. He also grants requests of individual family members for a private meeting.

The creation of a Coordination Office headed by an expert with a doctorate in psychology and staffed with more than eighteen members with specializations in public relations, psychology, theology, and Islamic education to monitor the cases of detainees and their families who have been released inside or outside the kingdom, as well as the families of terrorists killed in security operations.

Their functions and responsibilities include:

a) Receiving the families of detainees, persons who have been released, and the families of terrorists who have been killed.

b) Informing the families of detainees of the reason for their relatives' detention and the location where they are being held.

c) Scheduling interviews with the minister of interior or his representative and current detainees and/or their families.

d) Providing free travel and housing arrangements for families living outside of Riyadh to meet with HRH Prince Muhammad or his representative.

e) Issuing instructions to grant financial assistance and medical treatment to needy family members inside and outside of the kingdom.

f) Following up solutions to problems of detainees and their families, including marriage, employment, completion of education, and coordinating with the General Investigation Directorate on urgent and important matters.

g) Monitoring and treating special cases to ensure that those who have been released will not revert to their past conduct.

THE RIGHTS OF THE DETAINEES' FAMILIES

The families of detainees have the right to be informed of the legal justification for their family member's detention.

As necessary, the families of detainees may be permitted to visit them outside regular visiting hours.

The detainee may be transferred from his place of detention to a location closer to his family in order to facilitate family visits.

The authorities take into consideration the crime of the detainee and the hardship that his detention may cause in breaking up his family or depriving his parents of the care that he may have provided.

To alleviate the suffering of the family due to the detention of the terrorist, the authorities may provide medical treatment for his wife, his children, his parents, and relatives at a place of their choice in or outside of the kingdom.

Various programs are available to families of detainees, such as monthly family allowances, lump-sum assistance, and settlement of debts to help them lead a life free from want.

The authorities may consider direct requests for employment from family members of detainees in order for them to provide for their families.

THE PERSONAL RIGHTS OF DETAINEES

Detainees may not be arbitrarily fired by their employers or expelled from any institution where they may have been studying, including university, because of their detention. To the contrary, they are encouraged to continue their studies during their incarceration. Provisions are made for them to attend classes and to take exams at the school itself, when feasible, or for reading and other assignments sent to them in a timely fashion.

Marriages of detainees to non-Saudi women are legalized so that their wives can be brought to the kingdom.

Detainees may be permitted to receive conjugal visits under privacy conditions.

THE RIGHTS OF RELEASED DETAINEES

Financial assistance is provided to help them reestablish a law-abiding and stable life and to avoid reverting to their past illegal conduct.

Allowances are paid to them and their families for fixed periods of time until they are able to find suitable employment.

To enable them to marry, they are provided financial assistance, including payment of the dowry and other marriage-related expenses.

THE RIGHTS OF FAMILIES OF KILLED TERRORISTS

The ministry of interior is aware that families of terrorists who have been killed are innocent of the personal conduct of criminal family members. It provides them the following assistance:

94

a) Visits to the family by a committee of specialists to study all aspects of its situation and provide them with any psychological and social support that they may need.

b) Alleviation of the family's suffering, including his wife, children, parents, and relatives through monthly allowances, lump-sum assistance, and payment of their debts to ensure them a decent life.

c) Identification and provision of solutions to pressing problems caused by the acts of the deceased and coordination with the competent authorities to facilitate their solution.

To date the ministry of interior has spent more than 400 million riyals on prisoners convicted of terrorism and their families

CONDITIONS OF DETENTION AND REHABILITATION

There are no secret detention centers in the kingdom. Prisons and places of detention are regulated by law and subject to continuous control and inspection by the Bureau of Investigation and Public Prosecution.[86] The code also provides for unannounced visits to ensure that no person is unlawfully detained.[87]

To protect the human rights of detainees and put the minds of their families at rest, each detention center is equipped with more than 1,500 surveillance cameras to monitor the manner in which the detainees are treated by the supervisory staff. In the event of a complaint submitted by the detainee's family, a review of the video

86 Article 36, Law of Criminal Procedure states: "No person shall be detained or imprisoned except in the places designated for that purpose by law. The administration of any prison or detention center shall not receive any person except pursuant to an order specifying the reasons and period for such imprisonment duly signed by the competent authority. The accused shall not remain in custody following the expiration of the period specified in that order.

87 Article 37, Law of Criminal Procedure. Members of the Bureau of Investigation and Public Prosecution shall, at any time and without regard to official hours, visit the prison and other places of detention...to ensure that no person is unlawfully imprisoned or detained."

recording is made with the detainee's family or representative to determine the accuracy of the complaints.

The bureau can be notified through its official website of any person who is unlawfully imprisoned. Members of the division responsible for the inspection of prisons investigate all complaints. The kingdom's Human Rights Commission and the National Society for Human Rights can also visit public prisons and detention centers as well as centers run by the General Investigation Directorate at any time and without seeking permission from the competent authority in order to ascertain conditions of detention, interview prisoners freely, record their comments, and discuss them with the competent authorities.[88]

Understandably, some sections of Saudi society have indirectly characterized the government's rehabilitation programs as catering and pampering to terrorists. However, the government has held steadfast to its conviction that these programs serve the national interest and it has no intention of discontinuing or diminishing them.

---

88 In my opinion, the Saudi government, or any government for that matter, would be irresponsible if it never detained any suspect secretly for a short period of time. However, unlike other countries where suspects are imprisoned and held indefinitely and their families are not informed of their whereabouts, in Saudi Arabia this is neither good police work nor good public relations. Given the rigidly close ties between members of nuclear families, extended families, and tribal relationships in Saudi Arabia, the government would have no compelling reason to detain any individual for any meaningful length of time without the knowledge of his family because the government needs the family to be part of the solution, not part of the problem. As Doctor Al-Ansary points out in his paper, "Allegations concerning secret detentions are refuted by the social solidarity that characterizes Saudi society. If any such cases existed, they would be rapidly discovered by the public..."Al-Ansary, 10.

I also appreciated the Crown Prince's assurance that Saudi Arabia condemns terror." "He's[Crown Prince] been very strong about condemning those who committed those murders...Right after 9/11, he was one of the strongest voices of condemnation.

President George W. Bush,
Crawford, Texas, April 26 , 2002.

CHAPTER 8

PREVENTION:
HARD AND SOFT MEASURES OF
COMBATING TERRORIST ACTIVITIES

Terrorists depend on funding to conduct their operations, their ability to slip across international borders to carry out their terrorist operations and escape the law, and on lax security at public places, especially at airports, diplomatic missions, and high-profile public places. To restrict the movements of terrorists internationally, Saudi Arabia has signed numerous extradition agreements and accords to share and exchange sensitive information with the United States of America and other countries, including Britain, France, India, Morocco, and Turkey, to name a few.

The antiterrorist cooperation with the United States, as enumerated above, encompasses exchange of critical security information, extradition of wanted individuals, monitoring of money laundering, and mutual cooperation on terrorist issues that go far beyond agreements made with other countries. For example, newly published reports and photos (not officially confirmed by the United States or Saudi Arabia) allege that the two countries have opened a state-of-the-art drone base in the vast Empty Quarter of Saudi Arabia to carry out antiterrorist attacks against operatives of Al-Qaeda in the Arabian Peninsula. American-born Yemeni terrorist Anwar Al-Aulaqi and his son were reputedly killed by a drone launched from this base.[89]

> Britain's antiterrorism cooperation with Saudi Arabia is disrupting and degrading AQAP based in Yemen. Saudi Arabia is a key ally for the Yemeni government in its struggle against AQAP, making Yemen a safer country for its citizens and reducing the threat to the UK and our allies. British-Saudi collaboration has resulted in the foiling of AQAP terrorist attacks, which would have caused substantial destruction and loss of life, including the provision of information to protect British interests. An example of this cooperation was the discovery at East Midlands airport of a "printer bomb" onboard a US-bound flight in October 2010. The initial alert came from the Saudi authorities, who have been quick to provide information to protect British interests on many other occasions.[90]

Significantly, because of its special relationship with Pakistan, the kingdom has accelerated its cooperation with India. "These developments include the deportation of a top Lashkar-e-Taiba (LeT) operative and the detention of a wanted Indian Mujahideen (IM) suspect. After a long period in custody, Saudi authorities deported Syed Zabihuddin Ansari (aka Abu Jundal) to India on

89 Noah Schactman, "Is this secret drone base in Saudi Arabia?" Wired Inside Magazine, February 7, 2013.
90 "UK's relations with Saudi Arabia and Bahrain." www.parliament.uk,, session 2012-2013.

June 22. Ansari is a top-ranking Indian operative in the LeT and one of the key conspirators in the November 2008 Mumbai terrorist attacks. The deportation itself brings a much needed breakthrough in the otherwise slow-paced Mumbai terror-attack investigation."[91]

Not surprisingly, given their extensive cooperation, Morocco's efforts to combat terrorism on its soil greatly reflect the influence of Saudi Arabia. According to a report:

> To counter radical Islamism, Morocco also has exerted control over religious leaders and institutions, created theological councils, supervised and retrained imams, closed unregulated mosques, retrained and rehabilitated some individuals convicted of terror-related crimes to correct their understanding of Islam, and launched radio and television stations and a website to transmit Moroccan religious values of tolerance.[92]

There are unconfirmed reports vigorously denied by the Saudi government that it authorizes its antiterrorists experts to meets discreetly with Israeli antiterrorist officials to discuss ways of combating mutual terrorists threats to their countries. None of these reports have been supported by the slightest evidence, but even if true, they would represent the normal behavior of two common enemies beset by the same but more dangerous enemy.

The Saudi program directed at preventing potential terrorist acts is based on four major objectives, through the imposition of rigid controls on:

(1) Financial institutions, transfer of money, enforcement of strict procedures that govern institutions, public and private, that collect money for the poor and needy.

(2) Increased supervision and monitoring of religious activity to ensure that religion is not used as a tool to deliberately or inadvertently enhance terrorist activities.

---

91   The Jamestown Foundation, "A Challenge to Pakistan." *Terrorism Monitor* 10, no. 15, July 26, 2012

92   Alexis Ashrieff, "Morocco: Current Issues." Congressional Research Service, June 20, 2012.

(3) The review of current curriculum and books used at educational institutions to ensure that they are free from radical material.

(4) The institution of new educational programs aimed specifically at young students, male and female alike.

In compliance with UN resolution 1373, Saudi Arabia established a Permanent Counter-Terrorism Committee (PCTC) comprised of experts, consultants, and specialists from the following agencies: Ministry of Interior, Ministry of Foreign Affairs; General Intelligence Agency, and the Saudi Monetary Agency. These agencies are charged with: 1) taking appropriate action on requests received from foreign countries with regard to combating terrorism and financing and (2) preparing reports on initiatives taken by Saudi Arabia in respect to combating terrorism for submission to the UN Council Committees in according with resolutions 1371, 1390, 1642, and other relevant resolutions; identifying issues that require the kingdom to take legislative and executive procedures and providing appropriate recommendations.

These tasks include studying all issues submitted to the committee that are related to combating terrorism, studying reports submitted by the PCTC, and making suggestions and recommendations regarding procedures that should be taken in matters concerning the combating of terrorism in order to take necessary measures.

The Empowering of the PCTC to perform any other tasks concerning combating terrorism.

FINANCIAL
COMBATING MONEY LAUNDERING AND FINANCING OF TERRORISM
AT THE INTERNATIONAL LEVEL [93]

To cut off terrorist funding, the Kingdom of Saudi Arabia has enacted a number of fiscal regulations that limit terrorists' capability to

93 Abdullah F. Ansary and Omar S. Al-Zahrani. "Combating Money Laundering and Terrorism Financing: The Law and Practice of the Kingdom of Saudi Arabia." unpublished paper, Salvador, Brazil, April 12–19, 2010, with the permission of Dr. Al-Ansary.

amass funds both at the domestic level and at the international level in cooperation with other countries. The government put tight controls on the transfer of money, both domestically and internationally and charged the Saudi embassies to oversee part of this responsibility. In late 2005, the government enacted stricter regulations on the cross-border movement of money and precious metals. Money and gold valued in excess of $16,000 must be declared upon entry and exit from the country. [94]

The Saudi government has embarked on a sophisticated plan to cut off funding for the terrorists domestically and in cooperation with the international community. This has been very successful for the most part, but because of the large number of Saudis holding substantial bank accounts abroad, it has not stopped all funds from reaching terrorists, deliberately or inadvertently, through charitable institutions or by personal donations.

To combat illegal funding to extremist groups, and to ensure that charitable donations are actually used for purposes for which they were intended, the government has issued numerous decrees and has created new institutions to monitor Islamic charities. For example, one of the ways that Al-Qaida raised money was to put collection boxes bearing the names of fictitious charities in mosques, ostensibly to appeal for money to donate to the needy so that they could purchase lambs for the Feast of the Sacrifice Eid (Al-Adha) at the conclusion of the Pilgrimage (Hajj). To circumvent this, the Saudis removed all collection boxes from houses of worship and, as an alternative, created a program whereby donors could buy a coupon from the government for the price of the lamb, and it would then arrange for the lamb to be purchased and given to a poor or needy family.

> The Saudi government and the United States have jointly designated several organizations as financiers of terrorism under United Nations Security Council Resolution 1267, including: the Bosnia based Vazir and the Liechtenstein-based Hochburg AG; four branch offices of the Al-Haramain Foundation (Kenya, Tanzania,

---

94   http://www.state.gov/s/ct/rls/crt/2006/82733.htm

Pakistan and Indonesia); and, five additional branch offices of Al-Haramain, an organization which is now dissolved.[95]

Saudi Arabia has implemented all relevant Security Council Resolutions concerning the combating of terrorism and its financing, including resolutions regarding the freezing of funds and financial assets belonging to persons and entities listed in the consolidated List of the Sanction Committee of the Security Council, in particular, Security Council Resolutions 1373 (2001), 1368 (2001), and 1455 (2003); Resolutions Regarding Threats to International Peace and Security Caused by Terrorist Acts: 1390 (2002), regarding the situation in Afghanistan; (1456) regarding Combating Terrorism.

In implementing these specific resolutions, the kingdom has frozen the funds and financial assets belonging to the Taliban in accordance with resolution 1267 (1999) and those belonging to persons named in lists of resolution 1333 (2000). In 1994, it was among the first countries to freeze the funds and financial assets of Osama bin Laden and those associated with him.

Saudi Arabia has established contact points to coordinate its efforts with international organizations, associations, and other countries to combat the financing of terrorism through the ministry of foreign affairs and the Saudi Permanent Delegation to the United Nations.

Saudi Arabia hosted the first Regional Asian conference in the Middle East in cooperation with the executive law agencies and banking establishments. It was held from January 28–30, 2002 at the banking Institute of the Saudi Arabian Monetary Agency in cooperation with the ministry of interior.

In 2004, a global conference was held at Al Imam Mohammad Bin Sa'ud Islamic University to discuss issues of terrorism violence and extremism.

Saudi Arabia was an active participant in the meetings of the Group of Twenty (G-20) and implemented the G-20 Action Plan

---

95 "The Kingdom of Saudi Arabia Initiatives and Actions to Combat Terrorism." Royal Embasssy of Saudi Arabia, Information Office, November 2012.

for Terrorist Financing. It is a member of the Gulf Cooperation Council (GCC), which is a full member of the Financial Action Task Force (FATF), as well as a founding member of the Middle East-North Africa Financial Action Task Force (MENA-FATF). This group was created in November 2004 with the purpose of promoting and implementing international anti-money laundering, combating terrorist financing, and adopting the FATF 40-+9 recommendations on anti-money laundering and combating terrorist financing.

In September 2003, Saudi Arabia completed the Mutual Evaluation by a team of FATF assessors based on the 30+8 FATF recommendations and was one of the first countries evaluated under this new methodology. The evaluation discussed in February 2004 at the plenary meeting in Paris was highly positive. Saudi Arabia also cooperated with the FATF to hold the first conference outside of its headquarters in 1994 at the banking Institute in Riyadh.

The kingdom concurred with the International Monetary Fund (IMF) on implementing the Financial Sector Assessment Program (FSAP) in Saudi Arabia during the first quarter of 2004, which included the evaluation of the efforts of Saudi Arabia in combating financing of terrorism and money laundering.

Saudi Arabia has organized and hosted several international events with regard to combating terrorism. These included:

The International Conference in Combating Terrorism, which was held in Riyadh from August 5–8, 2005, during which important recommendations were made regarding the relation between terrorism and money laundering and arms and drug trafficking. This conference concluded its sessions by making the following recommendation to the participating countries:

a) To fully implement the provisions of the existing Anti-Money Laundering/Countering the Financing of Terrorism (AML/CFT), in particular the FATF 40+9 and the recommendations of the relevant United Nations Conventions and the Security Council Resolutions;

b) To strengthen the efforts of the IMF and World Bank in AML/CFT;

c) Encouraged countries not subject to mutual evaluation by FATF or FATF style regional bodies (FSRBs) to volunteer for assessment by the International Monetary Fund and World Bank;

d) Encouraged all countries to develop Financial Intelligence Units (FI) that meet the criterion of Egmont Group Definitions and Standards and to have them join the Egmont Group to share their experience, expertise and operational information; and [96]

e) Proposed the establishment of an International Counter Terrorism Program under the auspices of the UN that is still under consideration.

THE ROLE OF THE SAUDI ARABIAN MONETARY AGENCY (SAMA)

The SAMA has been in the vanguard of controlling funds that could possibly be used to finance terrorist activities. These include the creation of special programs to train bank employees, members of the Bureau of Investigation and Public Prosecution, of Saudi Customs, and of other government authorities. It is holding training programs in cooperation with Naif Arab University for Security Sciences and the King Fahd Security College, and Training Institute of the Department of Public Security. All of these training programs were prepared by experts of SAMA in the fields of money laundering and terrorism financing. SAMA also issued a number of other regulations in support of its efforts to combat money laundering, terrorist financing, and other financial crime activities. As early as 1990, SAMA issued the Charitable Institutions and Associations By-Laws with which all domestic charities had to comply in order to ensure that contributions were actually used for charitable purposes.

---

96 The Egmont Group was formed in Belgium in 1995 to monitor suspicious financial activity, such as money laundering and funding for terrorists. It took its name from the Egmont Palace in Brussels, where the first meeting convened.

In 1991, it issued the Operational Rules that governed the By-Laws that required any activity involving raising donations and receiving charitable contributions to be registered at the ministry for social affairs. It also empowered the minister to disband any charitable group that deviated from its objectives, or that seriously violated its charter, or that used funds for purposes other than those allowed, or if its activities infringed upon the public manners or existing customs in the kingdom or in any way disturbed the public order.

Saudi Arabia implemented the forty recommendations for combating money laundering issued by the FATF in 1990, as well as the Task Force's nine recommendations concerning the combating of terrorism financing.

In November 1995, SAMA issued its first set of guidelines relating to anti-money laundering to all banks operating in the kingdom based on the forty recommendations of the FATF. SAMA further enhanced these guidelines by issuing a more extensive set of requirement in its rules governing Anti-Money Laundering & Combating Terrorism financing in May 2003.

In July 1996, SAMA issued Guidelines for Banks in Saudi Arabia for organizing audit committees.

In May 2002, SAMA issued its first set of Rules Governing Opening of Bank Accounts and General Operational Guidelines. In addition to consolidating all previous SAMA circulars on the subject, these rules provided new requirements that facilitated the implementation of and conformity with the best international banking practices in accordance with the Basel committee principles. And these guidelines were subsequently updated in 2003, 2007, and 2008.

In 2003, Saudi Arabia enacted the Anti–Money-Laundering Law that criminalized terrorism financing and provided for severe punishments for its infractions including incarceration, the imposition of fines, and the confiscation of funds and proceeds of those found guilty. To combat money laundering through drug trafficking, Saudi Arabia enacted the Law on Combating Narcotics and Psychotropic Substances in 2003. This law provided for Saudi Arabia to cooperate with other states in the area to apply punishment, among the most severe in the world, including capital punishment, for convicted drug smugglers and dealers. In 2004, Saudi Arabia established by royal decree a charity foundation named The Saudi National Commission for Foreign Relief and Charity Work Abroad and designated it as the sole Saudi body licensed to perform charity activities abroad. All other charitable entities were banned from any charity activities abroad including donations or financial aid except through the aforesaid Commission. It also provided that any person or entity in violation of these terms would be subject to prosecution.

In April 2005, it issued qualification requirements for appointment to senior positions to banks.

In April 2008, it issued the Guidelines for Combating Embezzlement and Fraudulent transactions. Other relevant SAMA regulatory circulars issued on different dates included the prohibition of nonresidents of the kingdom from opening of bank accounts without prior approval from SAMA and subject to justification.

Administrative and Organizational Units

SAMA established an anti-money-laundering unit staffed with highly trained and qualified employees. Similar units were established at the ministry of justice and the ministry of commerce and industry.

SAMA also established a Permanent Anti-Money Laundering Committee with representatives from seven relevant government ministries and agencies that deal with money laundering.

A Financial Investigations Unit (SAFIU) was established in 2002 at the ministry of interior to deal with money laundering and terrorism-financing cases and coordinating with the money laundering unit of SAMA. The SAFIU joined the Egmont Group in 2009.

Each bank or money exchanger operating in Saudi Arabia must establish a Money Laundering Control Unit or appoint a designated compliance officer with the bank or money exchanger responsible for internal reporting and informing SAFIU and SAMA when money laundering or terrorist financing activities are suspected.

Saudi banks have been directed to pay special attention to money laundering operations and report any information regarding suspicious operations and fraud to the various committees in these banks, operations, managers, in order to exchange information and work together.

Saudi laws and regulations require that persons leaving or entering the kingdom who have more than SR 60,000 or its equivalent must complete a cash declaration form that is to be presented to Saudi customs. Failure to comply is a punishable offense.

The coordination and cooperation and exchange of information with other states regarding the combating of terrorist and its financing have been improved.

The promotion and support of specialized security studies and research in the field of combating the financing of terrorism.

THE HARAMIN FOUNDATION

Saudi Arabia and the United States have jointly designated certain Islamic charities as financiers of terrorism and have blocked their accounts. Both countries have listed nine branches of the Al-Haramain Islamic Foundation as terrorist financiers under the 1999 United Nations Security Council Resolution 1267.[97]

On February 1, 2004, US Treasury's Office of Foreign Assets Control (OFAC) added Al Haramain charities in six countries to its list of Specially Designated Global Terrorists (SDGT). Those based in Oregon and Saudi Arabia were not on the list. Then on February 18, 2004, federal law-enforcement agents, warrant in hand, searched the office of Al-Haramain Islamic Foundation, Oregon, (AHIF-OR) as part of an investigation into financial crimes. On February 19, 2004 the (OFAC) froze the assets of (AHIF-OR) and issued a press release announcing the freeze but did not have a court order

---

97   http://www.saudiembassy.net/files/PDF/Reports/Saudi—chronology-08.pdf

authorizing it. This started a long legal battle that worked its way through the courts over whether AHIF-OR was a cover charity that was funding terrorist organizations. The question was settled by the Ninth Court of Appeals on September 23, 2011 that upheld a lower court decision that declared that the government's seizure of AHIF-OR assets and funds was unconstitutional and amounted to unlawful confiscation of property under the Fourth Amendment. It rejected the government's contention that Al-Haramain was a terrorist organization under the meaning of US law and, therefore, the seizure was necessary in order to protect the country's national security.

EDUCATIONAL REFORM THE CURRICULUM

For years the Saudi government had been urged by some of its own educational experts to revise some of the curricula in the schools, including but not limited to social and religious instruction in the lower grades and in the technical/scientific curriculum at universities. Their recommendation was based on the need to prepare Saudi students to compete more successfully with foreign students at the international level. However, not much was done to carry out these reforms due to the objections and opposition of a large body of conservative local public opinion that had been persuaded that these reforms were anti-Islamic and, therefore, against Saudi values. The extremists and the terrorists exploited and promoted this belief as they too accused the Saudi government of contaminating much of Saudi-Islamic culture and society by increased Westernization.

In the wake of 9/11, in which fifteen of the nineteen culprits were allegedly Saudis, the US government prevailed on some Middle East governments, including the Saudi government, to review and to reform their school curricula with regard to teachings that were said to justify the killing of non-Muslims and even some Muslims who were not of the Wahhabi persuasion.

In 2003, after Saudi terrorists targeted Saudi Government buildings and the residences of expatriates causing considerable casualties and destruction, the Saudis, themselves, were moved to look more closely at the undergraduate curricula and to implement recommended changes.

The ministry of education conducted an audit of school textbooks and curricula to ensure that teachers do not advocate intolerance and extremism. While most of the material found in Saudi textbooks is carefully selected, the ministry found it necessary to correct the conduct of some teachers who substitute other books that carry radical views. With this in mind the ministry is providing special training programs for men and women teachers of Islamic studies to promote religious tolerance.

In 2003, a study was undertaken by former Saudi judge Sheikh Abdel Aziz Al-Qassem and Saudi journalist Ibrahim Al-Sakran of three important elements of the curricula, namely the traditions of the prophet (hadith), religious law and ritual (al-fikh) and matters of religious belief (al-tawhid). This study was presented at the Second Forum for National Dialogue that met in Saudi Arabia in late December 2003 under the patronage of then Crown Prince Abdullah bin Abdel Aziz and published early the following year. It found that the curriculum "encourages violence toward others and misguides the pupils into believing that in order to safeguard their own religion they must violently repress and even physically eliminate the other." [98]

On February 12, 2007, the Council of Ministers approved a six-year $2.3 billion project to develop Saudi Arabia's public education. It includes upgrading curricula and improving the educational environment and teacher training.

A major problem in revising the curricula is the teachers, themselves, many of whom are not convinced that the government is really serious about change in education and is only responding to pressure from the West. These teachers ignore the fact that revising the curriculum also speaks to the need to train the

---

98   Nina Shea, "This is a Saudi Textbook:Saudi Arabia's Curriculum of Intolerance" with excerpts from the Saudi Ministry of Education Textbooks for Religious Studies." *Center for Religious Tolerance, 2006,*" The Washington Post, May 21, 2006.   Shea argues that the textbooks were still replete with prejudices against non-Islamic religions, including non-Wahhabi forms of Islam, from first to the twelfth grades in Saudi schools.

younger generation to meet the demands of higher standards of competition in the developing workforce. It is not only the course content that requires serious revision but also the teaching method of rote learning and where the instructors assign exercises that are useless. For example, one task for an eighth-grade class was "to discuss the problem of staying up late, its causes, effects, and cure." One young Saudi complained that the curriculum and the teaching methodology were not preparing him to compete in the job market.[99]

According to Naif Al-Roumy, who heads a corporation charged with reforming the Saudi education system, ten thousand teachers have already been retrained to work in dozens of model schools around the country, and eventually the entire teaching force of 500,000 will be retrained.[100]

Prince Faisal bin Abdullah, the son-in-law of the king, was appointed minister of education in 2009. A known reformist, he is determined to change the educational system after several slow starts, and to work to persuade the religious conservatives who oppose it, "that the reforms are not incompatible with Islamic teachings."[101] Since taking office, he has launched dialogue workshops with teachers, parents, students, and clerics to explain the plans. "Resistance to change happens when people do not understand what we are doing," Faisal al-Muammar, deputy education minister, told the Financial Times.[102] He envisions an overhaul of education into a kind of holding company, like Sabic or Maaden, the kingdom's petrochemical and mining companies.

"But the Prince faces an uphill battle. After a meeting between clerics and Prince Faisal, Sheikh Yousef Al-Ahmed, a radical cleric, threatened to persuade families to sue the minister, accusing him of overseeing a project to "corrupt female students and promote mingling of sexes."[103]

---

99 Crossroads Arabia "Education Reform: In Process." *The New York Times*, February 10, 2011.

100 Kelley McEvers, "Changing the ways Saudis Learn: Angry Teachers and Empty Libraries." *Slate*, September 9, 2009.

101   100 Shea, Op. cit.

102   Abeer Allam, "Saudi Education Reforms Face Resistance."*Financial Times,* April 25, 2011.

103   Ibid.

RELIGIOUS PRONOUNCEMENTS AND DECISIONS ON TERRORISM[104]

Several Saudi religious scholars have founded or acted as cofounders of Islamic counseling programs in Britain. The fruits of this effort were unveiled in an important grassroots effort directed against radicalization in the UK. The Radical Middle Way Program is an initiative aimed at articulating a mainstream understanding of Islam that is dynamic and relevant especially to young British Muslims.

The Ministry of Islamic Affairs has dismissed 353 imams, preachers, and muezzins (those who call to prayer) for their extreme views and placed 1,367 on suspension. The latter were ordered to join an enlightenment program over several years. It has also instituted a program to impose electronic monitoring of all mosques in the country using the Geographic Information Systems (GIS). This allows the ministry to monitor day-to-day activities in any mosque, including prayers and ceremonies, with great accuracy.

Between 1996 and 2006, the Council of Senior Ulema', the highest institution in the official religious establishment of Saudi Arabia, stressed that acts of subversion, bombing, killing, and destruction of property are serious crimes that require punishment in accordance with Islamic Law. In June 2004, it issued a fatwa stating that acts of terrorism disrupt the security of the country, shed innocent blood, destroy property, and terrorize people. It called upon the people to be vigilant and inform the authorities of any information they may have regarding individuals who are planning to carry out terrorist acts.

At its sixteenth session held in January 2002, the Islamic Fiqh Council of the Muslim World League in Mecca stressed the fact that terrorism has absolutely no connection to Islam; the Islamic Summit Conference held in December 2005 condemned terrorism in all of its forms and stated the need to criminalize all terrorist practices including those that provide financial support.

---

104   See Appendix C.,

On October 1, 2007, Sheikh Abd- Al-Aziz Al Al-Sheikh, the Saudi Mufti, issued a fatwa prohibiting Saudi youth from traveling abroad to engage in jihad without authorization by the ruler.

The Council of Senior Ulema' has launched an official website for fatwas. It is intended to provide quick access to fatwas issued by authorized scholars. The move is intended to ensure that authorized fatwas are readily available to the public in order to avoid confusion with those issued by unqualified scholars.

The Saudi authorities have recognized that some radical clerics in the kingdom have abused their rights under freedom of religion and expression to spread religious views that conflict with Islamic doctrine in general and specifically with the Wahabbi expression that prevails in the kingdom. Some preachers, imams, religious scholars (ulema'), and muezzin, among others were found to be publicly promoting, encouraging, and even advocating acts of terrorism against foreigners and privately condemning the Saudi regime for its cooperation with the West.

The religious establishment in the kingdom is a separate autonomous body within the Saudi government. The authorities in the domain of religion alone and not the political authorities decide questions of faith and morals, and issue official edicts (fatwas) on questions of religious legitimacy that are binding on all citizens without exception. There exists in Islam a compendium of Islamic rulings (fatwa) that have been issued over the past 1,400 years and used as precedents and guidelines for Muslims throughout the world whether they live in predominantly Islamic or non-Islamic countries. They govern virtually every aspect of life, from birth to marriage. However, in cases where no precedents exist or where misinterpretations of established precedents can mislead the Islamic community, the religious body of scholars (ulema') decides the issue through consensus. Some of their decrees are accepted in other countries as guidelines or in totality as definitive.

Among topics which have been challenged most recently by the Islamist practitioners of terrorism are the concepts of terror (irhab) and striving (jihad). For many centuries their meanings were established by fatwas as to what they meant and when they could be properly exercised. However, recently some radical Islamic scholars out of the mainstream have pronounced their own interpretations on these concepts which contradict traditional Islamic practices to justify their own terrorist activities or the activities of others and to recruit adherents to their cause.

Muslims at home and abroad have raised funds under guise of charitable donations that were subsequently used, deliberately or inadvertently, to finance terrorist activities. As a result, on March 23, 2010, HRH King Abdullah instructed the Senior Clerics Council and of the Standing Committee for Fatwa in Saudi Arabia to issue a religious ruling on the funding of terrorism.

Subsequently the Mufti of Saudi Arabia, Abdel Aziz bin Abdullah bin Muhammad Al Al-Sheikh, informed the king that in response to this instruction the Senior Clerics Council met in extraordinary session and issued ruling No. 239 of April 12, 2010, that "determined that the funding and planning of terror are forbidden, and are punishable according to religious law, whether (the act in question is) providing funds, collecting funds, or taking part in these activities, in any way. The Council emphasizes that the prohibition on funding terror does not apply to support for charity programs providing livelihood, care or education for the poor..."[105]

International reaction to the fatwa has been generally positive, but there has been some criticism.

Daoud Al-Shiryan, deputy secretary-general of Al-Arabiya TV praised the Senior Clerics Council for clearly condemning terrorism while many other clerics failed to do so. Sheikh Yousef Al-Qaradhawi, head of the International Union of Muslim Scholars, also praised the decision.

Army General David H. Petraeus, former chief of Central Command "lauded the Council of Senior Scholars in Saudi Arabia's recent issuance of a fatwa that, for the first time, specifically condemns and outlaws the financing of terrorism as a violation of Islamic law."[106]

---

105   The Middle East Media Research Institute, May 10, 2010. Special Dispatch. See appendix for full English text of Fatwa.

106   Donna Miles, American Forces Press Service, United States Central Command, "Petraeus Praises Saudi fatwa condemning terror financing." Washington, DC, May 22, 2010.

Rejecting the reaction of some writers that approved the fatwa but felt that it should have been issued much earlier, the Saudi Mufti replied that the issue was weighty and required careful consideration. He said the council would send its conclusions to other legal authorities around the world.[107]

According to the *Saudi Daily* published in Riyadh, Saudi Arabia intends to use the fatwa as a legal basis for fighting domestic terrorism and also intends to promote international laws against the funding of terrorism and to submit initiatives on the matter at international forums.[108]

On January 29, 2002, Dr. Abdullah al-Mutlaq, a member of the Senior Scholars Council and of the Standing Committee for Fatwa in Saudi Arabia, spoke at King Faisal Hall for Conferences under the topic of "Terrorism and Islam's Position Regarding It."[109] According to Dr.Al-Mutlaq, the concepts of terrorism can best be conveyed in Arabic by the term "irhab," meaning "to dread," "be frightened," and "be horrified." However, Islamic Law has not defined it as idiomatically as it is defined nowadays. He pointed out that "it was mentioned in the Qur'an as well as in the traditions of the Prophet...in its lexical meaning, not as arbitrarily defined and used at the present time." He mentions that scholastic and legal bodies, as well the official definitions of countries throughout the world, differ on the definition and define it to suit their own self-interests. His preference is that devised by the ministers of interior of the Arab World, which condemned terrorism "regardless of the place or the perpetrators, with the exception of violence against legitimate opposition to foreign occupation". A four-day conference of religious scholars and experts in Saudi Arabia in April 2010 ended with a similar declaration. But it also recommended the adoption of a definition of terrorism as agreed upon by a meeting of Arab ministers a month earlier, a definition that "emphasized the need

---

107   Ibid.

108   Rantburg.   June   15,   2010,   http://www.rantburg.com/poparticle. php?D=2010-06-15&ID=298888.

109   Abdullah Al-Mutlaq,."Terrorists are Neither Heroes nor Martyrs but Criminals and Deserve the Hirabah Punishment." Original Arabic and official English translation in the possession of the author.

to differentiate between terrorism and the legitimate struggle of people against occupation[110]."

He asserts that while the different definitions of terrorism found in the literature differ greatly, they all agree on three of its characteristics: (1) it is an illegal use of violence; (2) it brings about public horror; and (3) its aims are political. The Qur'an, he says, describes it as corruption on earth (fasadu fil-ardh), prohibits it, and punishes its perpetrators with severe punishment in this world and in the next.

This type of terror excludes common crimes, such as robbery and homicide. The latter crimes are restricted to a limited number of persons in a specific context, while terrorism uses "exploding and setting fire to public properties" meant to terrify the public or covert acts, such as the sale of illegal arms and spreading of narcotics aimed at subverting public security and morality. This is strictly forbidden in Islam, according to many citations in the hadith.[111]

Al-Mutlaq points out that terrorism exists in Western and Eastern countries and that it is not limited to a specific religion, but he does not consider national resistance as terrorism because it is the exercise of a fundamental human right to remove injustice and to achieve and maintain self-determination, which is specifically approved in the Qur'an. However, he does not include in this category Nazi and fascist groups and others such as the Red Brigades, Direct Action, and the Tupamaros.[112]

Al-Mutlaq said that Islam has prescribed five ways to protect against terrorism.

First, rulers and leaders must be just, if not God will punish them on the Day of Judgment. Many practitioners of terrorism justify their activity because they claim that they have been treated unfairly.

Second, those in power must properly educate the people, because misunderstanding is a cause of some terrorism. For

---

110   "Almost Ten years after 9/11, UN Still Grappling to Define Terrorism." CNS New. com, April 21, 2011.

111   Compilations of sayings of the Prophet Mohammed compiled by renown Hadith authority, Muslim.

112   Sura 39.

example, they read the Qur'an but misinterpret it, and that leads them to implementing its exhortations incorrectly.

Third, God commands that the people must obey their Muslim rulers. He prohibited rebellion against them unless they demonstrably act against the revelations in the Qur'an. Rebellion is not permissible, even if the ruler commits grievances, because it brings greater injustices and harm to the people than his misdeeds. Thus, God has ordered the people to be patient and the religious scholars to intervene with the ruler on their behalf but not to break the ranks of Muslim unity.

Fourth, Islam's constitution, the Qur'an and the Traditions of the Prophet (hadith), mention in different places that Islam is the religion of mercy and of doing good, and that is manifestly the opposite of terrorism.

Fifth, God has prohibited any action or activity that may support or spread terrorism, such as bestowing praise upon criminals and justifying crimes as being legal and calling them heroes and martyrs. This is contrary to what God, Himself, has ordered, namely to do good and avoid evil.

Islam's history has many examples of those righteous leaders who worked hard to convince those who have gone astray to return to the path of good sense and to the straight path and to avoid fighting brother Muslims. They discussed with these dissenters their mutual differences and ultimately some of them changed their minds.

The exclusive use of force to deal with deviant behavior is much less effective than using the mind. Force alone creates more deviant ideas that will turn against the existing regime. Thus, the mind should first be used to combat deviant behavior, and only when that proves ineffective should force be used.

In conclusion, then, one of the best ways to prevent terrorism as established under Islamic principles is to dialogue with your opponents, listen to what they have to say and point out the truth to them. God has allowed this with nonbelievers as well as with believers.

For the recalcitrant who terrorize kill, and threaten the innocent and for those who destroys their security, God has decreed the

Hirabah punishment if he rejects dialogue and persists in his deviant ways. Thus, those who murder and take property will be crucified and killed; those who take property but do not murder, his hands and feet will be cut from opposite sides; and those who have not killed or taken property will be exiled from the land. The majority of Muslims scholars believe that these punishments must be carried out exactly in the way mentioned. However, Imam Malik of Medina believed that the ruler can choose among these punishments in whatever way he sees fit. Al-Mutlaq appears to agree with Imam Malik that the ruler has the discretion to apply whatever punishment he chooses.[113]

The prophet himself enforced this kind of worldly punishment and, as severe as it seems, the punishment rendered on the Day of Judgment for these same crimes will be even more severe and longer lasting.

THE DIFFERENCE BETWEEN JIHAD AND TERRORISM

Dr. Al-Mutlaq rejected the idea that Islam condones terrorism, as some people have claimed, citing various verses from the Qur'an, particularly Anfal: 60. He maintained that this verse must be read in its linguistic not idiomatic usage, namely in the context of the military doctrine of deterrence. In that verse God ordered the Muslims to prepare themselves militarily against enemies that may want to do them harm. When the enemies know that Muslims have the power to fight back, they will not harm the Muslims. And he gives the example of some countries that were not attacked because their enemies knew that they had the capacity for nuclear deterrence

Jihad, a doctrine that Islam upholds, differs from terrorism as the word is used today in different ways.

First, jihad exists in order to support the call to God (Al-Da'wah), which is primarily based on persuading through dialogue. It is intended to restore justice, help the oppressed, and place humanity

---

113   Al-Mutlaq, op. cit. p. 11.

on the righteous path. God allowed the Muslims to fight when they were wronged, but He did not permit monasteries, churches, synagogues, mosques, and other places where God is worshipped to be pulled down. [114]

Second, jihad is authorized in order to safeguard against intrigue that intends to keep truth away from the people and to lead them astray from God's path. It may not be used to dominate one race over the other. God allows fighting aggressors but not to initiate hostilities.

Third, jihad is authorized to destroy the power of those who are corrupt and who spread corruption among others. They expel people from their homelands and unjustly confiscate their possession. But during the act of jihad, it is forbidden to kill the innocent children, women, old people, and those who do not participate in the fighting, and the prophet made it a point to remind his commanders of this before he sent them out on jihad. This is quite different from terrorism that is based on the principle of indiscriminate killing in order to spread terror and violate security. Terrorism claims the lives of the innocent and destroys the public infrastructure.

Fourth, the supreme motto of jihad is "neither treachery nor breach of agreement." Islam orders it followers to strictly respect pledges and treaties and to prohibit infidelity and treachery. Thus, it is not permitted to attack anyone who believes that he still has a covenant with you. In contrast, terrorism never respects any covenant or any commitments and is characterized by unexpected and treacherous acts.[115]

THE NATIONAL DIALOGUE CAMPAIGN

On December 13, 2004, Islam Online invited Saudi writer and researcher Jafar Mohamed Al-Shayeb to speak on "National Dialogue in Saudi Arabia: Prospects and Results." He is also an American-educated businessman, a social activist who is concerned with and

---

114   Al-Mutlaq. op. cit. (Surat al Hajj 39-41.
115   Ibid.

has written on civil society and human rights issues. He is founder of Althulatha Cultural Forum in Qatif, Saudi Arabia.

Al-Shayeb commented that the idea of national dialogue was first greeted by serious doubts among the public. The reasons being that (1) there was no tradition of national dialogue, (2) the cultural and religious differences were too many, and (3) there was no common ground on which to base it. These were compounded by the fact that social development and change had not kept pace with the great changes in the realms of economics and finance. However, things began to change after the fourth national conference held on December 6–8, 2004, most notably because they had been officially sponsored by the government. The title of the conference was "Youth Issues: Reality and Anticipation". It was preceded by workshops for young people in different Saudi cities and attended by more than 650 youth, male and female. They discussed issues of importance to them, education, work, culture and society, and citizenship. The youth represent 65 percent of the total population of the country.

Sixty young men and women were invited to attend the Fourth Conference in addition to forty intellectuals, academics, businessmen, and scholars. They all discussed these issues as well as those of particular interest to themselves and made appropriate recommendations on how to deal with them.

Al-Shayeb has now concluded that the national dialogue is an excellent step in the right direction. The differences among the extremists in religion and education are too great to expect that they can be overcome within the short time that is necessary to bring Saudi society where it should be. He noted that dialogue is an essential part of Islam and that the Qur'an and the Sunnah both encourage it.[116]

CYBER TERRORISM

On December 2, 2002, the Saudi Information Agency reported that the grand Mufti of Saudi Arabia, Shaikh Abdel Aziz Al Al-Shaikh,

---

116 "National Dialogue in Saudi Arabia," *Islam Online*, December 13, 2003, see also Al-Shayeb.org.

the highest official cleric in the country, issued a fatwa approving the combating of anti-Islamic material by planting viruses on these websites on the internet. He added that it would be better to try to dialogue with the writers but that if this was not possible then it would be legitimate to try to destroy them with viruses. [117]

The law to fight cyber-crime imposes a maximum sentence of ten years imprisonment and/or a fine of a maximum of $1.3 million on anyone convicted of creating a website for a terrorist organization or on any computer device that promotes radical views, such as providing information on how to make explosives.

The Saudi Information Technology and National Security Conference meeting in Riyadh on December 11, 2007, asked the United Nations to encourage its members to introduce new laws that criminalize the use of communications technology to spread terrorist activities. Three thousand security intelligence personnel and information technology experts attended this conference. Prince Sultan bin Abdel Aziz told delegates his intelligence organization had identified thousands of websites, which fuel Al-Qaeda ideology. He stressed the need for immediate action to cull the rampant growth of cyber-terrorism, which he said increases by some 9,000 websites per year. [118]

117   "Exclusive: Saudi Grand Mufti Ok's Cyber Terrorism," *Saudi Information Agency*, December 2, 2001, http://www.arabianews.org/english/article.cfm?qid=19&sid=6.

118   "Cyber-terror makes a comeback in the news." *Zeid Nasser,'s Tech Blog*, December 11, 2007, http://zeidnasser.blogspot.com/2007/12/cyber-terror-makes-comeback-in-news.html.

"This joint designation makes a new level of coordination in the international cooperation that has characterized the fight against terrorism, and I want to thank the Saudi leadership for taking the step with us , and I hope that this is only the first of many."

Paul O'Neill, Secretary,
Department of the Treasury, Press Room, March 7, 2002:

CHAPTER 9

REHABILITATION

A key element in the Saudi rehabilitation program of terrorism is the indoctrination of its participants in the orthodox practices of Islam. The program makes a special effort to spread moderate Islam through daily lectures in mosques, through educational reform especially in primary and secondary schools, through visits of religious sheikhs to educational institutions, and through the distribution of books and TV programs especially crafted for this purpose. This latter effort included a special book distribution program near the Yemeni border. In some cases visits to sites where terrorist operations occurred were arranged.

Under the rehabilitation program, a hundred classes are taught in five areas in the kingdom, Riyadh, Jidda, Dammam, Qatif, and Abha. Attendance at rehabilitation programs is voluntary.

University professors or religious sheikhs teach classes, as the case may be. The classes are conducted in a friendly non-adversarial manner. The courses require much study and last from six to ten weeks. Instructions include the study of permissible jihad, the true meaning of takfir, relationships with non-Muslims, and psychology. The participants are required to take a final exam at the conclusion of the course.

The age of the students is early to mid-twenties, with the average age twenty-two; however, a small number of students range from sixteen to forty-six years of age.

As of May 2009, a total of ten thousand individuals were arrested and detained for interrogation. Of these, four thousand are still in prison, including two thousand sympathizers of al-Qaeda. Two thousand teachers have been removed from classrooms for their extremist views in the past five years, and four hundred are in prison.[119]

New Detention Centers

An obstacle to the rehabilitation program was the mixing of terrorists and common criminals. To avoid this problem, a rapid program has been undertaken to build five prisons that are specially designed to house terrorists; the first was opened in 2004. Their locations are Riyadh, Qassim, Abha, Dammam, and Jidda. They are state-of-the art buildings expressly built for rehabilitation, not for punishment. Each prison has the capacity to house up to 1,200 individuals. These new facilities are better able to meet and to accommodate the special type of relationship between the officials and the detainees that was not possible in ordinary prisons. They also enable the separation of committed terrorists and militants from those who are more amenable to dialogue and of petty thieves from common hardened criminals and from those who are wont to spread their violent religious beliefs to others.

---

119 Christopher Bouchek, *"Counter-Terrorism from Within, Assessing Saudi Arabia's Religious Rehabilitation and Disengagement Program."* RI, December 19, 2008.

American researcher Christopher Boucek and Canadian journalist for CBC Nancy Durham both made escorted visits to the new prison at Ha'ir. Mr. Boucek published his report on January 28, 2008, and Ms. Durham published her account on December 18, 2007. It is worthwhile to read their separate accounts, which are reproduced here virtually verbatim but slightly edited to eliminate irrelevant subject matter.

Mr. Boucek wrote:

> The new Riyadh facility was built outside the city at the site of a pre-existing prison at al-Ha'ir, located approximately twenty-five miles south of Riyadh. The complex is made up of several existing facilities, including one for common criminals and another specially designated to house security offenders. A number of reported al-Qaeda figures are held at the maximum-security facility at al-Ha'ir and it has been said that this has made the prison a tempting target for militants. The new facility at al-Ha'ir is set off from the other pre-existing structures at the site and is surrounded with its own sophisticated security, including perimeter walls and fences, buried seismic cables and microwave detection systems.
>
> The new al-Ha'ir prison is comprised of two sections with different types of cells: one section of the prison has small group cells designed to house up to six prisoners, while the other section is made up of smaller individual cells. The individual cells can accommodate up to two people. The facility also includes ten handicapped cells and ten larger single occupancy cells with desks and other amenities to facilitate advanced study. In total, there are 320 cells at the new facility at al-Ha'ir. In addition to the detainee and prisoner processing and intake areas, there are thirty-two individual interrogation rooms, as well as a prison infirmary.
>
> There are cameras throughout the new facility, including one in every cell and interrogation room. The video feeds first to the prison headquarters, then to the mabahith (General Investigations, the Saudi

internal security service), and ultimately to the ministry of the interior in Riyadh. This is intended to provide accountability and to prevent instances of abuse through the knowledge that no act of mistreatment will go unseen.

Each cell is designed in large part to be self-contained, each equipped with toilets, showers, sinks, and windows. This was intended to reduce the need for prisoners to be leaving their cells more than is necessary and lessening the level of interaction between guards and prisoners. The cells were also constructed to prevent inmates from communicating between cells; in older prisons inmates were able to use the pipes to speak with each other. Food is prepared centrally in the prison kitchen and then delivered to the each cell. After meal services, inmates can purchase tea and other sundries from someone who goes cell to cell.

Intercoms in each cell allow prisoners to communicate with the guard posts. Each corridor of cells has a dedicated and contained outdoor area for prisoner exercise or in the event of fire evacuation. In September 2003 there was a major fire at al-Ha'ir in which sixty-seven inmates died, and at least twenty more were injured. The furnishings and mattresses used in the cells are now fire proof.

Each cell is equipped with a television set, mounted within the wall above the cell door behind Plexiglas. The televisions are centrally controlled from guard posts at the end of each corridor. In addition to regular television broadcasts, these can also be used to transmit lectures and special programs designed or selected by the advisory committee.

One of the factors that distinguishes these new facilities from other prisons in the kingdom is the inclusion of special purpose-built space dedicated to the counseling program. This is centered on a large lecture hall and classroom space designed to accommodate up to fifty persons. This large space can be further divided into smaller rooms for more private discussion, as well as to accommodate female visitors. Lectures from here can be broadcast to individual cells in order to increase the reach of the clerics and scholars that come to work in the prison beyond the physical capacity of the hall but also to engage with those prisoners who may not yet be ready to interact with others. An important aspect of the Saudi rehabilitation program is that it does not just consist of religious lectures; dialogue and discussion is encouraged. To facilitate this, prisoners are able to ask questions via the intercom system in their cells. Networking the prisons together now allows lectures, sermons, and presentations to be broadcast simultaneously throughout the entire Saudi prison system.

Off of the lecture hall there are a number of smaller counseling rooms, each with windows and separate toilets. Elsewhere in the building there are a series of other spaces for families to accommodate visits and facilitate the inclusion of a detainee's family and larger social network in the rehabilitation process. This also includes rooms for conjugal visits for married prisoners, who are allowed several hours with their spouses. One of the keys to the Saudi program is that it does not just treat the individual but involves a detainee's whole family. Greater family involvement, such as through extended family visitations, shared meals, and other sessions with scholars creates opportunities for a detainee's family to learn about the plight of their loved one. Furthermore, it also allows the committee to learn more about a prisoner's unique social situation, data which in turn is used to help support the detainee's family while he is in custody and to help support his reintegration upon release.

Another essential aspect of the rehabilitation program is to demonstrate that cooperation with the authorities will result in a suspect being treated well. It is understood that this is needed not just to facilitate dialogue, but also to encourage others to take advantage of this and other programs offered by the government. As such it crucial to dispel rumors of abuse and to guarantee a program participant's welfare—these are vital steps in building the rapport and trust that the counseling process will eventually build upon.

These new prisons are part of the effort to demonstrate the compassion that will result from cooperation.[120]

Ms. Durham wrote:

Toward the end of my stay in Saudi Arabia, I asked my minder from the ministry of the interior if I could take some external shots of a prison where hard-core jihadis are locked up. I wanted to show the alternative for jihadis who refuse to recant their views.

In response, Major Omer Al-Khatami delivered an inside tour of the country's newest prison. It's located at Al Hear, south of Riyadh, next to the infamous older Al Hear prison. The new Al Hear is a sprawling compound on a bleak desert landscape and it is so new it didn't yet have inmates. No matter; for a journalist to see inside a Saudi prison is rare and I jumped at the opportunity.

When we arrived at sunset, an eager committee was there to welcome us. Our tour was led by a Lebanese architect, Mohammad Martini from Beirut, whose business card says "Project Manager, Security Buildings for the Ministry of Interior" (Saudi Arabia). He told me Al Hear is the most secure prison in the world, "more than maximum security."

Al Hear, built to accommodate 1,200 inmates, is bright, airy and filled with light. Even though we walked the long corridors at night I found the artificial lighting easy on my eyes and the high-ceilinged cells not at all claustrophobic. Each cell has a flat screen television, high up on the wall, with twenty available channels. An intercom allows inmates to buzz a guard to request a

---

120   Boucek, op.cit. Jailing Jihadis.

channel change. During my visit, a prayer channel was on, echoing throughout the empty prison.

This cell will hold four inmates. Al Haer is air-conditioned, has facilities for disabled inmates, and clean water in every cell. The toilet has a barricade for privacy. There is a window in each cell, high up. Again and again Mardini told me his design includes, "natural light and air ventilation, all according to Human Rights Watch" (HRW). I asked him if he had consulted with HRW; he said he had not, but that he does read their documents.

It is clear Mardini wants to provide the highest possible standard of living to inmates. Whether the Saudis will have human rights in mind when they make use of Al Haer's forty-two spacious and bright interrogation rooms is another matter.

This prison corridor at Al Haer shows its "cool" mauve theme.

The new prison at Al Haer is a world apart. For a prison, it is surprisingly serene. Cell doors and iron gates are painted mauve. Everything else is a soft creamy white. Mardini told me he chose mauve because it is a cool color, good for easing tensions. Never the colour red.

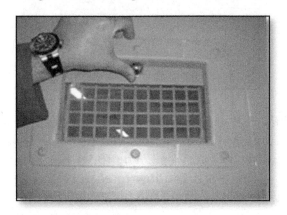

Prison project director Mardini shows a window that allows guards to see inside the cell)

Al Haer is equipped with what Mardini calls "mating rooms", for conjugal visits. They are furnished with double beds and comfortable chairs. Prisoners are allowed two 24-hour conjugal visits each month.

Mardini pointed to one cell and said it was a VIP cell. I assumed he was joking, proud of its spaciousness and relatively agreeable decor, but when he said it a second time I asked what he meant. "For members of the royal family" he said. Incredulous, I asked, "really"? He confirmed this adding, "We even have an apartment with rooms" for more senior family members.

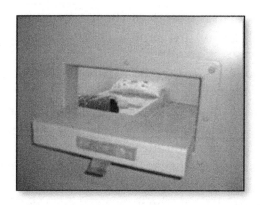

A view through the food delivery hatch into a cell.

State of the art security

Master control has twenty-five television screens to monitor inmates. There are cameras everywhere, except inside cells, and each camera stores fifteen days' memory. The perimeter wall is seven meters high, topped with barbed wire. Just inside the wall is the latest in perimeter security, an invisible microwave detection system that senses human movement. There are primary and secondary security systems, a back up for every eventuality.

Al Haer has a state-of-the-art master control room where all prison movement is monitored with twenty-five screens.

Although Al Haer is a state-of-the-art maximum-security facility, some inmates will stay for only a short time: for example, junior jihadis who show a willingness to change their outlook. However, all jihadis are eligible for religious rehabilitation classes inside the prison.

Those guilty of lesser, jihad-related crimes (e.g. attempting to join the insurgency in neighboring Iraq, or promoting jihad on the internet, as opposed to a violent attack upon the Kingdom itself) may find they're soon enrolled in a rehabilitation program at a relaxed detention center closer to Riyadh, where detainees continue with religious studies, participate in art therapy, swim and play volleyball. After a couple of months there, they will be free.

Inmates will be taught the Saudi government-approved version of the Koran in this prison classroom.

On the night I left Al Haer, Saudi authorities announced the arrest of 208 suspected terrorists in the Kingdom. Major Omer told me they will "definitely" be among the prison's first occupants."[121]

---

[121] Nancy Durham, "Where Saudis will send their most dangerous," December 18, 2007.
http://www.cbc.ca/news/reportsfromabroad/durham/20071218.html

In the new prisons, detainees are generally confined one or two persons to a cell. This is a sharp departure from ordinary Saudi prisons, where there are usually eight to ten and not infrequently up to thirty prisoners to a cell.

Under the prevention program any city may inform the authorities that it foresees a problem with the radicalization of the young and request help. The government responds by sending fifteen professors to the location and they distribute material and engage the elite of the community and tribal leaders. The professors then write up their findings, and submit reports that contain their recommendations.

Under the psychological and social program, the detainees are examined for mental health conditions. Families of the detainees are also visited to learn about the family backgrounds from which the prisoners come. Needy families are provided government support as required in order to deny Al-Qaeda and other radical groups the opportunity of supporting them.

The family is one of the greatest allies in its fight to rehabilitate radicals.

As an incentive to the public, contests are sponsored from time to time. In April 2009, several contests were held in the city of Yanbu. Two thousand and five hundred participated to win a prize of 85,000 Saudi riyals. Three women won prizes in each contest.

RECIDIVISM

Although the Saudis regard their antiterrorist program a success, they realize that it is not without its disappointment, one of which is recidivism. The Saudis claim an overall 80 to 90 percent success rate for the program. There are thirty-five acknowledged recidivists. Out of approximately three thousand individuals arrested and incarcerated, 1,400 have reportedly renounced their former ways and have been released. Another one thousand remain in the program.

Of 120 Saudi citizens sent to the rehabilitation program from the Guantanamo facility, 10 remain in the program. Of the 110 released,

6 have been rearrested on the charge of terrorism. In December, a wanted recidivist turned himself in to authorities, and another was killed after crossing the Yemeni border with an explosive vest. Eleven more are on Saudi Arabia's most wanted list.[122]

According to the Department of Defense (DOD), the terrorist recidivism rate in December 2008 was 11 percent, and in its April 2009 report 14 percent. In January 2010, DOD spokesperson reported the current figure to be closer to 20 percent, or the equivalent of one in five prisoners released is returning to the fight.

Pentagon sources acknowledge that calculating the rate of recidivism is an "inexact science." In April 2009, the DOD defined a recidivist as follows:

> Various former Guantanamo detainees [who] are known to have reengaged in terrorist activity associated with the al-Qaida network, and have been arrested for reengaging in terrorist activities including facilitating the travel of terrorists into war zones, providing funds to al-Qaida, and supporting and associating with known terrorists.

The calculation of recidivism is further complicated because, in addition to confirmed recidivists, some individuals return to jihad without being recognized. That raises the question as to whether these individuals have really returned to the fight if they were never formally convicted in the first place. [123]

"So, does rehab work? Recidivism figures come from the local governments, so they aren't particularly reliable. The Saudis claim that, since 2003, they have converted and released 1,400 participants; as of 2008, only 35 of them—or 2 percent—had been rearrested. Of the 121 or so prisoners repatriated from Guantanamo Bay to Saudi Arabia, 6 have been rearrested. These are, of course, cases of *known* recidivism. The real numbers may be much higher"[124].

---

122 Jennifer L. Hesterman, "Catch and Release Jihadist Recidivism." Police One.com, May 4, 2010, http://www.policeone.com/terrorism/articles/3295091-Catch-and-release-Jihadist-recidivism/

123 Ibid.

124 Christopher Beam, "Jihadis Anonymous: What happens in terrorist rehab?" *Slate*, January 23, 2009, http://www.slate.com/articles/news_and_politics/explainer/2009/01

According to Dr. Abdel Rahman Al-Hadlaq, Director General of the General Administration for Intellectual Security that oversees the rehabilitation program, twenty percent of the 120 Saudis who had been repatriated from at Guantanamo and passed the rehabilitation program have fled to Yemen and resumed their radical activities as compared to 9.5 percent who had not been at Guantanamo. He attributed this relapse to their torture at Guantanamo. "Those guys from other groups didn't suffer torture before, the non-Guantanamos (participants). Torturing is the most dangerous thing in radicalization. You have more extremist people if you have more torture."[125]

Not everyone is ready to give a modicum of credit to the Saudi antiterrorist program. Some, like Thomas Joceleyn, have made it very clear that no matter how effective the Saudi program may be in fighting terrorism and even in aborting terrorists' attacks on Western targets, the Saudis do this only for self-serving purposes.

After questioning the reliability of the rate of recidivism among the Saudis who have been rehabilitated and the efficacy of the program itself and questioning Saudi sincerity in its dealing with the United States vis-à-vis its fight against terrorism, Joceleyn concluded:

> Perhaps the most troubling aspect of the Saudi program is this: the rehabilitation course covers various religious topics, including takfir, loyalty, allegiance, terrorism, legal rules for jihad, and psychological instruction on self-esteem. The course does not address anti-Western/anti-US views, focusing only on the difference between Wahhabism, Saudi Arabia's conservative branch of Islam, and takfirism, the violent ideology espoused by Al-Qaeda...Got that? The Saudis are not all that troubled with the terrorists' anti-Americanism, which is typical of the xenophobic Wahhabis. The program is principally designed to guide their violent ambitions away from their fellow Muslims, that is, those residing in the Kingdom. This is consistent with Saudi Arabia's longstanding policy. The

---

125 "Saudi Gitmo Prisoners Return to Militancy." http://world-countries.net/archives/45839, June 18, 2010,

House of Saud has little trouble with directing the jihad elsewhere. The royals' only real concern is protecting their own necks, which is part of the reason (and only part) why the Kingdom's cooperation in what was previously called the "war on terror" has been so uneven.[126]

Another take on the rehabilitation program was given by Jessica Stern and Marisa Porges. Writing in *Foreign Affairs*, Marisa Porges and Jessica Stern considered how terrorists can and cannot be de-radicalized by state governments and drew on examples from the Saudi rehabilitation methodology:

Todeterminewhetherthesetacticsareeffectiveandworthyof support, the government should consider de-radicalization programs (which aim to reform terrorists in custody) separately from counter-radicalization efforts (which help prevent the radicalization of vulnerable populations in the first place). De-radicalization can thus be distinguished as a tool that supports broader counterterrorism and counter-radicalization strategies. Only then will policymakers appreciate why highly individualized programs that focus on rehabilitation and behavioral modification are the best approach for mitigating the potential future threat of detained terrorists.[127]

The program was created by the Saudi ministry of interior in an effort to re-educate extremists about the peaceful principles of Islam and reintegrate them to mainstream Saudi society. Although several of the program's graduates have reverted to terrorism the Saudi government will continue trying to rehabilitate terrorists.

---

126 Thomas Jocelyn, *"About that Saudi Rehabilitation Program."* Islam Daily, Augt 22, 2009,.

127 Marisa Porges and Jessica Stern. "Getting Deradicalization Right>" Foreign Affairs, May/June 2010. And Jessica Stern. "Mind Over Martyr." January/February 2010. Marisa L. Porges served as a counterterrorism policy adviser in the Departments of Defense and the Treasury; Jessica Stern consults with various government agencies on counterterrorism policy.

In a recent audio statement, Said Ali Al-Shehri, a citizen of Saudi Arabia, who was a prisoner at Guantanamo Bay and later graduated from a Saudi program designed to rehabilitate radical Muslims called on Muslims to attack Americans wherever they find them.After his completion of the program he traveled to Yemen and has been identified as a leader of the Yemeni branch of Al-Qaeda.

To get an idea of how the rehabilitation program works, consider the case of Mohammad Al-Awfi, a Saudi national. Shortly after the September 11, 2001 terrorist attacks in the US, Al-Awfi was arrested at the Afghanistan-Pakistan border on suspicion of aiding terrorist groups and was sent to Guantanamo where he spent six years. He was released in November 2007 and sent to the rehabilitation center just outside of Riyadh. Afterwards, he fled to Yemen and worked for Al-Qaeda in the Arabian Peninsula. Later he recrossed the border, returned to Saudi Arabia and gave himself up.[128] Turki al-Otayan, the rehabilitation center's lead psychologist and one of the first to evaluate Al-Awfi noted that "He hates Americans so much about what they have done to him" at Guantanamo.

"They put you in shorts in an area with extremely cold air-conditioning for months until you requested to see the interrogators and tell them things,.." "They destroyed me. They affect on me. They killed my brothers.' These kinds of things."

At the center, Awfi took classes in anger management, Islamic law, history, and art therapy.

Awfi graduated from the program in early 2008. Then, during the holy month of Ramadan, he decided he wanted revenge against the Americans. He fled to Yemen and joined Al-Qaida in the Arabian Peninsula. In 2009, he appeared in a video alongside the group's leaders.

"We warn our fellow prisoners about this rehabilitation program," Awfi says to the camera. "We were used. But thank God, we were able to escape their power."

Back in Saudi Arabia, psychologist Otayan and other officials from the center paid a visit to Awfi's family.

---

128 Kelley Mcevers, "A test for Saudi Arabia's Terrorist-Rehab Program." NPR, February 15, 2010

"They thought the security force would come to the house to search the house, to arrest some of them," Otayan says.

But instead, officials said they could help Awfi. Although he made a mistake, officials said they did not hate Awfi personally, only his behavior.

Oyatan says he asked for cooperation from Awfi's family for their protection and for Awfi's. And it was then that Awfi's relatives started making phone calls to him in Yemen.

Not long after, the Saudis say, Awfi turned himself in."[129]

At the rehabilitation center, inmates play soccer with guards. Inmate Ahmed Zuhair spent more than six years at Guantanamo for suspected terrorist activity in Bosnia and Afghanistan.

When Zuhair is released from the center, he says the government has promised to set him up with a new house and seed money to restart his business running a mini-market in the holy city of Mecca.

"OK, I change my life," Zuhair says. "I change my city; go another city, to forget everything. Now better my family. A new house. Good this."

Zuhair's story is similar to Awfi's. He says he is not guilty of terrorism, but he is mad at the Americans for holding him at Guantanamo for so long. But now that he is with his family, Zuhair promises to stay away from bad guys.

In both cases, Saudi authorities at the rehab center say they're less concerned with the truth about the detainee's past than they are about his behavior in the future. Whether he's fully rehabilitated or not, officials say."[130]

Christopher Boucek's summation of the Saudi rehabilitation plan is insightful. A Middle East expert at the Carnegie Endowment for International Peace, he says "it wasn't the classes that brought Awfi back into the fold, but the government's contacts with Awfi's family.

"In a society where you get everything from the government, it can be really powerful when the government comes and asks you to do something,"... "I think people understand the message being sent — You have a duty and responsibility, and we'll take care of you. We're doing our part; you need to do your part."[131]

---

129 Ibid.
130 Ibid.
131 Ibid.

THE TRANQUILITY CAMPAIGN

Although not a formal element of the Al-Munasahah campaign, the tranquility campaign has become an integral part of the rehabilitation program and has since been adopted by the government program. However, it is still is largely under the control of individual volunteers,

Started in 2004 by a small group of volunteers, today it is composed of more than sixty-six volunteers, including eleven women, all of whom have honed internet skills. These volunteers visit extremist websites, chat rooms, and other forums and engage in dialogue to contain the spread of radicalization and recruitment. The target audience of this campaign is the age group from sixteen to twenty-five. While the young are highly susceptible to the influence of deviant principles, they are also more open to change and with proper guidance more resistant to extremists' approaches.

Recently, Tranquility Campaign scholars broadened their audience target and challenged Ayman Al-Zawahiri and other Al-Qaeda leaders to a dialogue over their radical views of several major Islamic concepts. First, they visited the Al-Qaeda websites, such as Al-Sahab, Sawt-al-Jihad, and Al-Fajr, and others in order to identify the most active ones. Then they studied the characteristics and strategy that each website used to recruit and promote its ideas. Campaign volunteers did not ask the participants to renounce their views but focused on controversial questions about the Sharia in order to correct their misunderstanding of Sharia concepts.

In January of 2008, the Tranquility Campaign announced that it had convinced 722 male and 155 females to reject their radical ideology on 1,500 extremist websites. In March of 2007, that number was 690 and included individuals from Saudi Arabia and several other countries.

According to Khalid Al-Muhawwah, the chief of the campaign's public-relations office from 2005 to 2008, its volunteers have engaged approximately 1,600 individuals who had advanced extremist views on various Internet websites and instant text messaging. Of these 70 percent were from the Gulf States and 20 percent from other Arab countries and individuals from Western countries.

The campaign systematically covers 600 websites and forums. Those that renounced their extremist views are subject to numerous studies by the research section to determine how they were led astray.

In support of the Tranquility Campaign, the ministry of Islamic affairs has established the Media Preaching Commission, composed of scholars and members of the media, to monitor extreme ideology and violations of established principles in Islam. It has also established a confidential hotline that takes phone calls from family members who discuss the suspect behavior of their children or their children's friends.

The ministry of religious endowments and Islamic affairs monitors and defines the policy and activity of this campaign in an advisory role.

The scientific section of this campaign is composed of religious scholars and sociologists who engage in dialogue with the extremists.

The psychosocial section is composed of psychiatrists and sociologists who study the psychological and social dimensions of the extremist groups.

The monitoring section keeps track of all internet forums, websites, chat rooms, and other venues that circulate information over the internet.

The publishing section disseminates fatwas, opinions, advice, and tapes in various electronic news groups.

Other sections include the design, service-site, the public-relations, and the supervision and planning sections.

THE RELIGIOUS AUTHORITY CAMPAIGN

Senior members of the kingdom's religious establishment have issued public condemnations of terrorism. Between 1996 and 2006, the Council of Senior Ulama', the highest institution in the official religious establishment of Saudi Arabia, stressed that acts of subversion, bombing, killing, and destruction of property are serious crimes that require punishment in accordance with Islamic Law. In June 2004, it issued a fatwa stating that acts of terrorism disrupt the security of the country, shed innocent blood, destroy property, and terrorize people. It called upon the people to be vigilant and inform the authorities of any information that they may have regarding individuals who are planning to carry out terrorist acts.

At its sixteenth session held in January 2002, the Islamic Fiqh Council of the Muslim world League in Mecca stressed the fact that terrorism has absolutely no connection to Islam, while the Islamic Summit Conference held in December 2005 condemned terrorist in all of its forms and stated the need to criminalize all terrorist practices including those that provide financial support.

On October 1, 2007, Sheikh Abdel-Aziz Al Al-Sheikh, the Saudi Mufti, issued a fatwa prohibiting Saudi youth from traveling abroad to engage in jihad without authorization by the ruler.

The Council of senior Ulama' has launched an official website for fatwas. It is intended to provide quick access to fatwas issued by authorized scholars. The move is intended to ensure that authorized fatwas are readily available.

We're very satisfied with Saudi cooperation. They've been with us in many areas of this coalition and many of the steps that need to be taken. You know, they've helped to isolate the Taliban diplomatically. They've worked with us on a number of military requests that we've had. And we're working together in the financial area as well. So we're very satisfied with the cooperation. We've found that they've been together on everything we've asked.

Richard Boucher, spokesman,
Department of State Daily Press Briefing, October 11, 2001:

CHAPTER 10

WHAT WE CAN LEARN FROM IT

Saudi Arabia's war against terrorism, like ours, is one of necessity, not choice. It is a war to protect its own national independence and safeguard its Islamic and Arab character and institutions. It is designed to combat terrorism at home and beyond its own borders because it knows that terrorism does not stop at national frontiers.

What have we learned from the Saudi experience? A number of things.

The Saudis have demonstrated that torture is not a suitable technique for combating terrorism if the objective is to eliminate it or to extract viable intelligence to combat it. They have shown torture to be counterproductive. As Mansour Al-Turki noted, almost every terrorist who resumed terrorist activities after having completed the intensive Saudi antiterrorist program had been tortured at Guantanamo or elsewhere and carried the scars with them. They became virtually immune to rehabilitation; the memory of what had been done to them was entrenched in their being and was almost inextricable. Some of them have gone so far as to acknowledge that rehabilitation enabled them to renounce the errors that led them to engage in terrorism in the first place, but it could not efface the scars of torture.

That violence was unrequited.

The Saudis have also demonstrated that genuine humane treatment of prisoners, for example, providing them and their spouses with the basic humane need of privacy and time together alone combined with the strict application of laws to punish the terrorists for their unlawful deeds results in respect for the private individuals and also for the official authorities. In sharp contrast, the absence of the accommodation of personal privacy with one's spouse that characterizes prisons in the West breeds unnatural sexual activity and violence. Because most prisons in the West are so overcrowded, criminals—violent and less so—are released prior to completing their sentences or even without serving any time whatsoever in order to make room for the new batch of condemned prisoners. As a result the rehabilitation of the individual suffers, and the power of the authorities is diminished.

For example, the medical doctor who was found guilty for the death of Michael Jackson was sentenced to four years in prison. Hardly had the judge slammed down the gavel to announce the sentence when legal pundits were already betting that the sentence would be served at home, under house, arrest because of the lack of prison space.

The Saudi program provides the incentive for rehabilitated terrorists to redeem themselves by alerting the authorities to an impending terrorist attack. The passengers on a plane from the Netherlands to Detroit on Christmas Day 2010 can thank a former terrorist who completed the Saudi antiterrorist program for their well-being. He alerted Prince Naif bin Abdel Aziz to a terrorist plot to detonate a bomb on a flight from Amsterdam to Detroit. The prince informed American authorities who acted just in time to thwart the attack and arrest the terrorist on the plane in possession of the bomb that he would have detonated in-flight.

The program has shown that the harnessing of the capabilities of existing organizations, such as churches, synagogues, mosques, and social organizations, can contribute immensely to the combat of terrorism by sponsoring lectures, antiterrorism campaigns, and similar public activities.

The Saudi program has also shown that the expenditure of millions of dollars to rehabilitate criminals may be a far better investment for society than expending the same amount on prison security. In California it costs about $47,102.00[132] to incarcerate a prisoner for one year, a sum considerably higher than the annual cost for a college education at a first class institution.

Part of the problem here is the ongoing debate between those who insist on punishment as retribution for yesterday's past errors as opposed to those who believe that rehabilitation better serves society today.

Undeniably all these efforts have earned the gratitude of the Saudi people and the admiration of the international community. However, they can only keep the proverbial wolf from blowing down the door. Unless they get rid of the wolf that is still lurking outside, they will only be stop-gap measures at best and this for several reasons.

First, the number of potential terrorists is all but infinite. It is not as if there were a static number of terrorists and the task was simply to target them until they were all eliminated in one way or another—killed, incarcerated, or rehabilitated. In fact, for every one put down, another activist is ready to replace him.

Second, we know from hard experience that it does not take hordes of terrorists to wreak havoc on the stability and tranquility of a state. The actual number of terrorists throughout the world that are sowing violence is small compared to the thousands of civilians and soldiers hunting and chasing them down. And the odds are stacked against the law-abiding citizens who must thwart every terrorist attempt in order to protect themselves from death and destruction while the terrorists win whenever they successfully complete a destructive mission.

---

132 Legislative Analyst's Office, California's fiscal and PolicyAdvisor, http://www.lao.ca.gov/laoapp/laomen/sections/crim_justice/6_cj_inmatecost.aspx?catid=3

Third, while some foot soldiers among the terrorists come from poor and less educated classes, a large percentage of the leadership and their ardent followers are trained and seasoned professionals, for example medical doctors, university professors, engineers, and writers. In addition to being well educated, they are highly motivated.

Some, like Ayman Al-Zawahiri, were reared in upper middle-class homes, and others, such as Osama bin Laden, came from very wealthy families. They abandoned lives of ease and forfeited lucrative situations to follow lives replete with physical danger and insurgency. The political, religious, and economic goals that they advocate and that cause them to use violence must not be dismissed as having no saving grace however vile the methodology used to achieve them. Very often their unacceptable method of delivering the messages with invective conceals the fundamental realities that are shared by the masses. It is just this confluence of ideas that garner support for them among ordinary law-abiding citizens even as the latter, themselves, eschew the use of violence. It is precisely the memory of irredentist problems kept alive over many years and centuries that ultimately turns individuals to seek redemption in violence.

It is one thing for the Saudi government, or any government for that matter, to persuade the purveyors of terrorism that religion prohibits the use of violence except in self-defense, that their violent actions harm their own families, disrupt the common good and therefore they must renounce their violent ways. It is quite another to provide them with permissible, meaningful alternatives to pursue their legitimate objectives whether they be political, economic, social, legal, and so on. That this question is on the mind of law abiding, rational people was clear in the question and answer exchange between Dr, Al-Mutlaq and members of his audience.

For example, the moderator of the lecture asked him, "The legal resistance in Palestine is considered by some western media as terrorism, whereas the demolition, destruction, and corruption that Sharon does against our brothers are called self-defense." Dr. Mohammed Abbas also asked, "You have discussed terrorism that Muslims engage in, but what about the terrorism that Jews and

Americans carry out against Muslims all over the Islamic World? What is the Islamic response to it?"[133]

Dr. Khadeem Bakki from Senegal also expressed similar questions directly to Dr. Al-Mutlaq. He mentioned that some Islamic countries were being held back from fully developing their own self-determination by powerful foreign countries who were looking to serve their own self-interest.[134]Another member of the audience, Dr. Baha'Al-Deen Arabi, asked "What is the solution that your honor suggests to us in regard to this aggression, and what can we do to resist it?"

Dr. Al-Mutlaq gave the standard reply that all governments use, namely "trust the government to do the right thing," an understandable reply because all governments are prey to the reality that they must survive in a jungle of conflicting and complementary national and international security interests. But it is not likely to dissuade activists who are motivated by injustice from continuing their acts of terrorism, even though they become part of the same international constraints if and when they succeed to power and assume control of the government. It is a vicious circle.

Certainly, the promise of a productive job, a new house, a wife, and a reformed life are all essential first steps in the process of rehabilitating actual terrorists and deterring them from actually committing terrorist crimes. They are excellent beginnings, but they do not fill the void of resentment that many terrorists feel toward Westerners who mock their religion, exploit their resources, and violate their rights to self-determination and deny them the right to be masters in their own homes. Material incentives may encourage radicals to abandon their evil ways, but they do not necessarily eliminate the fundamental logic that led them there in the first place or inhibit them from keeping these ideas alive through discussions with others after they, themselves, have renounced the practice of violence.

Part of the solution is in the creation of incisive, imaginative programs at the international level that attack terrorism at its roots in ways similar to the Saudi antiterrorist preventive program:

---

133   Ibid.
134   Al-Mutlaq.op.cit. 11.

retribution, rehabilitation, and reintegration of the offenders into society.

We have seen that such programs are feasible. Saudi-like programs have already been adopted in such culturally diverse areas as Algeria, Egypt, Jordan, Yemen, Singapore, Indonesia, and Malaysia. Even the American military has adopted some of them. In 2007, Major-General Douglas Stone, the commander of the detention facilities in Iraq introduced religious-education programs for detainees that are modeled on the Counseling Program in Saudi Arabia. Its Counseling Program employs Muslim clerics to rebut extremist views and offer job programs for captives, literacy efforts, case reviews, and potential early release from prison to those who demonstrate a willingness to renounce violent behavior. Britain also has undertaken several initiatives modeled after the Saudi programs.

All these are positive steps that should be emulated to the extent possible given the wide cultural, social, and religious differences between the various countries throughout the international community. The leaders of the international community must set the example for this.

Saudi society has the advantage over Western countries because of the strong family and tribal ties that still play an important role in its society. For example, adult men who have families of their own are likely to defer to their parents' wishes in family affairs out of a sense of deeply ingrained respect for them. For example, they are not likely to smoke tobacco in front of their parents and young males are likely to defer to parents on the selection of a wife. These traits are nonexistent in traditional American life. But we have our own national practices which can play a similar role in promoting antiterrorist activity if properly harnessed. Americans are renowned for sympathizing with and contributing to alleviate the hardships of others during catastrophes or calamities, whether they occur at home or in other parts of the world, both at the governmental and private levels. The American ingenuity to create new or to join existing private organizations that promote the advancement of national welfare goals can be used in the battle against terrorism. Programs similar to anti-smoking, anti-pollution, and anti-littering campaigns have succeeded beyond all initial expectations and have become second nature to most Americans.

Enhancing Americans' awareness of the dangers of terrorism in their private lives is a worthwhile goal of the federal, state, and municipal governments. This, together with determined governmental programs at all levels, could help bring the threat of terrorism, in all its forms, under control.

UNPUBLISHED OP-ED. "NEW YORK AND WASHINGTON: SEPTEMBER 11" ON ACCOUNTABILITY FOR TERRORISM, INTERNATIONAL HERALD TRIBUNE SEPTEMBER 21, 2001

---

135   John S. Habib, *New York and Washington,* Unpublished Op, Ed, New York Times September 21, 2001.

New York and Washington

September 11 2001

We are all outraged at the assaults on the World Trade Center in New York and the Pentagon in Washington, D. C. We were outraged to see Americans commandeered in the sky and used as lethal weapons to massacre their own people on their own soil.. The targets were chosen carefully.. The first visited our National Security Interests, our survival, our defense; the second our National Interests, the quality of life, how we live.

The two attacks shook our confidence as individuals and as a nation. The staggering loss of lives and the enormous number of injured was greater than the strongest among us could bear. Our material losses pale before this human sacrifice..

To characterize them as acts of war or terrorist acts is to clothe them in the garb of undeserved respectability. They were diabolical acts not in the sense of good or bad or light and darkness, but as insidious challenges that demand less brawn and more brain power....We must eschew the newly discovered logic of terrorist management that eradicates one virus and generates another.. This struggle demands will power, wit, cunning and heavy doses of fairness and justice

How did we the United States plunge from the most beloved, the most respected, the most esteemed nation in the world only fifty years ago to these depths wherein some of our closest European allies have characterized us as arrogant and insensitive, and former Asian allies called us the Great Satan?. From what planet did these American haters descend to unleash their fury on us? And why, of all the constellations in the universe did they select us? Or, if they are earthlings what moved them to strike now in this last decade and not before? What motivated them to exact this terrible pain? We need answers to these questions.

In this time of travail when national unity is essential, we must remain vigilant that national solidarity is not equated with blind acceptance of national policy and that closed ranks not become the intellectual equivalent of closed minds. Unquestioned policy, must never be the litmus test of loyalty or the gauge of love of country.

Yet even as the consequences of this awful tragedy are not fully known, the major television networks and the written media parade before us politicians and policy makers to lecture us on the perpetrators. Understandably they never suggest that their own incoherent and inconsistent foreign policies may have played some part in creating the environment that bred hatred and disrespect for our country. Unfortunately the media validates their silence by not raising the question of accountability..

Just as we must hold accountable those who perpetrated this appalling crime , we need accountability from those politicians that systematically led us down this tortured path, from the media that marginalized or would not print the views of competent American that opposed or questioned these policies, and from. members of Congress who sent one-size-fits all form letters instead of studied replies to constituents who questioned them on foreign policy issues.

Among the Americans that these politicians let down on that sunny morning of 11 September 2001 were :Buddhists, Christians, Jews, Muslims, agnostics, atheists, capitalists, laborers, the straight and the gay, the rich and the poor, the young and the old, all confident that their national leaders were doing the right thing by them when they left for work never to return, interred instead in a collective requiem, their blood and charred flesh aflame in one ecumenical holocaust..

We can redeem their deaths by remaining the most militarily powerful and the freest nation on earth and by leading a coalition that unites the world rather than divides it. A coalition to achieve justice and fairness is one worthy of American leadership. Nothing underscores the need for this more than the stark reality that our massive military force and immense material wealth combined with that of our most powerful allies cannot achieve our self-appointed mission to rid the world of terrorism without the help of the poorest, the smallest, the weakest of nations, where terrorism too often is a daily dose of injustice and humiliation....

In assessing where we have been and where we are headed, in our quest for justice and fairness, we must be vigilant. Hatred of us among some individuals and some governments, whatever the reasons, has taken a life of its own. Bent as they are on translating this hate into our death and destruction, they must be confronted forcefully.. But this kind of hate need not exist forever.. We proved this when we rehabilitated Germany and Japan after World War II despite their atrocities; and in Vietnam when we abandoned flawed policies, and reconciled with our adversaries in spite of 55,000 soldiers dead and thousands more wounded.

America must become once again a beacon of light and hope to all peoples.

America's security and survival require no more

The American people deserve no less.

APPENDIX B[136]

SOME EFFORTS AND PROCEDURES UNDERTAKEN BY THE KINGDOM OF SAUDI ARABIA IN COMBATING TERRORISM

INTRODUCTION

In the fight against terrorism, the Kingdom of Saudi Arabia confirmed on several occasions denouncing and condemning terrorism in all its forms and manifestations. It also played a very influential and

---

136 Ministry of Interior , Some Efforts and Procedures Undertaken by the Kingdom of Saudi Arabia in Combating Terrorism, 2111-2012, , MOI/Gov.SA (undated).

significant role in maintaining security and combating against any destroying operations. It has also taken many measures and actions needed to combat terrorism at all levels: domestic, regional, and international, and in various forms through security and intellectual confrontations, along with imposition of financial restrictions.

The Kingdom also confirms its full readiness to cooperate with all efforts to combat and condemn terrorism, whatever its origin or objectives, in all international forums. The Kingdom is fully prepared to join the international and regional antiterrorism efforts and strongly make a significant contribution within collective global efforts under the umbrella of the United Nations to combat terrorism in all its forms, structures, and objectives, notably, the Kingdom has already suffered from terrorist attacks in the past and worked for a long time to resist this dangerous scourge, specifically those attacks employing a variety of tactics, including kidnapping, bombing, and suicidal operations, along with the attack mirrored on al-Haram al-Sharif in Makkah on 01/01/1400 H 20, 11/1979.

It should be noted, though, that crimes against the security of the state and crimes of terrorism are subject to the terms of the actions of criminal procedure law, without any exception to the rule.

With regard to the determination of all disputes and crimes, including crimes of terrorism, the courts are competent to adjudicate in accordance with article (49) of the basic law, and article (26) of the justice system, which stated that Specialized courts may be established by a Royal Decree through a proposal of the Supreme Judicial Council.

With regard to defending the accused in such crimes, the advocacy system and the system of criminal procedure on the defendants' right to an attorney or agent at pretrial and trial stages and any other facilities as stated in Article (19) of the principles of legal profession, along with Articles (4,69,64,70,119) of the code of criminal procedure.

And implementation of the provisions contained in the Arab Convention against terrorism and in the Treaty of the Organization of the Islamic Conference on combating terrorism, which have been ratified by the Kingdom, terrorist crimes were included within the big issues deemed to be arrested in light of the ministerial decree No. (1245) of 07.23.1423 H., in accordance with Article (112) of the code of criminal procedure. The system is currently being prepared to fight crimes against the State and against terrorism. This system is still under study by component authorities in the Kingdom.

At the International Level, The Kingdom of Saudi Arabia has taken measures and actions in the fight against terrorism and its financing. Among the most important issues, the Kingdom:

- Strongly confirms rejecting, denouncing, condemning terrorism in all its forms and manifestations, whatever its origin or objectives in addition to cooperation, accession, and contribution of the kingdom to regional and global anti-terrorism in the fight against terrorism and terror financing.
- Commitment to the full implementation of the international resolutions issued by the Security Council under chapter VII of the Charter of the United Nations, as well as other instruments relevant to combating terrorism and its financing, including asset freeze, travel ban and arms embargo against all persons and entities included on the consolidated list of Security Council sanctions committee, and closer cooperation with states and international organizations to eradicate the phenomenon of terrorism, particularly cooperation with the United Nations committee and its specialized agencies concerned about terror fight against al-Qaeda and Taliban, which was established under resolution 1267 (in 1999) and its follow-up technical team, and Terrorism Committee, which was formally created under resolution 1373 in (2001) and its Executive Directorate.
- Encouraging international efforts to address the phenomenon of terrorism and to take advantage of the expertise and research and exchange of knowledge at the domestic, regional, and international levels.
- Calling to hold an international convention for combating terrorism through an international work agreed upon in the framework of the United Nations.
- Promoting Islamic Solidarity in the fight against air piracy.

- Establishment of a supreme committee to combat terrorism and a permanent committee for the same goal to receive and consider incoming requests to the Kingdom from other countries relevant to combating terrorism and taking the necessary actions while working on the implementation of relevant Security Council resolutions relating to combating terrorism and its financing.
- Establishment of communication channels to coordinate with the international organizations and bodies and other countries for cooperation in fight against terrorism and its financing through the Ministry of Foreign Affairs and the permanent delegation of the Kingdom to the United Nations.
- Participation in the work of the Sixth Committee (legal Committee) of the United Nations to discs the items raised under Measures leading to eliminate international terrorism since it had been included on the agenda of the General Assembly sessions in 1972.
- The Kingdom signed and joined a number of international and regional conventions to combat terrorism and its financing, as follows:

1. Convention on Offences and Certain Other Acts Committed on Board Aircraft (Tokyo, 1963).
2. Convention for the Suppression of Unlawful Seizure of Aircraft (Lahey, 1970).
3. Convention for the Suppression of Unlawful Acts against the Safety of Civil Aviation (Montreal, 1971).
4. Convention on the Prevention of Crimes against Internationally Protected Persons, including Diplomatic Agents and Punishment (New York, 1973).
5. International Convention against Taking of Hostages (New York, 1979).
6. Protocol for the Suppression of Unlawful Acts of Violence at Airports Serving International Civil Aviation attached to the Convention for the Suppression of Unlawful Acts against the Safety of Civil Aviation (Montreal, 1988).

7. Convention for the Suppression of Unlawful Acts against the Safety of Maritime prosecution (Rome, 1988).
8. Protocol for the Suppression of Unlawful Acts against the safety of the Fixed Platforms Located on the Continental Shelf (Rome 1988).
9. Convention on Marking of Plastic Explosives for Detection (Montreal, 1991).
10. International Convention for the Suppression of the Financing of Terrorism (New York, 1999).
11. International Convention for the Suppression of Terrorist Bombings (New York, 1997).
12. Convention of Suppression of Nuclear Terrorism (New York, 2005).
13. Convention on the Physical Protection of Nuclear Material (Vienna, 1980).
14. Amendments to the Convention on the Physical Protection of Nuclear Material.

The Kingdom also joined a number of regional conventions in the fight against terrorism, including:

- Convention of the Organization of the Islamic Conference on combating International Terrorism, 1999.
- Code of Conduct for Combating International Terrorism, adopted by the Organization of Islamic Conference in the Seventh Islamic Summit Conference in 1995.

-Arab Convention against Terrorism, 1998.
-Arab Strategy to Combat Terrorism, adopted in 1996 by the General Secretariat of the Council of Arab Interior Ministers.
-Convention for the Cooperation Council for the Gulf Arab States on combating terrorism, 2004.
Security Strategy for combating the phenomenon of extremism accompanied by terrorism-related extremism for the Corporation Council of the Gulf Arab States.
The Kingdom signed and ratified several security agreements with foreign countries, including:

1. Memorandum of Understanding between the Ministry of Interior of Saudi Arabia and the Ministry of Interior of the Republic of Italy against terrorism and engagement in illicit drugs, doping, and other forms of organized crime.
2. Convention on the verification of drug trafficking and the confiscation of the revenues of trafficking between the Kingdom of Saudi Arabia and Britain.
3. Memorandum of understanding for cooperation between Saudi Arabia and Britain in the field of terrorism, and counter-narcotics, and organized crime.

The Kingdom signed and ratified several security agreements with Asian countries, Islamic and Arab, including:

1. Memorandum of Understanding on combating crime between the Kingdom of Saudi Arabia and the Republic of India.
2. Agreement for security cooperation between Saudi Arabia and the Islamic Republic of Iran.
3. Agreement on Cooperation in the areas of security and the fight against narcotic drugs and psychotropic substances between the Government of the Kingdom of Saudi Arabia and the Government of the Republic of Turkey.
4. Agreement for security cooperation between Saudi Arabia and the Republic of Senegal.
5. Convention on extradition of criminals between the Kingdom of Saudi Arabia and Pakistan.
6. Agreement on Cooperation between the Ministry of Interior in the Kingdom of Saudi Arabia and the Tunisian Ministry of the Interior.
7. International border agreement between Saudi Arabia and the Sultanate of Oman and the annexes thereto.
8. Agreement of the Cooperation Agreement between the Ministry of Interior in the Kingdom of Saudi Arabia and the Ministry of Interior, Kingdom of Morocco.
9. Agreement for security cooperation between Saudi Arabia and the Great Socialist People's Libyan Arab Jamahiriya.

10. Agreement for security cooperation between Saudi Arabia and Yemen.
11. Cooperation Agreement between the Kingdom of Saudi Arabia and the Republic of Iraq in connection to specialty of the ministries of interior in the two countries.
12. Cooperation agreement between the security of Saudi Arabia and the Hashemite Kingdom of Jordan.
13. Security Cooperation Agreement between Saudi Arabia and the Sudan.

The Kingdom submitted its periodic reports (the first, second, third, fourth, and fifth supplementary) to the Commission of the Security Council Counter-Terrorism Committee established under Security Council resolution 1373 H (2001).

Organization of many international conferences, including the Counter Terrorism International Conference held in Riyadh February 58, 2005, and hosting the First Asian Regional Meeting in the Middle East on cooperation between law-enforcement authorities and banking institutions January 28–30, 2002, at the Institute of Banking of the Saudi Arabian Monetary Agency in cooperation with the Ministry of Interior (Saudi Arabia Interpol), as well as holding an international conference under Terrorism from Islamic Perspective at Al- Imam Muhammad bin Saud Islamic University to address issues of terrorism, violence and extremism (1425 H, 2004), as well as participation in many meetings, seminars, and conferences on combating terrorism, including active participation in Monitoring Team meetings.

- Participation of the Kingdom effectively in meetings of the Group of Twenty (G-20) as well as the implementation of the recommendations of this group on combating the financing of terrorism.
- The Kingdom was subjected to the Mutual evaluation of the Financial Action Task Force (FATF) in September 2003 and passed the assessment at its meeting in Paris in February 2004, and a second assessment took place in March 2009.

- Cooperation has also been achieved with the Financial Action Task Force (FATF) to convene the first conference for the team outside its headquarters in 1994 at the Institute of Banking in Riyadh.
- The Kingdom approved an agreement with the International Monetary Fund (IMF) on the implementation of the Financial Sector Assessment program (FSAP) in the Kingdom during the first quarter of 2004, where the program included evaluation of the Kingdom's efforts in combating the financing of terrorism and money laundering.

ACTIONS AND SECURITY MEASURES AT THE NATIONAL LEVEL'

- Updating and inventing security devices on counter-terrorism
- Unifying the Security Commanding Agencies under His Royal Highness Assistant to Minister of interior for security affairs to promote cooperation and coordination between various security agencies and non-security in addressing the phenomenon of terrorism.
- Develop regulatory systems and regulations related to combating terrorism and terrorist crimes.
- Standing firmly with perpetrators of terrorist crimes, track them down, and taking legal and judicial procedures in accordance with the provisions of Islamic law and the kingdom's obligations internationally, regionally, and bilaterally.
- Development of severe restrictions on the manufacture, import, sale, possession, trading, acquisition of weapons, ammunition, equipment, or spare parts according to the system of arms and ammunition in the Kingdom of Saudi Arabia issued in 1981 and updated in 2005. The system has set procedures on control of possession of carrying weapons

by individuals and stated specific conditions requirements that determine the right to bear arms.

- Tightening border controls to prevent infiltration and smuggling, as most of the weapons and explosives seized from the possession of terrorist groups are believed to have entered the Kingdom via some neighboring countries, so the Kingdom has strengthened border security measures and provided the necessary support staff and equipments in addition to applying the border security system of border security system and executive regulations as punishment to violators.

- Publishing of wanted lists of the people believed to be involved in terrorist actions to intensify the search for them and pursuing with the involvement of citizens in the fight against terrorism, which threatens their lives, properties, and peace. For that reason, the Ministry of Interior offered financial rewards to both who give information, or report on the members of the deviant group, or contribute to setting off a terrorist act by disclosing the cell or those who are planning to handle the act.

- Appreciating workers' effort in their terrorism-fighting efforts and their achievements while saluting with honor the martyrs and the injured and providing support for their families. A treat, which has had a significant impact upon the hearts of the security services and contributed to the doubling of efforts to combat terrorism.

- Recovering from the effects that occur because of confrontations with the deviant group that may lead to killing innocent people or damaging property, which should be faced appropriate procedures.

- Providing all humanitarian and social services for terror arrest suspects, their relatives, and the released, which provides a great value to the requirements of the intellectual and behavioral reform. It is worth mentioning that the Kingdom has spent on those arrested and released until 30/03/1430 H.. a total of (326,936,927,98) three hundred and twenty-six million and nine hundred And thirty-six thousand, nine hundred and twenty-seven riyals.

- Imposing severe restrictions on the chemicals that enter in the installation of explosive materials and not allowed to be imported, except after studying product by chemists and security specialists to determine the need for it, together with the enforcement of the law of explosion on the violators.
- Strengthening security measures on housing compounds inhabited by targeted foreigners and compelling owners to take precautions and the security controls required.
- Identifying target sites (whether residential or oil installations or vital facilities, industrial installations, government departments, shopping malls, restaurants, parks or others and to assigning security committees competent to assess the regular security measures and promoting actions and taking key security measures to protect them.
- Issuing System combating cyber computer crimes and electronic transactions to achieve information security protect the public interest, and ethics, and morals.
- Enforcing the disclosure system for the traveler who carries cash, or convertible securities, or precious metals exceeding 60,000 Saudi riyals or equivalent to ($16,000.

Measures and procedures to protect strategically important buildings, particularly headquarters of oil installations:

- Establishment of a high ministerial committee to protect oil and industrial installations chaired by The Crown Prince, Deputy Premier and Minister of Interior, His Royal Highness Prince Naïf bin Abdulaziz, to discs matters related to providing security protection to those facilities and develop plans to achieve goals.
- Establishment of a monitoring committee under the chairmanship of His Royal Highness the Assistant of the Interior Minister for Security Committee branching of the Supreme Committee and involving officials from all

military sectors to follow the operational procedures of the components of the necessary security protection in the field in order to achieve unity of command between the various military departments.

- Creation of several subcommittees emanating from the main Follow-up Committee comprising representatives of all the security sectors of the Ministry of Interior and military departments in order to assess the situation around the clock and monitor the implementation of engineering and regulatory actions on the ground.
- Organizing the outsourcing and military facilities of all petroleum, industrial, and important services and privacy according to their importance and their geographical locations.
- Coordinating with companies and petroleum Industry, industrial and service bodies to qualifying industrial security personnel associated with those facilities, and increasing their numbers according to the need of each type of facility.
- Supporting the security forces of installations with 35,000 different military positions to enable them to ensure the protection of armed security for all oil industrial and service installations in the Kingdom.
- Coordination with the vital installations and economic key points to modernize and develop all procedures and security and engineering necessary precautions to protect those facilities.
- Promoting security measures, human patrolling and robotic (air, land and sea) of all pipelines and oil facilities.
- Promoting coordination and procedural requirements between Joint Security Operations, Military rooms, and Security for Office Communication, military and security offices of the petroleum and industrial facilities for follow-up field work around the clock.
- Updating and developing the security devices and security administrations of industrial facilities to suit the requirements against the terrorist threats.

- Updating and developing engineering, construction, and regulation codes applied to facilities attached to establishment to suit the requirements of the prevention of terrorist threats.
- Activating channels of communication between the Secretariat of Supreme Commission of Industrial Security and security departments of industrial establishments connected with petroleum and industrial products and security agencies to pass new information about terrorism and terrorists.
- Updating emergency plans and evacuation from petroleum facilities and important industrial oil to meet the current terrorist threats, and conduct mock experiments to verify their suitability on an ongoing basis.
- Conducting training and joint exercises between the industrial security of petroleum, industrial facilities, and government security forces to increase capacity of efficiency to identify needs and fill gaps, if any.
- Developing and updating communications equipment and channels between security sectors and oil installations, industrial and service, to provide the necessary information and deliver them to the persons concerned, around the clock.
- Intensifying awareness raising through outreach programs, bulletins, and audiovisual communication aiming to raise the sense of security among citizens and employees of oil and industrial installations in order to continue participating actively in maintaining the security and safety of vital installations.
- Permanent cooperation and exchange of technical and safety expertise with some friendly countries regarding the protection of oil installations, industrial and important service of which signing of the agreement on technical cooperation between the United States of America and the Kingdom on 11/5/1429 H to protect infrastructure and enhance security measures.
- Application of the requirements of the international Code for the security of international ships and port facilities (ISPS Code) issued by the International Maritime Organization

(IMO) at all ports, of industrial and commercial. These instructions contributed to raise the level of security for offshore installations or those located on the coast, especially in the areas of security plans and the Automatic Identification System (AIS) to find Marine's units and conduct training and joint exercises as well.

FINANCIAL MEASURES AND PROCEDURES FOR BANKING

- Creating a channel of communication between the Ministry of Interior and the Saudi Arabian Monetary Agency to facilitate cooperation and communication for the purpose of combating terrorist financing and money laundering.
- Establishment of a permanent committee for combating money laundering composed of representatives from a number of government agencies to examine all issues related to money laundering.
- Establishment of units to combat money laundering in Saudi Monetary Agency (Central Bank) and in local Saudi banks to make sure they not engaging in money laundering or terrorist financing and to inform the competent authorities in case of suspicion.
- Issuance of the Anti-Money Laundering Law of August 2003 and its implementing regulations to criminalize the financing of terrorism.
- Establishment of a Financial Intelligence Unit (FIU) within the Ministry of the Interior, whose task is to deal with issues relating to financing of terrorism, and money laundering, and coordination with the unit of money laundering at the Saudi Arabian Monetary Agency. This unit has joined the Saudi government (group on Tuesday, 06.02.1430, corresponding to 26/05/2009 during the annual meeting in the city of Doha, Qatar.

- Application of the Forty Recommendations on money laundering and the special nine recommendations (SR) on combating the financing of terrorism issued by the Financial Action Task Force (FATF).
- The Kingdom of Saudi Arabia has established legislation and regulations for the banking and financial sectors to make sure to take into account the principle of caution and that its internal procedures will be able to determine the identity of clients, activities, and processes that they do it; also the Kingdom has taken several measures to support the legal framework.
- In 1995 the Saudi Arabian Monetary Agency issued a manual to all Saudi banks for prevention and control of money-laundering activities. These instructions are derived from what is stated in the forty recommendations, including: monitoring of suspicious transactions, reporting suspicious activities to security forces, and sending a notice to the Saudi Arabian Monetary Agency. These guidelines are being harmonized with the principles of Basel's Committee on Banking Supervision and international practices in the banking sector. These guidelines have been updated and issued under a circulation by the Saudi Arabian Monetary Agency as rules to fighting money laundering and terrorist financing.
- Rules for opening accounts at commercial banks and the general regulations concerning operation have been issued on 05/14 2002 including the contents of the relevant international standards for identifying bank accounts such the principle of "know your customer" and terms form the standards of contractual obligations between the customers and the banks issued by the Basel's Committee in order to protect the banking sector in the face of economic and financial crimes and money laundering. Some other extra rules were added on 08/022003.
- Banks are not permitted to open bank accounts for non-Saudi residents or companies before taking approval from the Saudi Arabian Monetary Agency and on reasonable grounds to have.

- Implementation of training programs, especially for banks, public prosecution, Customs Department, governmental bodies, and any other government departments in addition to holding training programs in cooperation with Naïf Arab University for Security Sciences, King Fahd Security College, and the Public Security Training city, and all those training programs have been Provided by experts from the Saudi Arabian Monetary Agency in the atmospheres of money laundering and terrorist financing.

MEASURES AND PROCEDURES FOR ORGANIZING CHARITY WORK

- Several actions and measures have been taken to organize charity work at the Kingdom, of which there are 498 associations under the supervision of the Ministry of Social Affairs, where these associations are subject to specified conditions of associations and charitable institutions under decision No. (107) issued by the Council of Ministers on 25/6/1410 H (1990). The provisions of these Regulations included the following:

  - These associations are prohibited from engaging in any assistance or cooperate with any charitable agencies outside the Kingdom.
  - Each established association is required to clarify the geographical scope within the Kingdom, in other words demonstrates service areas so as not to interfere within the scope of other services.
  - An accountant from the Ministry of Social Affairs will visit these organizations to follow up the exchange of aid to the needy and make sure they are always by check and not cash in order to protect the Association and

to preserve the rights of the beneficiaries. The review process will be through financial documents.

- The Ministry of Social Affairs issued many circulars to prevent dealing or exchanging cash assistance.
- Forms of assistance provided by these associations to the needy are numerous, including food, electrical appliances, and clothing, and the like, and sometimes cash-assistance checks issued and acted mostly for orphans, widows, divorced women, the elderly, and the needy.
- To ensure easy monitoring of cash expenses and to regulate the use of donations and disbursement of aid to beneficiaries, a number of circulars have been issued directing to the important use of checks and of boxes or coupons.
- The Ministry of Social Affairs contracted with five accredited accounting offices to provide quarterly reports on the documentary cycle of the charity work in the kingdom.

- Issuance of many controls over charity associations in order to avoid any potentially illegal activities in practice.
- Necessity of legal accountant for each institution to report issues regarding accounting and present an annual accurate budget.
- Prevention of charities and individuals from collecting donations in mosques and prevention and removal of Boxes, along with directing prayer leaders (imams) and preachers to do so and follow-up.
- Prevention of Cash Transfer
- In terms of cash fund-raising, the orders and instructions prohibit collecting personal donations, except through licensed entities. In response to violation of this kind, bank accounts will be frozen, and transactions will be preserved. Furthermore, the General Security Service will have the capacity to investigate, and if anyone is up to something

suspicious, the General Investigation will take the necessary corrective actions.

- Several cases of exploitation of charitable work had been detected, and the perpetrators announcement has been declared through the media to fortify and protect the community from falling victim to such exploitation.

INTELLECTUAL MEASURES AND MEDIA PROCEDURES'

- In 1999 senior scholars (Ulema') in Saudi Arabia issued a statement (Fatwa) against terrorism denied all terrorist acts. Also the Kingdom's Mufty and the official bodies and other religious sectors condemned the acts of terrorism and stressed that such acts are prohibited and are considered one of the major sins and are not in conformity with the provisions of Islamic Shariah, which fights terrorism in all forms and related names.
- Appeal directed to all concerned departments in the government and civil-society organizations and the private sector to draw attention to the youth welfare and paying attention to their issues and Immunizing them from intellectual breakthroughs and tendencies of extremism, violence and extremism and behavioral deviation in its various forms, methods accompanied with deepening the impact of the level of religious and national commitment.
- Educating the society by raising the security and intellectual levels toward the phenomenon of terrorism and its real danger, the various forms of media, also including counterterrorism topics in the curriculum for teaching at universities and colleges in the Kingdom.
- Inviting other government agencies with their various institutions and its educational and information security instruments to identify and clarify the duties of the citizens

and responsibilities of residents towards contributing effectively in maintaining security and discipline due to the fact that intellectual security is a comprehensive national claim, and the responsibility for the protection of society is dictated by solidarity.

- Encouraging the competent authorities for book printing, publications, and tapes issue and CD-ROMs that refute deviant thoughts in order to be distributed to members of the community and the detained, along with coordination with the competent authorities to monitor what is being published as books, audio, and video related to thinking and prevent from dissemination, distribution and trading, to wipe out the roots of deviant thought; in addition to supporting and encouraging specialized studies and security research specialized in the fight against terrorism.
- Initiating dissemination of media interviews and presentations with each of those repent and the instigator likewise. Also Call to repentance is extended to accommodate people wanting to surrender.
- Encouraging community members to cooperate with security people to track the leadership, members, and places of the deviant groups and to emphasize the importance of cooperation between citizens and the security services based on mutual responsibility in the application of the concept that security is everyone's responsibility.
- Consolidating and enhancing interaction between departments of security, citizens, and residents and raising the morale of the security people in the service of the nation and generating the confidence of belonging to the community that appreciates their efforts of security services and stands complementing the security men in achieving safety of this society and the preservation of its components.
- Adopting an information approach based on transparency by disclosing the identity of the wanted by authority along with the deviant groups through different media statements,

ensuring that these statements confirm that the Ministry of Interior is intended and determined to prosecute the elements of crime and work to root out all terrorist cells with their tools and symbols to be known that the Ministry will not tolerate or condone those who are embracing, supporting, or funding terrorism.

- Establishment of public administration fostering intellectual security, which aims to address and combat intellectual aberrations that lead to extremism and terrorism.
- Establishment of an advisory committee in order to fight through reshaping dialogues of mind revealing the suspicions of the deviant groups and refute them relying upon the top scholars of the society.
- Implementation of a faith-based rehabilitation program for prisoners called the Care Program applied to those who are near completing the period of their sentences, seeking to provide intensified directive guidance will be transferred to the arrested, to ensure the safety of their intellectual though and the stability of emotions together with readiness for living within the members of the community as law-abiding citizens focusing with others on community building not nation destroying
- Application of a program called Post-care Program, which designed to help those being released after a drastic change by providing humanitarian and social services, giving them opportunities to communicate with families, relatives, and enjoy visits.
- Facilitating meetings to interested people of religious authority (Ulema') to approach the deviant groups to talk to them and reform deviant thought.

Appendix One

APPENDIX C

COUNCIL OF SENIOR SAUDI ULEMA' FATWA ON TERRORISM,[137]

R esolution 239 dated 27 Rabi al-Thani 1431 H [April 12, 2010] All Praise to Allah, the Lord of the world; and May peace and prayers be upon our Prophet and his family and companions; and thus:

The Council of Senior Ulema [Council of Senior Scholars] in its twentieth extraordinary session help in Riyadh, Saturday 25 Rabi al-Thani 1431 H [10 April 2010], refers to its previous decisions and statements concerning crimes committed by the corrupters on earth by undermining the security and causing grave violations of sanctity in Muslim and other countries, such as the decision of

---

137 "Council of Senior Ulema Fatwa on Terror-Financing, April 12, 2010, Royal Embassy of Saudi Arabia, Washington, D.C., May 7, 2010 http://www.saudiembassy. net/announcement/announcement05071001.aspx

12 Muharram 1409 H [25 August 1988] and the statements of 22 Jumada al-Thani 1416 H [16 November 1995]; 13 Safar 1417 H [30 June 1996]; 14 Jumada al-Thani 1424 H [12 August 2003].

The Council considers the ruling on the "financing of terrorism" by judging that "terrorism" is a crime aiming at destabilizing security, and constitutes a grave offense against innocent lives, as well as against properties, whether public or private,; such as: blowing up of dwellings, schools, hospitals, factories, bridges, airplanes (including hijacking), oil and pipelines, or any similar acts of destruction or subversion outlawed by the Islamic Shariah [law]. It also regards the financing of such terrorist acts as a form of complicity to these acts that leads only to bring accessory to them and to bring a conduit for sustaining and spreading of such evil acts.

The Council also looked into textual evidences from the Qur'an, the Sunnah (sayings and deeds of the Prophet Muhammad), and the rules of Shariah that "incriminate the financing of terrorism." Of these evidences are the Sayings of the Almighty: *"...and help you one another in Al-Birr and At-Taqwa* (virtue, righteousness and piety); *but do not help one another in sin and transgression. And fear Allah. Verily, Allah is Severe in punishment* [Surah Al-Ma'idah, verse 2]. He also Said: *And of mankind there is he whose speech may please you, in this worldly life, and he calls Allah to witness as to that which is in his heart, yet he is the most quarrelsome of the opponents. And when he turns away, his effort in the land is to make mischief therein and to destroy the crops and the cattle, and Allah likes not mischief"* [Surah Al-Baqarah, verses 204-205]. He, the Almighty, also said: *"And do not do mischief on earth after it has been set in order"* [Surah Al-A'raf, verse 56].

Al-Hafiz ibn Hajar, may Allah have mercy on him, said in Fath al-Bari: "the perpetrator and the one who provides cover for him are equal in sin."

Furthermore, it is the established rules of Islamic Shariah: for the means is the ruling of ends. Add to this ruling the general Shariah provisions for safeguarding and protecting rights, vows, and commitments in Islamic or other countries.

Thus, the council rules that the financing of terrorism, the inception, help, or attempt to commit a terrorist act, whatever kind or dimension, is forbidden by Islamic Shariah and constitutes a punishable crime thereby; this includes gathering or providing of finance for that end or providing help or participating in it in any form or manner, including financial or non-financial assets, regardless whether these assets are originated from legal or illegal sources.

He who committees such a crime intentionally, commits a forbidden act and has been in a flagrant violation of Shariah that calls for a punishment according to its law.

The Council also affirms that the incrimination of the financing of terrorism does not extend to ways of supporting legitimate charity to help the poor people and alleviate their sufferings or pay for their treatment and education, hence, this Allah ruling on the money of the rich to be paid to the poor.

The Council, by declaring this ruling, call upon all Muslims to adhere to the teaching of their religion and the righteous path of our Prophet, may peace and prayer be upon him, and to refrain of any act that might cause any harm to other people or transgress on them.

We invoke Allah Almighty for the good, the safeguarding, the unity, and prosperity of this country, the Kingdom of Saudi Arabia, other Muslim countries, and also to improve the lives of all mankind and to help spread virtue and justice all over the world. Allah is the guide and director to the righteous path. May peace and prayer be upon our Prophet, his family, and companions.

The Council of Senior Ulema

Abdulaziz bin Abdullah bin Mohammad Al-Asheikh, Chairman of the Council of Senior Ulema

Saleh bin Muhammed Al-Luhaidan
Dr. Abdullah bin Abdulrahman Alghidayan (did not attend due to illness)

Abdullah bin Solaiman bin Moneea'
Dr. Saleh bin Fawzan bin Alfawzan
Dr. Abdullah bin Abdulmohsin Alturki
Dr. Abdulwahab bin Ibrahim Abu Solaiman
Dr. Abdullah bin Mohammad Al-Alshaikh (did not attend due to foreign travel)
Dr. Saleh bin Abdullah bin Homaid
Dr. Ahmad bin Ali Sirr Mubaraki
Dr. Abdullah bin Mohammad Almotlaq
Dr. Mohammed bin Abdulkarim bin Abdulaziz Al-Issa
Saleh bin Abdulrahman Al-Hussein
Abdullah bin Mohammed bin Saad Alkhinain
Dr. Mohammed bin Hasan bin Abdulrahman bin Abdulatif Al-Alshaikh
Dr. Yaqub bin Abdulwahab bin Yosef Al-BaHussein
Dr. Abdulkarim bin Abdullah bin Abdulrahman Al-Khudair
Dr. Ali bin Abbas bin Othman Hakami
Dr. Qais bin Mohammed bin Abdullatif

APPENDIX D[138]

OFFICIAL SAUDI ANNOTATED PROFILES OF SAUDI TERRORISTS

audi Arabia names 47 most-wanted terrorists
Saudi Arabia's interior ministry has issued a new list of 47 most-wanted Saudi terrorists linked to Al-Qaeda. All of the 47 most-wanted leaders and fighters belonging to Al-Qaeda are outside of the Saudi kingdom. Mansour al Turki, the spokesman for the ministry of interior, announced the names of most-wanted Saudis at a press conference in Riyadh on Jan 9. A list was sent to Interpol last week.

---

138   Bill Roggio, "Saudi Arabia Names 47 Most-Wanted Terrorists" , The Long War Journal, January 10, 2011

Turki said the Saudis (terrorists) are "extremely dangerous," according to The Saudi Gazette, which also published the photos of the 47 wanted terrorists.

"They have had training in the e of arms, and some of them have had leadership roles in Al-Qaeda," Turki said.

According to Turki, none of the 47 Al-Qaeda operatives are in the kingdom. Twenty-seven of them are thought to be in Pakistan and Afghanistan, 16 are thought to be in Yemen, and four more are believed to be in Iraq. The spokesman said the ministry had received information that 16 of them are in Yemen, 27 in Afghanistan and Pakistan, and four in Iraq," He said the suspects are aged between 18 and 40. We have got information that some of the suspects were playing a leadership role in Al-Qaeda. We have not listed Ahmed bin Abdul Aziz Al-Jasser, who is No. 1 on the new list, in any previous list because we list people only after receiving enough evidence about their role in the terror network," he added...Al-Turki referred to Al-Qaeda's efforts to recruit children, including orphans to carry out terrorist operations inside and outside the Kingdom. He disclosed the ministry's plan to present a television program on how Al-Qaeda recruited two orphans.

He also downplayed suggestions that family ties were the main factor in helping Al-Qaeda recruitment.

He highlighted the role of the Internet in spreading Al-Qaeda's deviant ideology. "According to one study, the first step for joining Al-Qaeda and subscribing to its ideology is the Internet," he said.

Missing from the current list of most-wanted Saudis are some of the top leaders of Al-Qaeda, including Osama bin Laden, his sons, Mohammed, Said, and Hamza bin Laden, both of whom hold senior leadership positions; Sheikh Saeed al Saudi, Osama's brother-in-law and a senior Al-Qaeda leader; Said al Shihri, the deputy leader of Al-Qaeda in the Arabian Peninsula; and Shaikh Muhammad Abu Fa'id, a top financier and a manager for Shabaab, Al-Qaeda's affiliate in Somalia.

Several Saudi al-Qaeda leaders, some of whom were not on the kingdom's previous lists of most-wanted terrorists, have been killed in Afghanistan and Yemen over the past year. In a propaganda tape released last fall, Al-Qaeda announced the deaths of commanders

Abu abd al Rahman al Madani, Abu Salamah al Najdi, and Luqman al Makki. The three Saudis were said to have been killed in Afghanistan. An airstrike in Kumar province in September 2010 killed Salad Mohammad al Shahri, a longtime jihadist and the son of a retired Saudi colonel.

In December 2010, Yemeni security forces killed Abu Hamm am Qahtani, Al-Qaeda in the Arabian Peninsula's propagandist, who founded the terror group's media arm. Qatari was wanted by the Saudi government.

Saudi Arabia names 47 most-wanted terrorists

By Bill Roggio. January 10, 2011, Saudi Arabia's 47 most-wanted terrorists linked to al Qaeda. The Long War Journal from a list published at The Saudi Gazette.

Saudi Arabia's interior ministry has issued a new list of 47 most-wanted Saudi terrorists linked to al Qaeda. All of the 47 most-wanted leaders and fighters belonging to al Qaeda are outside of the Saudi kingdom.

Mansour al Turki, the spokesman for the Ministry of Interior, announced the names of most-wanted Saudis at a press conference in Riyadh on Jan. 9. A list was sent to Interpol last week.

Turki said the Saudis are "extremely dangerous," according to The Saudi Gazette, which also published the photos of the 47 wanted terrorists.

"They have had training in the use of arms, and some of them have had leadership roles in al Qaeda," Turki said.

According to Turki, none of the 47 al Qaeda operatives are in the Kingdom. Twenty-seven of them are thought to be in Pakistan and Afghanistan, 16 are thought to be in Yemen, and four more are believed to be in Iraq.

Missing from the current list of most-wanted Saudis are some of the top leaders of al Qaeda, including Osama bin Laden, the leader of al Qaeda; Osama's sons, Mohammed, Said, and Hamza bin Laden, both of whom hold senior leadership positions; Sheikh

Saeed al Saudi, Osama's brother-in-law and a senior al Qaeda leader; Said al Shihri, the deputy leader of al Qaeda in the Arabian Peninsula; and Shaykh Muhammad Abu Fa'id, a top financier and a manager for Shabaab, al Qaeda's affiliate in Somalia.

Several Saudi al Qaeda leaders, some of whom were not on the kingdom's previous lists of most-wanted terrorists, have been killed in Afghanistan and Yemen over the past year. In a propaganda tape released last fall, al Qaeda announced the deaths of commanders Abu abd al Rahman al Madani, Abu Salamah al Najdi, and Luqman al Makki. The three Saudis were said to have been killed in Afghanistan. A airstrike in Kunar province in September 2010 killed Sa'ad Mohammad al Shahri, a longtime jihadist and the son of a retired Saudi colonel.

In December 2010, Yemeni security forces killed Abu Hammam Qahtani, al Qaeda in the Arabian Peninsula's propagandist, who founded the terror group's media arm. Qahtani was wanted by the Saudi government.

Photos of the 47 Most Wanted

Ahmad Abdul Aziz Jassir Al-Jassir — Ahmad Muhammad Abdul Aziz Al-Suwaid — Anas Ali Abdul Aziz Al-Nashwan — Basim Salim Irad Al-Subail — Basim Muhammad Hamed Al-Fazia Al-Juhani — Bassam Ibrahim Yahya Al-Sulaimani — Bandar Mushil Sha'an Al-Shaibani Al-Otaibi — Turki Sa'ad Muhammad Oulais Al-Shahrani — Turki Hadi Sa'ad Al-Atifi Al-Qahtani — Hussein Saleh Dhafir Aal Bahri

Hamza Muhammad Hassan Draishi — Khalid Ali Abdul Rahman Al-Jubaili Al-Qahtani — Khalid Radhal Abdullah Al-Atifi Al-Qahtani — Za'am Saeed Farhan Al-Shaibani Al-Otaibi — Sa'ad Qa'ed Muq'id Al-Maqiati — Solaiman Ahmad Turaikhim Al-Hamdan — Saleh Abdul Aziz Ramad Al-Luhaib — Adil Radhi Sagr Al-Wahabi Al-Harbi — Adil Saleh Ahmad Al-Qumashi — Abdul Rahman Abdul Aziz Rashid Al-Farraj

Abdul Majeed Faisal Muhammad al-Jubairi Al-Shehri — Amr Sckaiman Ali Al-Ali — Fahd Awaiyedh Mu'tiq Al-Ma'badi — Fawwaz Ayedh Jaman Al-Masoudi Al-Otaibi — Fawwaz Awaiyedh Mu'tiq Al-Ma'badi — Faisal Mu'tad Mutjhl Al-Muraikhan Al-Harbi — Mu'tib Hamad Muhammad Al-Ju'aiwi — Mu'tib Saeed Muhammad Al-Amri — Muhammad Saleem Saeed Buraikan — Muhammad Farhan Salman Al-Malki

Muhammad Mutrih Muhammad Al-Adwani Al-Zehrani — Maran Farhan Ghazi Al-Shaibani Al-Otaibi — Mu'jib Muhammad Jamal Al-Qahtani — Hashim Muhammad Ibrahim Al-Hindi — Waleed Jarbou' Eid Al-Julaidi Al-Harbi — Waleed Humayyed Hameed Al-Waladi — Yasser Dakheel Nafi' Al-Wahabi Al-Harbi

On May 7, 2003, the Saudi Interior Ministry announced a list of 19 names who it said were planning to carry out subversive activities. On May 12, 2003 Riyadh compound bombings took place.

ENGLISH/ARABIC

1. **Turki Nasir Al-Dandani** تركي ناصر الدندني died by suicide July 2003 in al-Jawf
2. **Ali A. Al-Ghamdi** علي عبد الرحمن الفقعسي الغامدي surrendered 26 June 2003
3. **Khalid al-Juhani** خالد محمد الجهني one of twelve dead perpetrators of the Riyadh compound bombings.
4. **Saleh M. al-Oufi** صالح محمد عوض الله العلوي العوفي became the leader after al-Muqrin death, killed 17 or 18 August 2005 in Madinah
5. **Abdel Aziz al-Muqrin** عبد العزيز عيسى المقرن became the leader after Al-'Uyayri death, killed in Riyadh 18 June 2004[
6. **Abdulrahman M. Yazji** عبدالرحمن محمد جيازي killed 6 April 2005
7. **Hani S. Al-Ghamdi** هاني سعيد الغامدي
8. **Mohammed O. Al-Waleedi Al-Shihri** حمد عثمان الوليدي الشهري [1
9. **Rakan M. Al-Saikhan** راكان محسن الصيخان killed 12 April 2004 in Riyadh
10. **Yousif S. Al-'Uyayri** (or Ayyiri or etc.) aka al-Battar يوسف صالح العييري الملقب بالبتار first operational leader of AQAP, author, and webmaster, killed June 2003 in Saudi Arabia
11. **Othman H. Al Maqboul al-'Amari** عثمان هادي آل مقبول العمري recanted, under an amnesty deal, 28 June 2004
12. **Bandar A. Al-Ghamdi** بندر عبد الرحمن الغامدي captured September 2003 **in Yemen and extradited to KSA**
13. **Ahmad N. Al-Dakheel** أحمد ناصر الدخيل killed on July 28 in a police raid on a farm in Al-Qassim Province[
14. **Hamid F. Al-Asalmi al-Shammri**

15. **Faisal A. Al-Dakheel** لدخيلا عبدالرحمن فيصل killed with al-Muqrin[
16. **Sultan J. Al-Qahtani alias Zubayr Al-Rimi** سلطان جبران القحطاني q.v., killed 23 September 2003 in Jizan
17. **Jubran A. Hakami** حكمي علي جران [
18. **Abdul-Rahman M. Jabarah** بارةج منصور عبدالرحمن "Canadian-Kuwaiti of Iraqi origin" dead according to al-Qaeda; brother of Kuwaiti-Canadian Mohamed Mansour Jabarah
19. **Khalid A. Hajj** حاج علي بن علي خالد leader, killed in Riyadh March or April 2004

LIST OF DECEMBER 6, 2003

A list published on December 5, 2003 contained twenty-six names. When a new list was published in February 2009 Carol Rosenberg, writing in the Miami Herald, reported that all but one of the captives had been killed or captured.

Rank	Name	Nationality
1.	Abdulaziz Abdulmuhsin Almughrin	Saudi
2.	Rakan Muhsin Mohammad Alsaykhan	Saudi
3.	Khalid Ali Ali-Haj	Yemeni
4.	Kareem Altohami Almojati	Moroccan
5.	Salih Mohammad Awadallah Alalawy Aloafi	Saudi
6.	Ibrahim Mohammad Abdullah Alrayis	Saudi
7.	Saud Homood Obaid Alqotaini Alotaibi	Saudi
8.	Ahmad Abdul-Rahman Saqr al-Fadhli	Saudi
9.	Sultan Bjad So'doon Alotaibi	Saudi
10.	Abdullah Saud Abunayan Alsobaie'e	Saudi
11.	Faisal Abdulrahman Abdullah Aldakheel	Saudi
12.	Faris Ahmed Jamaan al-Showeel al-Zahrani	Saudi
13.	Khalid Mobarak Habeeb-Allah Alqurashi	Saudi
14.	Mansoor Mohammad Ahmad Faqeeh	Saudi
15.	Isa Saad Mohammad bin O'ooshan	Saudi
16.	Talib Saud Abdullah Al Talib	Saudi

17.	Mostafa Ibrahim Mohammad Mobaraki	Saudi
18.	Abulmajeed Mohammad Abdullah Almoneea'	Saudi
19.	Nasir Rashid Nasir Alrashid	Saudi
20.	Bandar Abdulrahman Abdullah Aldakheel	Saudi
21.	Othman Hadi Al Maqboul al-Amri	Saudi
22.	Talal A'nbar Ahmad A'nbari	Saudi
23.	A'amir Mohsin Moreef Al Zaidan Alshihri	Saudi
24.	Abdullah Mohammad Rashid Alroshood	Saudi
25.	Abdulrahman Mohammad Mohammad Yazji	Saudi
26.	Hosain Mohammad Alhasaki	Moroccan

LIST OF JUNE 28, 2005[139]

The list of June 28, 2005 contained thirty-six names.[The Saudi government encouraged those named on the list to surrender, and promised lenient treatment. By April 7, 2007 the Saudi government reported that twenty-three of those individuals had been killed or captured. 36 individuals wanted by Saudi Arabia on 2005-06.

SUSPECTS WHO ARE WANTED FOR THEIR ROLE IN DOMESTIC TERRORIST ACTIVITIES BUT INFORMATION SAYS THEY ARE ABROAD:

Rank	Name	Nationality
(1)	Noor Mohamed Mosa, 21	Chadian
(2)	Manour Mohamed Yousef, 24	Chadian
(3)	Othman Mohamed Kourani, 23	Chadian
(4)	Mohsen Ayed Al-Fadhli, 25	Kuwaiti
(5)	Abdullah Walad Mohamed Sayyed, 37	Mauritanian
(6)	Zaid Hassan Humaid, 34	Yemeni
(7)	Fahd Saleh Al-Mahyani, 24	Saudi
(8)	Adnan Abdullah Al-Sharief, 28	Saudi

139 Raid Qti & Samir Al-Saadi," New Saudi Most-Wanted List, Kingdom Issues New List of Terrorists , Arab News , Crossroads Arabia, War on Terror: June 28, 2005,

(9)	Marzouq Faisal Al-Otaibi, 32	Saudi
(10)	Adel Abdullateef Al-Sanie, 27	Saudi
(11)	Mohamed Abdul Rahman Al-Dhait, 21	Saudi
(12)	Sultan Sunaitan Al-Dhait, 24	Saudi
(13)	Saleh Saeed Al-Ghamdi, 40	Saudi
(14)	Faiz Ibrahim Ayub, 30	Saudi
(15)	Khaled Mohamed Al-Harbi, 29	Saudi
(16)	Mohamed Othman Al-Zahrani, 44	Saudi
(17)	Abdullah Mohamed Al-Rumayan, 27	Saudi
(18)	Mohamed Saleh Al-Rashoudi, 24	Saudi
(19)	Saad Mohamed Al-Shahry, 31	Saudi
(20)	Ali Matir Al-Osaimy, 23	Saudi
(21)	Faris Abdullah Al-Dhahiry, 22	Saudi

- **Younis Mohammed Ibrahim al-Hayari.** 2005-07-03 KIA 36-year-old Moroccan. Overstayed his visa when on the Hajj in 1991; hid out with his wife and daughter; killed in a shootout in Rawda; described as the head of Al-Qaeda in Saudi Arabia.
- **Fahd Farraj Mohammed Aljawair.** 2006-02-27 KIA 35-year-old Saudi national.
- **Zaid Saad Zaid Alsammari** , KIA Killed in raid September 4–7, 2005.
- **Abdulrahman Salih Abdulrahman Almit'eb** , 2005-12-27 KIA a 26-year-old Saudi
- **Salih Mansour Mohsin Alfiraidi Alharbi**, KIA a 22-year-old Saudi[. Killed in raid September 4–7, 2005
- **Sultan Salih Hosan Alhasri**, KIA a 26-year-old Saudi;[killed in raid September 4–7, 2005
- **Mohammed Abdulrahman Alsuwailmi**, 2005-12-27 KIA a 23-year-old Saudi.
- **Mohammed Salih Mohammed Alghaith**, 2006-02-24 KIA a 23-year-old Saudi.
- **Abdullah Abdulaziz Ibrahim Altuwaijri** ,2006-02-24 KIA a 21-year-old Saudi.
- **Mohammed Saeed Mohammed Alsiyam Alamri**,2005-07-25 Arrested a 25-year-old Saudi.

- **Ibrahim Abdullah Ibrahim Almateer,** 2006-02-27 KIA a 21-year-old Saudi[.
- **Waleed Mutlaq Salim Alraddadi** a 21-year-old Saudi.
- **Naif Farhan Jalal Aljihaishi Alshammari** ,2005-09-07 KIA a 24-year-old Saudi. killed in raid September 4–7, 2005
- **Majed Hamid Abdullah Alhasiri,**2005-08-18 KIA a 29-year-old Saudi. Reportedly exploded a suicide belt, during an attempt to capture him by Saudi security officials.[
- **Abdullah Mohayya Shalash Alsilaiti Alshammari** ,2006-02-27 KIA a 24-year-old Saudi.
- **Noor Mohammed Ma** a 21-year-old Chadian national.[
- **Manoor Mohammed Yousef** a 24-year-old Chadian national.[

UNDER ARREST IN YEMEN

- **Fahd Salih Rizqallah Almohayyani** a 24-year-old Saudi.
- **Adnan bin Abdullah bin Faris al Omari**, 2005-11-08 Extradited a 28-year-old Saudi.

TRANSFERRED TO SAUDI ARABIA ON SEPTEMBER 11, 2005.

- **Marzooq Faisal Marzooq Alotaibi** a 32-year-old Saudi.
- **Adel Abdullatif Ibrahim Alsaneea'** a 27-year-old Saudi.
- **Mohammed Abdulrahman Mohammed Aldeet** a 21-year-old Saudi.
- **Sultan Sinaitan Mohammed Aldeet** a 24-year-old Saudi.
- **Salih Saeed Albitaih Alghamdi** a 40-year-old Saudi.
- **Fayez Ibrahim Omer Ayyoub** 2005-07-01 Surrendered a 30-year-old Saudi.
- **Khalid Mohammed Abbas Alharbi** a 29-year-old Saudi.

- **Mohammed Othman Mufreh Alzahrani**   a 44-year-old Saudi.
- **Abdullah Mohammed Salih Alramyan**   a 27-year-old Saudi.
- **Mohammed Salih Sulaiman Alrhoodi**   a 24-year-old Saudi[
- **Saad Mohammed Mubarak Alj**ubairi Alshihri   a 31-year-old Saudi
- **Ali Mater Ibrahim Alosaimi**   a 23-year-old Saudi.
- **Faris Abdullah Salim Aldhahiri Alharbi** a 22-year-old Saudi. His younger brother Rayed Abdullah Salem Al Harbi was killed in a shootout with Saudi police, in October 2009, while dressed in a head-to-toe women's garment, and while wearing an explosive suicide belt.

LIST OF FEBRUARY 3, 2009.

It listed 85 individuals, 83 of whom were Saudis, and two from Yemen. Carol Rosenberg, reporting in the Miami Herald, wrote that six of the men on the new most-wanted list were former Guantanamo captives. Robert Worth, reporting in the New York Times, wrote that fourteen Saudis, formerly held in Guantanamo, had fallen under suspicion of supporting terrorism following their release. The men were all believed to be living outside of Saudi Arabia, some of them receiving militant training. They were promised lenient treatment, and encouraged to turn themselves in at the nearest Saudi embassy.

Those on the new list include three Saudis who appeared in a threatening Al-Qaeda video: Said Ali al-Shihri, Abu Hareth Muhammad al-Awfi, and Nasir al-Wuhayshi, and another individual named Abdullah al-Qarawi. Al-Wuhayshi claims he is the leader of Al-Qaida in the Arabian Peninsula. Al-Qarawi is reported to be the leader of Al-Qaida in the Persian Gulf. Al-Shihri and Al-Awfi are former Guantanamo captives, and Al-Shihri stated he is Al-Wuhayshi's deputy.

The Saudi Gazette reported that Saudi security officials identified an individual named Saleh Al-Qaraawi as the leader of Al-Qaeda in Saudi Arabia.

An article published in Asharq Alawsat on February 6, 2009, noted the range in age among the suspects—from seventeen to fifty-two. This article named Abdullah El Qarawi, who it described as the "most dangerous" individual on the list, as the leader of Al-Qaeda operations in the Persian Gulf. According to the article, Abdullah El Qarawi is just 26 years old. The article listed the names and ages of fifteen other individuals.

Another article in the Asharq Alawsat identified other individuals from the list, including: Abdullah al-Abaed, wanted for the assassination of a senior police official, and Mohamed Abul-Khair, one of Osama bin Laden's bodyguards, and one of his sons-in-law.

On February 7, 2009, the Saudi Gazette reported some details of some of the wanted men. The article named seven men it identified as former Guantanamo captives, and five other most- wanted suspected terrorists it did not identify as former Guantanamo captives.

Those on the new list include three Saudis who appeared in a threatening Al-Qaeda video: Said Ali al-Shihri, Abu Hareth Muhammad al-Awfi and Nasir al-Wuhayshi, and another individual named Abdullah al-Qarawi. Al-Wuhayshi claims he is the leader of Al-Qaida in the Arabian Peninsula. Al-Qarawi is reported to be the leader of Al-Qaida in the Persian Gulf. Al-Shihri and Al-Awfi are former Guantanamo captives, and Al-Shihri stated he is Al-Wuyashi's deputy.

The Saudi Gazette reported that Saudi security officials identified an individual named Saleh Al-Qaraawi as the leader of Al-Qaeda in Saudi Arabia.

INDIVIDUALS SAID TO BE NAMED ON THE FEBRUARY 2009 LIST

- **Mish'al Muhammad Rashid Al-Shedocky.** Repatriated on May 14, 2003—one of the first captives to be repatriated. His repatriation was reported to have been part of an exchange of prisoners that resulted in the release of five United Kingdom citizens.

- **Adnan Muhammed Ali Al Saigh**. Repatriated on May 19, 2006. The Saudi Gazette reported he is believed to have traveled to a neighboring country with his brother-in-law, fellow suspect and fellow former Guantanamo captive, Othman al-Ghamdi, leaving behind his wife and son.
- **Yousuf Mohammed Mubarak Al Jubairi Al Shahri.** Possibly the brother in law of fellow suspect and former Guantanamo captive Sa'id Ali Jabir Al Khathim Al Shihri. Repatriated to Saudi Arabia on November 9, 2007. Killed in a firefight with Saudi police on October 18, 2009 together with Rayed Abdullah Salem Al Harbi.
- **Fahd Salih Sulayman Al Jutayli**. According to his mother he was living openly in Saudi Arabia just days prior to the publication of the most wanted list. Reported to have been killed by Yemeni security officials in September 2009.
- **Othman Ahmad Othman al-Ghamdi**. Repatriated on June 24, 2006. Worked as a car dealer following his release. The Saudi Gazette reported he is believed to have traveled to a neighboring country with his brother-in-law, fellow suspect and fellow former Guantanamo captive, Adnan Al-Sayegh, leaving behind his wife and son.
- **Turki Mash Awi Zayid Al Asiri**. Repatriated to Saudi custody on November 9, 2007, with thirteen other men. Name and age are a close match to former Guantanamo captive Turki Mash Awi Zayid Al Asiri.
- **Murtadha al Said Makram**. Repatriated to Saudi Arabia on November 9, 2007 Repatriated in spite of the annual review procedures recommending his continued detention.
- **Jabir Jubran Al Fayfi**. Identified as a former captive Jaber Al-Faifi. Repatriated on February 21, 2007. Repatriated in spite of the annual review procedures recommending his continued detention.
- **Ibrahim Sulayman Muhammad Arbaysh.** Repatriated on December 14, 2006 with sixteen other men.

- **Mohamed Atiq Awayd Al Harbi.** Repatriated to Saudi Arabia on November 9, 2007. Appeared in a threatening video from Al-Qaida in the Arabian Peninsula. Also identified as Mohamed Atiq Awayd Al Harbi. Repatriated in spite of the annual review procedures recommending his continued detention. Reported to have turned himself in Saudi Authorities on February 18, 2009.
- **Said Ali al-Shihri.** Repatriated to Saudi Arabia on November 9, 2007. Claims he is the leader of Al-Qaida in the Arabian Peninsula. Repatriated in spite of the annual review procedures recommending his continued detention.
- **Nasir al-Wuhayshi.** Appeared in a threatening video from Al-Qaida in the Arabian Peninsula. Claims he is the leader of Al-Qaida in the Arabian Peninsula.
- **Mohamed Abul-Khair.** Reported to be Osama bin Laden's son-in-law. Reportedly a link to Ramzi bin al-ShiBush. Nephew of fellow suspect Yousuf Al Jebairi Al Shahri. Reportedly smuggled into Yemen, by his uncle, to join al Qaida.
- **Baheij Al-Buheajy**
- **Rayed Abdullah Salem Al Harbi**. Killed in a firefight with Saudi police on October 18, 2009 together with Yousef Al Shiı Naif Mohamed Al Qahtani.
- **Hamd Hussein Nasser Al Hussein.**
- **Hassan Ibrahim Hamd Al Shaban**.
- **Abdullah al-Asiri.** Attempted to assassinate Saudi Prince Muhammad bin Nayef with a suicide bomb. Al Aseery told security officials he wanted to surrender, but asked to meet the Prince personally.
- **Abdullah El Qarawi.** Reportedly the leader of Al-Qaeda in the Persian Gulf. Described as the "most dangerous" individual on the list.
- **Saleh Al-Qaraawi.** Reportedly the leader of Al-Qaeda in Saudi Arabia.
- **Ahmed Abdullah Al Zahrani.**
- **Ibrahim al-Asiri.**
- **Badr Al Oufi Al Harbi**
- **Abdullah Abdul-Rahman Al Harbi**

- **Hussein Abdu Mohamed**
- **Abdulmohsin Al-Sharikh** The Saudi Gazette reports he is the brother to two former Guantanamo captives — Abdulhadi Al-Sharikh and Abdulrazzaq Al-Sharikh.
- **Abdullah Al-Juwair**. The Saudi Gazette reports he is the brother to Fahd Al-Juwair who was killed in a shootout with Saudi security officials, following an attempt to blow up a petroleum facility. His brother Fahd was listed on and earlier most wanted list.
- **Ahmad Al-Shiha.** Was studying Shariah law at University, when he disappeared.
- **Aqil Al-Mutairi.** Disappeared unexpectedly three years ago—believed to have gone to Iraq.
- **Faiz Al-Harbi.** Disappeared five months ago—had recently told his mother he was thinking of seeking an Islamic education outside of Saudi Arabia—but he hadn't said where. Also transliterated as Fayez Ghuneim Hameed Al-Hijri Al-Harbi.
- **Qasim al-Raymi**. One of the two Yemenis on the list. Alleged to (sic) be linked to: "a plot targeting the ambassador in San'a."
- **Obaida Abdul-Rahman Al Otaibi**. A journalist with Saudi Al-Jazirah; Attended Imam Mohamed Bin Saud University where he earned a degree in media; Attended the same high school as "Eisa Al-Awsham, a former Al-Qaeda commander. "Accused of "planning to target vital infrastructure within Saudi Arabia."
- **Sultan Radi al-Utaibi**. His family reports that he was killed fighting Americans in Baghdad in January 2007. The Saudi Interior Ministry assert DNA tests confirm he was killed in a skirmish with Yemeni security officials, on September 14, 2009.
- **Abdullah Mohammed Abdullah al-Ayad.** He was profiled as a deceased martyr in a propaganda video in 2008.
- **Ahmed Owaidan Al-Harbi.** Reportedly captured in Yemen in early 2009, described as "wanted" by Saudi security officials.

- **Mohammed Otaik Owaid Al-Aufi Al-Harbi.**
- **Khaled Saleem Owaid Al-Luhaibi Al-Harbi**.
- **Abdullah Thabet.** Alleged to hold Osama bin Laden as a hero. Alleged to have entered "clandestine cells" that launched raids against "non-believers". Alleged to have written a novel entitled "The 20th hijacker" about his jihadist years.
- **Fahd Raggad Samir Al-Ruwaili.** On March 26, 2009, Al-Arabiya television reported he surrendered to Saudi authorities. ABC News transliterates his name as "Fahad al-Ruwaily", and reports: "A news Web site close to the ministry said Thursday that al-Ruwaily was a key figure in al-Qaida training camps along Syria's border with Iraq."
- **Badr Mohammed Nasser al-Shihri.** Al-Shihri's surrender was reported on October 19, 2010. Al-Shihri was reported to have surrendered when he was living in Pakistan. The Associated Press reported that Saudi officials allowed al-Shihri to be released into the custody of his family, following his repatriation.

LIST OF JANUARY 2011

Saudi security officials published a list of 47 most wanted terrorist suspects in January 2011. According to the Saudi Gazette the list had been published by Interpol on January 5 2011. They reported one of the wanted men was between 20 and 30, and the remaining 12 were between 30 and 40. The list of 47 suspects included the following individuals:

Rank	Name
1.	Ahmad Abdul Aziz Jassir Al-Jassir
2.	Ahmad Muhammada Abdul Aziz Al-Suwaid
3.	Anas Ali Abdul Aziz Al-Nashwan
4.	Basim Salim Inad Al-Subail
5.	Basim Muhammad Hamid Al-Fazzi Al-Juhani

6.	Bassam Ibrahim Yahya Al-Sulaimani
7.	Bandar Mhil Shai'an Al-Shaibani Al-Otaibi
8.	Turki Sa'ad Muhammad Qulais Al-Shahrani
9.	Turki Hadi Sa'ad Al-Atifi Al-Qahtani
10.	Hussein Saleh Dhafir Aal Bahri
11.	Hamza Muhammad Hassan Uraishi
12.	Khalid Ali Abdul Rahman Al-Jubaili Al-Qahtani
13.	Khalid Hadhal Abdullah Al-Atifi Al-Qahtani
14.	Za'am Saeed Farhan Al-Shaibani Al-Otaibi
15.	Sa'ad Qa'ed Muq'id Al-Maqqati
16.	Solaiman Ahmad Turaikhim Al-Hamdan
17.	Saleh Abdul Aziz Hamad Al-Luhaib
18.	Adil Radhi Saqr Al-Wahabi Al-Harbi
19.	Adil Salhe Ahmad Al-Qumaishi
20.	Abdul Rahman Abdul Aziz Rashid Al-Farraj
21.	Abdul Majeed Faisal Muhammad Al-Jubairi Al-Shehri
22.	Amr Solaiman Ali Al-Ali
23.	Fahd Awaiyedh Mu'tiq Al-Ma'badi
24.	Fawwaz Ayedh Jaman Al-Masoudi Al-Otaibi
25.	Fawwaz Awaiyedh Mu'tiq Al-Ma-badi
26.	Faisal Mu'tad Muqbil Al-Muraikhan Al-Harbi
27.	Mu'tib Hamad Muhammad Al-Juraiwi
28.	Mu'tib Saeed Humammad Al-Amri
29.	Muhammad Saleem Saeed Buraikan
30.	Muhammad Farhan Salman Al-Maliki
31.	Nuhammad Mufrih Muhammad Al-Adwani Al-Zahrani
32.	Mu'jib Muhammad Jamal Al-Qahtani
33.	Hashim Muhammad Ibrahim Al-Hindi
34.	Waleed Jarbou' Edi Al-Julaidi Al-Harbi
35.	Waleed Humayeed Hameed Al-Waladi
36.	Yasser Dahheel Nafi' Al-Wahabi Al-Harbi

Suspects who remain at large, or otherwise unaccounted

Comprehensive List Of Terrorists Killed, Captured, Suicide[140]

Abdullah Ahmed Abdullah
Aafia Siddiqui (captured, killed)
Abd Al Aziz Awda
'Abd al-Hadi al-Iraqi (captured, killed)
Abd al-Rahman, Atiyah (captured, killed)
'Abd al-Rahman, 'Umar (captured, killed)
Abdelkarim Hussein Mohamed Al-Nasser
Abderraouf Jdey
Abdul Basit man
Addul Rahman S. Taha
Abdul Rahman Said Yasin
Abdul Rahim, Jamal
Abdullah, Abdullah
Abdullah al-Rimi
Abu Khabab al-Masri (captured, killed)
Abu Faraj al-Libi (captured, killed)
Abu Layth al-Libi (captured, killed)
Abu M'ab al-Zarqawi (captured, killed)
Abu Omran (Al-Mughassil, Ahmad Ibrahim)
Abu Solaiman (captured, killed)
Abu Yahya al-Libi
Abu Zubaydah (captured, killed)
Adam Pearlman
Adam Yahiye Gadahn
Adnan G. El-Shukrijumah
Ahmad Ibrahim Al-Mughassil
Ahmed Mohammed Hamad Ali
Ahmed the Tall (Swedan, Ahmed) (captured, killed)
al-Adel, Saif
al-Badawi, Jamal Mohammad
al-Bakri, Ali Sayyid Muhamed Mustafa

---

140 "Al-Qa'ida in the Arabian Peninsul," The National Counterterrorism Center, Counterterrorism Calendar 2011.

Ali Atwa
Ali Saed Bin Ali El-Hoorie
Ali Sayyid Muhamed Mustafa al-Bakri
al-Iraqi, 'Abd al-Hadi (captured, killed)
al-Kini, ama (captured, killed)
al-Libi, Abu Faraj (captured, killed)
al-Libi, Abu Yahya
al-Libi, Abu Layth (captured, killed)
al-Liby, Anas
Ally Msalam (captured, killed)
Al-Masri, Abu Khabab (captured, killed)
Al-Mughassil, Ahmad Ibrahim
Al-Munawar, Muhammad Ahmed
al-Nasser, Abdelkarim Hussein Mohammed
al-Qo, Fahd Mohammed Ahmed
Al-Rahman, Atiyah Abd
Al-Rimi, Abdullah
Al-Turki, Wadoud Muhammad Hafiz
Al-Umari, Hayn Muhammad
al-Yacoub, Ibrahim Salih Mohammed
al-Zarqawi, Abu M'ab (captured, killed)
al-Zawahiri, Ayman
Amer El-Maati
Ammar Mansour Bolim (Ali Atwa)
Anas Al-Liby
Ar-Rahayyal, Muhammad Abdullah Khalil Hsain
Atif, Muhammad (captured, killed)
Atif, Muhammed (captured, killed)
Atiyah Abd al-Rahman (captured, killed)
Atwa, Ali
Atwah, Muhsin (captured, killed)
Awda, Abd Al Aziz
Ayman al-Zawahiri
Azahari Bin Hin (captured, killed)
Azzam al-Amriki
Azzam the American
Baitullah Mahsud (captured, killed)

Ja'far al-Tayar
Jabar A. Elbaneh
Jamal Mohammad al-Badawi
Jamal Saeed Abdul Rahim
Janjalani, Khadafi (captured, killed)
Jdey, Abderraouf
Joko (Dulmatin) (captured, killed)
Kansi, Mir Amal (captured, killed)
Khadafi Janjalani (captured, killed)
Khair Mundos
Khalid Abdul Wadood (Abdullah Amed Abdullah)
Khalid Shaikh Muhammad (captured, killed)
KSM (captured, killed)
Laden
Laden
Libi, Abu Faraj (captured, killed)
Liby

Mahsud, Baitullah (captured, killed)
Mehsud, Hakimullah
Mir Amal Kansi (captured, killed)
Mohammed Ali Hamadei
Mugniyah, 'Imad (captured, killed)
Muhammad Abdullah Khalil Hsain ar-Rahayyal
Muhammad Ahmed al-Munawar
Muhammad, Khalid (captured, killed)
Muhammed Atef (captured, killed)
Muhsin Ma Matwali Atwah (captured, killed)
Mullah Omar
Mugniyah, 'Imad (captured, killed)
Mundos, Khair
Mustafa Setmariam Nasar (captured, killed)
Nasar, Mustafa Setmariam (captured, killed)
Noordin Mohammad Top (captured, killed)
Omar, Mullah
Patek, Umar
Pearlman, Adam

Most Wanted

$25 Million Reward Ayman al-Zawahiri:
$ 5 Million Reward Adnan G. el Shukrijumah
$ 5 Million Reward Hakimullah Mehsud
$ 5 Million Reward Saif al-Adel
$ 5 Million Reward Sirajuddin Haqqani
$ Million Reward Wali Ur Rehman
$ 5 Million Reward Adam Yahiye Gadahn
$ 1 Million Reward Abu Yahya al-Libi
$ 1 Million Reward Mullah Omar

TIME LINE OF TERRORIST INCIDENTS IN SAUDI ARABIA.

This timeline of the militant incidents in Saudi Arabia was derived from reports in the Saudi media and other sources

The attacks have killed 91 foreigners and Saudi civilians and wounded 510 people, according to the Saudi government. 41 security force members have been killed and 218 wounded, while 112 militants have been killed and 25 wounded.

The most serious violence to take place was a series of bomb blasts in Riyadh in late 1966 and early 1967. The bombings, which caused no known casualties, were claimed by the North Yemen-based Nasserite organization Union of the People of the Arabian

---

141 Wikipedia, "List of Militant Incidents in Saudi Arabia". As of April 29, 2013. Accessed 19 July 3013.

Peninsula ittihad sha'b al-jazira al-'arabiyya (UPAP). After the attacks, Saudi authorities arrested several hundred Yemenis, executed 17 of them and expelled the rest.

20 November– 4 December (See Grand Mosque Seizure) - number of militants took over the Masjid al-Haram in Mecca to protest the House of Saud's policies of westernization. The militants were well organized and armed and were initially able to repel attempts by the Saudi National Guard to storm the complex. The Saudis eventually brought in French and Pakistani GIGN commandos to help their forces retake the Mosque. Non-Muslim commandos underwent nominal conversion to Islam before being allowed into the Mosque. Eventually the Mosque was retaken and the 63 or 67 surviving male militants were executed. The number of people killed in the siege and the total number of militants involved are disputed. Official sources put the death toll at 255, but others suggest that it was higher. Ruhollah Khomeini addressed on Radio regarding the seizure of the Mosque on 21 November.

1988

30 September - four Shi'ite men are beheaded for blowing up fuel storage tanks at the Saudi Petrochemical Company (SADAF) facility in Jubail. They had entered the plant by cutting a hole in the perimeter fence. One tank happened to be empty, but another was full and burned for several days. Eventually the fire was extinguished when a firefighting team literally plugged the hole in the tank.

1995

13 November - a car bomb killed five citizens and two Indians at the offices of the Saudi National Guard in Riyadh.

1996

25 June (See Khobar Towers bombing) - the Khobar Towers apartment complex in Khobar, near Dhahran, is hit by a large truck bomb. Nineteen airmen are killed and 372 wounded by the blast.

William Perry, who was the United States Secretary of Defense at the time that this bombing happened, said in an interview in June 2007 that "he now believes al-Qaida rather than Iran was behind a 1996 truck bombing at an American military base."

2003

12 May (See Riyadh Compound Bombings) 35 are killed and over 200 wounded during a suicide attack on the Vinnell Compound in Riyadh. There is a rumor that National Guard collision was involved; however, there is no proof or credible source to support that claim.

31 May 2 police officers and a militant are killed.

14 June Security forces raided a building in the Khalidiya neighborhood of Makkah. Two Saudi police officers and five suspects were killed in a shootout. Twelve suspects were arrested including two from Chad and one Egyptian.

28 July Six militants — four Saudis and two Chadians — and two police officers were killed in a police raid on a farm outside of Al-Qasim. The four Saudis were identified as Ahmad Al-Dakheel, Kareem Olayyan Al-Ramusthan Al-Harbi, Saud Aamir Suleiman Al-Qurashi, and Muhammad Ghazi Saleem Al-Harbi. The Chadians were Isa Kamal Yousef Khater and Isa Saleh Ali Ahmed. Another Saudi wanted person, identified as Ibrahim ibn Abdullah Khalaf Al-Harbi, was arrested after he being injured.

14 June Security forces raided a building in the Khalidiya neighborhood of Makkah. Two Saudi police officers and five suspects were killed in a shootout. Twelve suspects were arrested including two from Chad and one Egyptian.

28 July Six militants — four Saudis and two Chadians — and two police officers were killed in a police raid on a farm outside of Al-Qasim. The four Saudis were identified as Ahmad Al-Dakheel,

Kareem Olayyan Al-Ramusthan Al-Harbi, Saud Aamir Suleiman Al-Qurashi, and Muhammad Ghazi Saleem Al-Harbi. The Chadians were Isa Kamal Yousef Khater and Isa Saleh Ali Ahmed. Another Saudi wanted person, identified as Ibrahim ibn Abdullah Khalaf Al-Harbi, was arrested after he being injured.

2004

19 January Shootout in Al-Nassim District (Riyadh)

29 January One unnamed gunman captured and five police officers killed in a shootout in the Al-Nassim District of Riyadh. April United States Embassy issues a travel advisory for the kingdom and urges all citizens to leave.

5 April An unnamed militant is reported killed in a car chase in Riyadh.

12 April A police officer and one militant are killed in a shootout in Riyadh. Rakan ibn Moshen Al-Seikhan and Nasser ibn Rashid Al-Rashid are wounded and escaped. Both are reported dead on 4 July.

13 April Four police officers are killed in two attacks by militants. Several car bombs are found and defused.

15 April The United States orders all governmental dependents and nonessential personnel out of the kingdom as a security measure.

21 April A suicide bomber detonates a car bomb in Riyadh at the gates of a building used as the headquarters of the traffic police and emergency services. Five people die and 148 are injured.

22 April Three unnamed militants are killed by police in Jidda in an incident in the Al-Fayha district.

1 May (See: Black Saturday (2004)) Seven people (two citizens, two Britons, an Australian, a Canadian, and a Saudi) are killed in a rampage at the premises of a petroleum company in Yanbu by three brothers. All the attackers, dressed in military uniforms, are killed.

22 May German chef Hermann Dengl is shot and killed at a Jarir Bookstore in Riyadh a fake police checkpoint in Riyadh.

29 May 2004 Al-Khobar massacres) 22 are killed during an attack on the Oasis Compound in Al-Khobar. After a siege the gunmen escape. 19 of those killed are foreigners.

6 June Simon Cumbers, an Irish cameraman for the BBC, is killed and the reporter Frank Gardner very severely wounded by gunshots to his head in Riyadh.

8 June Robert Jacobs, a citizen working for Vinnel Corp., is killed at his villa in Riyadh.

13 June One expatriate Kenneth Scroggs is killed and another Paul Johnson working for Lockheed Martin is kidnapped at also discovered on this date.

18 June citizen Paul Johnson is beheaded in Riyadh. His body is found some time later. A few hours later security services kill five militants (Abdul Aziz Al-Muqrin, Turki Al-Muteri, Ibahim Al-Durayhim and two others). A dozen are reported captured.

23 June Saudi government offers a thirty-day limited amnesty to "terrorists".

1 July Abdullah ibn Ahmed Al-Rashoud is killed in shootout east of the capital. Bandar Al-Dakheel escapes. Two policemen (Bandar Al-Qahtani and Humoud Abdullah Al-Harbi) are killed.

4 July The bodies of Moshen Al-Seikhan and Nasser ibn Rashid Al-Rashid are discovered. One had had his leg crudely amputated. Both seem to have been wounded in fights with the security services and died later.

13 July Khaled al-Harbi, who is listed on the government's most-wanted list, surrenders in Iran, is flown to Saudi Arabia.

14 July Ibrahim al-Harb surrenders himself in Syria.

20 July Shootout in Riyadh. Eisa ibn Saad Al-Awshan (number 13 on the list of the 26 most-wanted militants) is killed. Saleh al-Oufi , the head of Al-Qaeda in the kingdom escapes from the raid on the compound where he had been living with his extended family.

23 July Amnesty offer expires. Six wanted people had turned themselves in.

4 August Tony , an Irish expatriate, is shot and killed at his desk in Riyadh.

5 August Faris Ahmed Jamaan al-Showeel al-Zahrani (#11 on the government's list of most-wanted) is captured in Abha without a fight.

30 August An unnamed government employee is shot at while leaving a bank in Jidda. No injuries.

11 September Two small bombs go off in Jidda near the Saudi British and Saudi American Banks. Nobody is injured.

15 September Edward Smith, a British expatriate working for Marconi, is shot dead at a supermarket in Riyadh. No arrests are made.

26 September Laurent Barbot, a French employee of a defense electronics firm, is shot dead in his car in Jidda. Five Chadians confessed to the crime in June 2005.

4 November Unnamed 'deviant' is arrested in a shoot-out at an Internet café in Buraidah, Qasim region. Two policemen are injured.

9 November Shootout in Jidda. On Al-Amal Al-Saleh Street, police capture four unnamed militants and seize eight AKs and hundreds of locally-made bombs. No deaths are reported.

10 November Government announces the interception of 44,000 rounds of ammunition being smuggled in from Yemen. One Saudi waiting for the shipment is arrested.

13 November Five unnamed militants arrested in Riyadh and Zulfi. A number of machine guns and other weapons are captured. Nobody is hurt in the gunfight.

17 November A police officer (Private Fahd Al-Olayan) is killed and eight are injured in a shootout in Unayzah, Qassim. Five persons of interest are detained. Computers, pipe bombs and SR38,000 are seized.

6 December Five employees are killed (a Yemeni, a Sudanese, a Filipino, a Pakistani and a Sri Lankan) as five militants invade the Consulate in Jidda. No citizens are killed.

16 December A call for kingdom-wide anti-government demonstrations by a London-based group fails.

29 December Two suicide car bombs explode in Riyadh. One outside the Interior Ministry Complex, the other near the Special Emergency Force training center. A passerby is killed and some

people are wounded. In a resulting gun battle, seven suspected militants are killed. Two (Sultan Al-Otabi and Faisal Al-Dakheel) were on the Kingdom's list of 26 Most Wanted.

2005

13 March Saudi security forces in Jidda conduct an early-morning raid that kills one (Saed al-Youbi) labeled as a terrorist. One civilian was also killed; five policemen were wounded. Three other suspects were arrested. One was thought to be Ibrahim al-Youbi.

3 April through 5 April Saudi security forces launch the major Ar Rass raids against a three-house compound, 320 kilometers south of the capital. Fifteen terrorists, including Saleh Al-Aufi, reportedly the Al-Qaeda leader for Saudi Arabia were killed along with Talib Saud Al-Talib, also on the list of the 26 most-wanted persons. The gunfight lasted for most of two days and included the e of rocket-propelled grenades, machine guns and other heavy weapons. Students at a nearby girl's school were in danger from the fire and were evacuated by police who broke down the rear wall to their building.[9]

7 April using information from the previous raid, security services killed Abdul Rahman Al-Yaziji, number four on the most-wanted list in a firefight in the Southern Industrial District of Riyadh. The newspapers report that only three men on the list of the 26 most-wanted are still at liberty. They are Saleh Al-Aufi, Talib Al-Talib and Abdullah al-Rashoud.

22 April A group of four insurgents dressed as women attempt to bluff their way past a security checkpoint near the holy city of Makkah. Women are forbidden to drive in Saudi Arabia. The police gave chase as the group fled in their car. They were surrounded in a hilly area near Umm Al-Joud southeast of the city. Two militants and two security officers were killed in the resulting shootout, an unknown number were wounded. The battle took place as

the Western Region of Saudi Arabia was conducting its first-ever elections for local government councils.

9 May Abdul Aziz ibn Rasheed Al-Inazi is arrested after a shoot-out in Riyadh. His is described in the press as a leader of the Religious Committee of the insurgency.

18 May The United States Embassy issues a message that revokes the travel advisory for Saudi Arabia that had been in effect for a year.

16 June Security services announce the arrest in Riyadh of five Chadians who were described as 'members of a deviant group.' The detainees, whose names were not given confessed to the murder of Laurent Barbot in September 2004 as well as a number of armed robberies.

19 June Lt Colonel Mubarak Al-Sawat, a senior police commander in Makkah, was killed outside his home as he got in his car on his way to work. Newspapers report the killing may have been a botched kidnapping attempt.

21 June The killers of Lt Colonel Mubarak Al-Sawat are killed by security forces after a long fire-fight on the Old Makkah Road in the Holy City. Mansour Al-Thubaity and Kamal Foudah, both Saudi nationals, were fired on while fleeing police in a car, took another car and finally were killed while hiding in a building in a residential area. Three policemen were injured, one of them seriously.

24 June An internet site linked to Al-Qaeda in Iraq reports that Abdullah al-Rashoud, one of the few persons on the list of 26 Saudis most wanted has been killed by a bomb. If true, this would leave only two persons (Saleh Al-Aufi, the alleged leader of Al-Qaeda in Saudi Arabia, and Taleb Al-Taleb) on that list unaccounted for.

29 June The security services issues two new lists of wanted persons.

List A includes 15 names of persons suspected of terrorist affiliations and who are thought to be in the Kingdom. List B is of 21 names of persons suspected of terrorist affiliation, who are thought to be outside the Kingdom.

List A

(1) Younus Mohamed Al-Hiyari, 36, Moroccan. Killed 3 July 2005.(2) Fahd Farraj Al-Juwair, 35, Saudi.(3) Zaid Saad Al-Samary, 31, Saudi.(4) Abdul Rahman Saleh Al-Miteb, 26, Saudi. (See entry for 28 December 2005)(5) Saleh Mansour Al-Harbi, 22, Saudi.(6) Sultan Saleh Al-Hasry, 26, Saudi.(7) Mohamed Abdul Rahman Al-Suwailemi, 23, Saudi.(8) Mohamed Saleh Al-Ghaith, 23, Saudi.(9) Abdullah Abdul Aziz Al-Tuwaijeri, 21, Saudi.(10) Mohamed Saeed Al-Amry, 25, Saudi. Captured 25 July 2005(11) Ibrahim Abdullah Al-Motair, 21, Saudi.(12) Walid Mutlaq Al-Radadi, 21, Saudi.(13) Naif Farhan Al-Shammary, 24, Saudi.(14) Majed Hamid Al-Hasry, 29, Saudi.(15) Abdullah Muhaya Al-Shammary, 24, Saudi

List B

(1) Noor Mohamed Mosa, 21, Chadian.(2) Manour Mohamed Yosef, 24, Chadian.(3) Othman Mohamed Kourani, 23, Chadian.(4) Mohsen Ayed Al-Fadhli, 25, Kuwaiti.(5) Abdullah Walad Mohamed Sayyed, 37, Mauritanian.(6) Zaid Hassan Humaid, 34, Yemeni. (7) Fahd Saleh Al-Mahyani, 24, Saudi.(8) Adnan Abdullah Al-Sharief, 28, Saudi.(9) Marzouq Faisal Al-Otaibi, 32, Saudi.(10) Adel Abdullateef Al-Sanie, 27, Saudi.(11) Mohamed Abdul Rahman Al-Dhait, 21, Saudi.(12) Sultan Sunaitan Al-Dhait, 24, Saudi.(13) Saleh Saeed Al-Ghamdi, 40, Saudi.(14) Faiz Ibrahim Ayub, 30, Saudi. (See entry for 1 July 2005)(15) Khaled Mohamed Al-Harbi, 29, Saudi.(16) Mohamed Othman Al-Zahrani, 44, Saudi.(17) Abdullah Mohamed Al-Rumayan, 27, Saudi.(18) Mohamed Saleh Al-Rashoudi, 24, Saudi.(19) Saad Mohamed Al-Shahry, 31, Saudi.(20) Ali Matir Al-Osaimy, 23, Saudi.(21) Faris Abdullah Al-Dhahiry, 22, Saudi. (See entry for 1 July 2005)

1 July Newspapers report that Faiz Ibrahim Ayub (name 14 on list B) turned himself to a Saudi embassy, perhaps in Beirut. The government denies this.

The family of Faris Abdullah Al-Dhahiry (Name 22 on list B) claim he had been killed in Iraq in November 2004.

3 July Youn Mohamed Al-Hiyari (The first name on List A) is killed in a shoot-out with police in eastern Riyadh. Six police officers were injured in the clash which included the e of homemade bombs by the militants. Three men were arrested, but their names were not immediately released.

19 July Saudi Security forces capture a weapons cache in Al-Kharj south of Riyadh. The store included 1,900 kg of fertilizer, 125 kg of ammonium nitrate, aluminum powder, potassium nitrate and other chemicals ed by suspected Al-Qaeda militants to make bombs.

20 July The Embassy warns citizens in Saudi Arabia to lower their profile and be on alert due to intelligence indicating preparations were being made for a terrorist attack.

25 July Mohamed Saeed Al-Amry (number ten on List A) is captured in Madinah along with two unnamed others. He was carrying an explosive device when he was captured.

The Embassy restricts the travel of military personnel in the Kingdom to home and office only in light of intelligence indicating planning for a militant strike.

8 August United States, United Kingdom, Australian and New Zealand embassies and consulates close for two days in response to intelligence. Reuters reports the British government believe a militant attack to be in the final stages of preparation. Saudi security forces increase activity across the kingdom with additional

checkpoints presence. Military facilities increase security also. No militant activity or arrests are reported in the press.

18 August Saudi Security Forces conducted six raids around the kingdom killing four and capturing an unknown number of fighters. During one of these actions, Saleh al-Oufi is reportedly killed in Madinah. He was the fourth name on the original list of 26 most-wanted persons and has been described as the Al-Qaeda chief in the kingdom. He had narrowly escaped capture last year. His death leaves on one person on that list unaccounted for.

Newspapers also reported that Farraj Al-Juwait was killed by police near exit five on the Ring Road in Riyadh. Reports mistakenly indicate that this name was on one of the recent lists of most-wanted militants.

3 December Seventeen unnamed "terror suspects" are arrested in a series of raids in Riyadh, Al-Kharj and Majmaa. The security services also claimed to have captured an undisclosed amount of explosives and weaponry.

28 December In separate incidents, Saudi security forces killed two wanted militants in Qassim. Abdul Rahman Saleh Al-Miteb, (#4 on List A) was killed in Um Khashba after a routine traffic stop led to his killing two highway patrolmen. This set off a running gunfight that killed three more police officers. He was killed by gunfire, his body was holding an automatic weapon and a hand grenade.

Abdul Rahman Al-Suwailemi died in custody from his wounds after being captured elsewhere in the region. He was described as a computer expert who managed insurgent websites.

2006

24 February Saudi security forces have thwarted an attempted suicide attack at an oil processing facility in eastern Saudi Arabia,

Saudi security sources told CNN. Two pick-up trucks carrying two would-be bombers tried to enter the side gate to the Abqaiq plant in the Eastern Province, the largest oil processing facilities in the world (more than 60% of Saudi production), but the attackers detonated their explosives after security guards fired on them, according to statements from Saudi's interior and oil ministries. According to Saudi sources, the plant was not damaged and only minor damage to one small (1.5 inch) pipeline was caused by splinters, along with serious injuries among security guards and minor injuries among a few Aramco plant workers.

The dead suspects were later named as Muhammed Al-Gaith and Abdullah Al-Tuwaijri. Two members of the security forces were also killed in the fight.

27 February In a series of predawn raids sparked by the attack on Abqaiq, Saudi security forces killed five unnamed militants (in Al-Yarmouk) and captured another (in Al-Rawabi). In addition, three people were killed by the police at a vehicle checkpoint. Initial reports indicate that the checkpoint incident was a mistake, as those killed were Filipino guest workers.

26 October Security services announce the arrest of 44 Saudi nationals in Riyadh, Al-Qassim and Hail.

2 December Security services announce the arrest of 136 Al-Qaeda suspects, including 115 Saudi nationals. Calling the arrests "preemptive," they claim that at least one cell of militants were on the verge of making a suicide attack in the Kingdom.

2007

26 February Three French nationals, including a teenager, murdered during a desert trip near the ancient city Madain Saleh. [4]

2008

2009

In August, an attempt was made on the life of Saudi Prince and counterintelligence chief Mohammed bin Nayef by Al-Qaeda operative Abdullah Hasan Tali al-Asiri, who died after detonating an underwear bomb.

2012

On 26 August 2012, a spokesman for the Interior Ministry announced the arrest of 2 Saudis and 6 Yemenis in Riyadh and Jidda who had been preparing explosives for attacks within the kingdom. One member of the cell had had fingers amputated from injuries stained by working on explosives. Materials for making bombs were found in a Riyadh mosque.

COMPREHENSIVE LIST OF
TERRORIST ACTS IN SAUDI ARABIA

1995

November 13, 1995 The Office of the Program Manager, Saudi Arabian National Guard Modernization Program was attacked by a car bomb in a parking lot in Riyadh. Six killed, including five Americans, and 60 injured. The "Tigers of the Gulf," "Islamist Movement for Change," and "Fighting Advocates of God" claimed responsibility. Saudi authorities arrested and executed the perpetrators.[1]

1996

June 25, 1996 A truck containing about 5000 pounds of explosives targeted against military Bachelor Officers Quarters (BOQ) in Khobar, resulting in 19 dead and about 500 wounded. I had often stayed at this BOQ as a professor for the University of Maryland, and I had just stayed there only a few weeks before the bombing. It was a complex of buildings originally built for Saudis who did not want to live there because the internal designs of the apartments were incompatible with Saudi living space. Security around the buildings was lax, and merchants and vendors selling every kind of merchandise and services had set up permanent shops and eateries or temporary stands, with little or no restrictions or permits required. After the explosion, there were mutual recriminations between the and Saudi Governments over which country was responsibility for the lax security. One American charge was that the Saudi Government refused its request to raise the height of a perimeter fence, but this was later refuted by an American officer who was assigned there at the time.[142] Subsequently the American soldier that sounded the alarm was a student in a seminar on International Terrorism that I was teaching at a military base in Germany. He recounted to the class how he hesitated at first to sound the alarm, because he feared having to face the wrath of the soldiers if it were a false alarm, and how he raced down to each floor and pounded on the door to alert the other soldiers to evacuate the building.[143]

2000

On November 17, in central Riyadh at the junction of Oruba/ Olaya road, a car bomb killed British national Rodway and injured his wife Jane. The bomb was placed underneath his vehicle and detonated as it approached a traffic signal.

---

142 For a short discsion of this dispute, see John S. Habib, *Saudi Arabia and the American National Interest*, 211.

143 A fourteen-chapter account of the Khobar Tower assault by Anthony Bruno is available on the internet at Al-KhobarBombing.mht, TruTv.

The following week, on November 22, in Riyadh close to the RSAF HQ, a car bomb detonated on a vehicle driven by British national Mark Payne. Although the driver and his three passengers were injured, all survived the attack.

Less than one month later, on December 15 in Al Khobar, a small IED in a juice carton left on the vehicle of British national David Brown exploded as he attempted to remove it. Brown survived but lost his sight and part of his right hand.

2001

On January 10, 2001: a small bomb exploded outside the Euromarche supermarket in Riyadh. There were no casualties.

A bomb placed in a waste bin outside the Jarir bookstore on Oleya Road in central Riyadh on March 15 injured British national Ron Jones, American Charles Bayer, and a Canadian national. Jones was taken from hospital and arrested by Saudi authorities. During detention, Jones was subjected to torture to extract a confession before being released without charge after 67 days.

On May 3, an American doctor Gary Hatch received injuries to his face and hands after opening a parcel bomb in his office in Al Khobar.

On the eve of the strike on Afghanistan on October 6, a pedestrian suicide bomber killed an American, Michael Gerard outside a shopping center in Al Khobar. One Briton and two Filipinos were injured in the attack.

UK CITIZEN INVOLVEMENT

Publicly, the Saudi authorities blamed the car bombing campaign on a small group of western expatriates, mainly British, whom they claimed were fighting a turf war over the illegal distribution of alcohol. All of those involved in the alcohol trade were arrested and detained. Despite the arrests, the attacks on western nationals continued.

Early in 2001, video taped confessions by William Sampson and Sandy Mitchell were aired on Saudi state TV channels. Apart from the confessions, which both men later retracted, there was no evidence to link any of the western detainees to the bombing campaign. Sampson and Mitchell were later sentenced to death but were eventually released (but not pardoned), along with several other British detainees in August 2003 in a prisoner-exchange deal brokered by the UK and United States for Saudi detainees from Guantanamo Bay. Both men maintain their innocence, citing torture was ed to extract confessions. Court action taken in the UK by the men since their release failed after the UK High Court supported Saudi Arabia's defense under the State Immunity Act of 1978.

In their interrogation of suspects and in charges brought against detainees, the Saudi Mabahith were wholly uninterested in alcohol trading and did not charge the men with alcohol offenses. Those charged with the murders were accused of carrying out the attacks on behalf of MI6, the British Secret Intelligence Service. Diplomats from the British Embassy in Riyadh were invested of any involvement. One of those investigated was Deputy Head of Mission in Riyadh, Simon McDonald, who was later appointed British Ambassador to Israel. Although British embassy officials in Riyadh were aware of the continuing abuse of detainees, they failed to secure the support of the Foreign and Commonwealth Office in London in pushing hard for their release.

2002

In May, a Sudanese national attempted to shoot down a fighter jet taking off from the Prince Sultan Air Base with an SA-7 missile. The attempt failed, and in June, the Saudis arrested several suspects.

A month later, on June 20 in the Riyadh suburb of Al Nakheel, a British national, Simon Veness, a 35 year-old bank employee, was killed after a bomb placed underneath his vehicle exploded a few seconds after he set off for work.

On June 29, a car bomb placed on the vehicle of an American couple in Riyadh was disarmed by Saudi authorities.

On September 29, a car bomb killed German national Max Graf in central Riyadh.

2003

On February 20, 2003: Robert Dent, an employee for BAE Systems was shot to death in his car while waiting at a traffic signal in the Granada district of Riyadh.

A Saudi was killed on March 18 in an explosion at a villa in the Al Jazira district of Riyadh, where police uncovered a cache of arms and explosives. It is believed that he was manufacturing a bomb at the time.

At a hoe in the same district of Riyadh on May 6, police were involved in a shoot-out with suspected militants. All nineteen suspects escaped, and police unearthed another large cache of arms and explosives.

The insurgency took a giant leap forward with the Riyadh Compound Bombings. On May 12, attackers drove three car bombs into residential compounds housing Westerners and others, killing 26 people. Nine bombers also died. The compound bombings led to a harsh crackdown against militants by the Saudi government who, until this point, had been in denial about the terrorist threat within the Kingdom. Police and National Guard troops were involved in hundreds of raids, seizing weapons and equipment ed by the militants. Throughout most of 2003, these helped in keeping the anti-foreigner attacks down.

On November 8, hours after the embassy issued a warning about attacks in Saudi Arabia, a truck bomb struck the al-Mohaya residential compound in Riyadh, killing 17 workers and injured more than 100. Most of the victims were Muslims, prompting outcry among Saudi citizens.

2004

After the Muhaya bombing, militants either halted or were prevented from committing their attacks. Security forces continued their raids and arrests. On April 21, a car bomb struck a building originally ed by the Saudi police, killing 5 and injuring 148. This marked the start of a new campaign by the militants.

On May 1, the 2004 Yanbu attack left six Westerners and a Saudi dead. The attackers were killed or captured.

On May 22, German chef Hermann Dengl was shot to death in Riyadh at an ATM machine by Panda exit 10.

On May 29, the militants staged one of their most complex attacks, known as the 29 May 2004, Al-Khobar massacres. Gunmen scaled a fence of the Oasis compound, which hoes the employees of foreign oil companies and took dozens hostage. They are said to have separated Christians and Muslims and shot the Christians. Of those killed, 19 were foreign civilians, the rest were Saudis. The gunmen escaped.

On June 6, gunmen shot and killed an Irish cameraman of the BBC, Simon Cumbers, and also wounded reporter Frank Gardner.

On June 8, American Robert Jacobs of Vinnell Corp. was shot in his Riyadh villa. Another American expatriate, Kenneth Scroggs, was shot to death by two gunmen outside his home in Riyadh on June 13, and an American working for Lockheed Martin, Paul Marshall Johnson, was kidnapped at a fake police checkpoint in Riyadh.

On June 18, Johnson was reported beheaded in a video released to the news media. On the same day, Saudi security forces killed Abdul Aziz al-Muqrin, at that time the country's most wanted man.

On August 3, Anthony Higgins, an Irish expatriate, was shot and killed at his desk at the Saudi-owned Rocky for Trade and Construction Company in the Al Rawda district of Riyadh. The attackers' e of silencers on the pistols led investigators to believe it was an act of premeditated murder and not simply an act terrorism aimed indiscriminately at the expatriate community. Tony, who had worked in the Kingdom for almost 25 years, had been an active member of Saudi Arabia's underground church, and although unconfirmed, most who knew him believe he was gunned down for his impassioned but indiscreet efforts to spread the Christian faith within Saudi Arabia.

On September 15, Edward Muirhead-Smith, a British man working for Marconi, was shot to death in his car outside a supermarket in Riyadh.

On September 26, Frenchman Laurent Barbot, an employee of a defense electronics firm, was shot to death in his car in Jidda.

On December 6, militants staged perhaps their most brazen attack, the storming of the American consulate in Jidda. They breached the compound's outer wall and began shooting, though they did not enter the consulate itself. A Yemeni, a Sudanese, a Filipino, a Pakistani, and a Sri Lankan—all employees of the consulate—were killed, and about ten others were wounded. All of the gunmen were killed.

On December 29, suicide car bombs exploded outside of the Saudi Interior Ministry and the Special Emergency Force training center, killing a passerby and wounding several others. Though damage to each building was incurred, the attacks did not result in large-scale casualties and was the last significant attack of the insurgency. Two suicide bombers were killed.

2005

Saudi security forces made a great deal of successes against insurgents. Many militants were captured and several killed, many by American forces in Iraq. One of these, Saleh al-Oufi, who was killed on August 18.

On December 28, Saudi security services killed Abdul Rahman Al-Suwailemi and Abdul Rahman ibn Salen Al-Miteb in separate incidents. In the morning, Al-Miteb was stopped by two policemen and opened fire, killing both. This set off a running firefight, during which three other policemen were killed. Automatic weapons, grenades, forged documents, and almost half a million riyals in cash were also seized.

Despite these successes, foreign governments still have travel warnings in effect for Saudi Arabia.

2006

While attacks by militants have decreased dramatically since late 2004, violent incidents still occasionally occur. On February 24, two explosive-laden cars tried to enter the Abqaiq oil plant, the largest such facility in the world and producer of 60% of Saudi Arabian oil. Both cars exploded when fired upon by guards, killing the two bombers and two guards. A successful attack could have seriously crippled oil production.

In June, six militants and a policeman were killed in a gun battle in Riyadh.

2007

On February 4, Saudi security forces arrested ten people suspected of fund-raising for suspicious groups that engage in terrorism. Interior Ministry spokesman Major-General Mansour Al-Turki said seven Saudi citizens and one foreign resident were arrested in Jidda while two Saudi citizens were arrested in Medinah. Al-Turki went on to say, "We know of the group's activity as a whole, but we also need to define the role of each of the arrested members." The Interior Ministry issued a statement saying, "Security forces, in the framework of their efforts to fight terrorism and its funding, have arrested a group of suspects believed to be responsible for collecting donations illegally and smuggling the money to suspicious groups that e it in deceiving the sons of this nation and dragging them to disturbed areas."[]

In March, lawyers for some of the accused defended their clients by stating they were simply peaceful reformists. A petition was delivered to King Abdullah, asking that he consider a constitutional monarchy and was signed by 100 prominent business leaders and academics.

On February 26, suspected militants attacked a group of nine French citizens who were returning from the historical site of Madain Saleh in the northwest of Saudi Arabia. The group, traveling in three vehicles, had been looking for remnants of the Kingdom of the Hejaz railway track and had apparently stopped for a rest approximately 90 km north of Madinah when three assailants traveling in a 4x4 vehicle stopped then singled out and shot all four males in the group. Two died at the scene, a third en route to hospital and the fourth, a sixteen-year-old boy, died the following day after undergoing surgery to remove a bullet from his lung. No group has claimed responsibility for the attack. On March 7, authorities announced the arrest of several suspects and stated that they were hunting two named individuals in connection with the attack.

On April 6, security forces were involved in a gun battle with militants at a property 20 km outside Medina. One of the militants, a Saudi national named as Waleed Ibn Mutlaq Al Radadi, was killed in the shoot-out. One police officer was also killed, and several were injured. Al Radadi had appeared on a list of 36 most-wanted terrorists in 2005. An Interior Ministry spokesman said that the shoot-out was linked to an investigation into the killings of the French expatriates in February.

On April 19, Saudi authorities announced the arrest of eight people who had allegedly aided and abetted in the killings of the French expatriates in February. They also stated that Al Radadi had been the mastermind behind the killings.

On April 27, the Saudi Interior Ministry announced the arrest of 172 terrorist suspects in a series of raids on seven cells in the Kingdom in an operation lasting several months. The largest of the cells numbered 61 members. Unprecedented amounts of explosives and weapons of various types where uncovered after being buried in the desert. Also recovered was over $5 million in cash. Some of the cells had trained as pilots and planned attacks on military and oil installations, as well as the assassinations of high-profile individuals. Most of the suspects were said to be Saudi nationals.

On November 28, security forces arrested 208 terrorist suspects across the country.

2008

On June 25, the Saudi Interior Ministry announced the arrest of 701 militants since the start of the year, however, 181 were later released because there was no proof linking them to the terror network.

TIMELINE OF AL-QAEDA RELATED TERRORIST ATTACKS[144]

1995

November 13: SANG HQ in Riyadh bombed. First of the new wave of terror attacks and the start of the wind down of the presence in KSA. 7 killed:1 military, 6 Civilians.

1996

June 25: Bomb kills 19 US soldiers, wounds nearly 400 people at military housing complex in Al Khobar.

144   Anthony H..Cordesman and Nawaf Ubaid, *Al-Qaeda in Saudi Arabia*, rev. ed., Asymmetric Threats and Islamist Extremists, 6–8, Working draft, revised January 26,2005, Center for Strategic and International Studies, Washington, D.C.

2003

May 12: Suicide bombers attack housing compounds for foreign workers in Riyadh. Thirty-five are killed, including nine bombers, and 200 wounded. Al Hamra, Vinnell and Jedewahl compounds.

June 14: Raid in Mecca kills five Islamic militants and two security agents.

July 28: Raid on farm in Al Qassim kills 6 militants and two police.

September 23: Raid in Jizan kills Al-Qaeda operative wanted by the FBI.

November 3: Clash with terrorists in Mecca kills two and finds large weapons cache.

November 8: Suicide bombers blow up Riyadh compound housing foreigners and Saudis, killing at least 18. Old B1 Boeing compound, now called Muhaya compound.

2004

January 28: Gun battle in Riyadh kills 1 Al-Qaeda and 5 police.

April 21: Suicide bomber kills 5, including 2 senior police officers in attack on government building in Riyadh. The al Haramain Brigades claim responsibility.

May 1: Gunmen kill five Westerners in attack on oil office in Yanbu; four attackers and one policeman die. Some 50 people are injured.

May 20: Police battle militants near Burada, killing 4.

May 22: Terrorists kill German expatriate Herman Dengel, head chef of Saudi Catering Company on a Riyadh street.

May 29–30: Militants attack oil Company and housing compounds in Khobar.

Seven Saudi policemen and 22 civilians are killed. 50 hostages are taken.

June 6: Simon Cumbers, an Irish cameraman working for the BBC, is shot dead in Riyadh.

June 8: Gunmen kill American Robert Jacob of Vinnell Corp. in Riyadh.

June 12: American Kenneth Scroggs is shot dead in Riyadh. Al-Qaeda claims responsibility.

June 18: Kidnappers behead Lockheed Martin employee Paul M. Johnson Jr. in Riyadh.

August 3: An Irish civil engineer, Tony , is shot dead in Riyadh.

August 30: Gunmen fire on Consulate vehicle in Jidda.

September 15: Edward Muirhead-Smith, a British engineer, is killed in Riyadh in an attack claimed by Al-Qaeda.

September 26: Frenchman Laurent Barbot is shot dead in Jidda.

October 18: Top-ranking militant Abdel Majed al Manaya is among 3 terrorists killed in Riyadh.

November 4: Saudi Security forces arrest seven people, including a wanted terrorist suspect. The seven were apprehended during a raid on a cyber café in Buraida. Two security personnel were wounded in a shootout preceding the arrest.

November 6: Twenty-six Saudi religious scholars sign and release an open letter calling on Iraqis to fight Americans and considering it jihad. Two days later, the Saudi Ambassador to the United States, Prince Bandar, released an official statement making it clear that the letter from these scholars represented neither the Government of Saudi Arabia nor the senior religious scholars of the country.

November 9: In a predawn raid, Security forces kill one wanted terrorists and capture three others after a shoot-out in Jidda. The daily *Al-Riyadh* quoted a witness as saying that Sultan Al-Otaibi, from Saudi Arabia's list of 26 most-wanted terrorists, was killed in the confrontation. A substantial arms cache was found in the hoe where the suspected terrorists were found. The cache include machine guns, hand grenades and various types of ammunition. According to local press reports, the four-member group planned to attack a Jidda compound coinciding with firework celebrations during Eid Al-Fitr. Additionally, Security forces arrest three suspects north of Riyadh on the highway to Qassim.

: The Interior Ministry announces that King Fahd ordered the release of those militants who surrendered to security authorities as a result of the June amnesty offer.

November 12: Saudi security forces arrested five suspected terrorists in two operations in Riyadh and Zulfi. Three of the suspects were detained in Riyadh and two in Zulfi. Weapons and ammunition were reportedly seized in these operations. The next day, an Interior Ministry spokesman stated that these individuals were not directly involved in violence but were suspected of supporting extremist thought.

November 13: The Embassy releases Warden Message to remind of security concerns surrounding the death of Palestinian Authority Chairman Yasser Arafat. (Author note: American Embassies world-wide has a network of wardens usually composed of responsible American citizens, Each warden is assigned the responsibility of maintaining contact with a specific section of the American expatriate community. The Embassy communicates to these warden special messages, usually, but not always related to security development in the host country or elsewhere in the world that could impact the local American community.)

November 17: A security officer is killed and eight officers wounded during a raid on a terrorist hideout in Qassim. Five suspects were arrested. Two of the suspects were wanted by authorities and linked to Al-Qaeda. One reportedly belonged to the list of the 26 most wanted. He was not identified by name.

November 27: Saudi security forces in Jidda kill a terrorist suspect later identified as Essam Siddiq Mubaraki. This man was linked to plotters of the al Mujaya housing compound attack last November in Riyadh. One additional suspect was arrested in conjunction with the killing of Mabaraki. Additionally, police found a cache of arms in Mabaraki's car.

December 2: Saudi Security forces announce arrest of four suspected terrorists in various parts of the country. Two suspects were arrested in Artawiya. The two others were captured in vicinity of Hafr Al Baten and Buraidah.

December 6: Militants storm the consulate in Jidda, killing five employees and three gunmen.

December 29: Ministry of Interior and special forces recruitment office bombed, a Bystander killed. Seven suspected Al-Qaeda shot dead later in the evening.

INDEX

Selected Bibliography

Interviews

Al-Ansari, Abdullah F. Dr. Riyadh, Saudi Arabia, Ministry of Interior, in May 2009 and April 2010.

Al-Hadlaq, Abd Al-Rahman. Riyadh, Saudi Arabia, Center for Terrorism Activity. May 2009.

Documents

Council of Senior Ulema'. Fatwa on terror–financing.

Resolution 239 dated 27 Rabi al-Thani 1431 H (April 12, 2010].

Balfour Memorandum respecting Syria, Palestine, and Mesopotamia, 11 August 11, 1919. Woodward and Rohan Butler, Documents on British Foreign Policy, 1919-1939, London.

Note by Captain Garland of the Arab Bureau, June 11, 1919. Public Record Office, MSS, Foreign Office, vol. No. 4146. Document document No. E 91521.

Saudi Arabian Ministry of Interior. "Some Efforts and Procedures Undertaken by the Kingdom of Saudi Arabia in Combating Terrorism." Undated report.

Saudi Arabian Ministry of Interior. Annotated Official Lists of Terrorists 2011-2012.

Saudi Arabian Ministry of Interior. Official Annotated List of Saudi Terrorists May 2002.

Saudi Ministry of Interior. Official Annotated List of Saudi Terrorists, January 10, 2011.

Declaration of Independence

Wikipedia, July 26. 2013. "The Sykes-Picot Agreement May 16, 1916".

Unpublished Papers

Al-Mutlaq, Dr. Abdullah. "Terrorists Are neither Heroes nor Martyrs But Criminals and Deserve the Hirabah Punishment." Lecture, King Faisal Hall for Conferences, 29 January 29, 2002, Riyadh, Saudi Arabia.

Al-Ansary, Abdullah F, Dr. "Law and Practice of the Kingdom of Saudi Arabia Concerning the Detention and Rehabilitation of Individuals in Terrorism Cases." Presented to the 12th Twelfth United Nations Congress on Crime Prevention and Criminal Justice, Salvador, Brazil, April 12–19, 2010.

Al-Ansary, Abdullah F.Dr. and Al-Zahrani, Omar S. "Combating Money Laundering and & Terrorism Financing : The Law and Practice of the Kingdom of Saudi Arabia." Presented to the 12th Twelfth United Nations Congress on Crime Prevention and Criminal Justice. Salvador, Brazil, April 12–19, 2010.

Habib, John S. Unpublished Op-Ed. "New York and Washington: September 11." New York International Herald Tribune Time, September 21, 2001.

Wikipedia July 26, 2013. The Hussein-MacMahon Correspondence. July 14, 1915–January 30. 1916.

Wikipedia, July 26. 2013. The Sykes-Picot Agreement May 16, 1916.

Books

Al-Bishr, Mohammed, Editor. *Saudi Arabia and Terror: Cross-Cultural Views.* Ghainaa Publications. First Edition. Riyadh, Saudi Arabia, 1426H/2005.

Al-Hageel, Suleiman, and Abdul Rahman. *Human Rights in Islam and Refutation of the Misconceived Allegations Associated with These Rights.* 2nd edition, 1420H-1959G. No publisher given.

Al-Qabesi, Mohyiddin, ed. *The Holy Quran & The Sword, Selected Addresses, Speeches, Memoranda and Interviews by HM the Late King Abdul Aziz Al-Saud Founder of the Kingdom of Saudi Arabia.* Modified Fourth Edition , Saudi Desert House. 1419H-1

Al-Rihani, Ameen. *Ibn Saoud of Arabia: His People and Land.* Caravan Books, Delmar. New York, 1983

Ayoob, Mohamed. *The Many Faces of Political Islam: Religion and Politics in the Muslim World.* University of Michigan Press, August 07, 2007.

Eddy, William A. *FDR Meets Ibn Saud.* America-Mideast Educational & Training Services, Inc., 1954.

Gold, Dore. *Hatred's Kingdom: How Saudi Arabia Supports the New Global Terrorism.* Regnery Publishing, February, 2003.

Habib, John S. *Saudi Arabia and the American National Interest.* Universal Press, Florida, 2003.

Habib, John S. *Ibn Sa'ud's Warriors of Islam: The Ikhwan of Najd and Their Role in the Creation of the Sa'udi Kingdom, 1910-1930.* Leiden, E. J. Brill, 1978

Ingrams, Doreen. *Palestine Papers: Seeds of Conflict 1917-1922.* John Murray Publishers, Ltd. June, 1972.

Kramer, Gudrin. *The Jews in Modern Egypt, 1914-1952.* I.B. Tauris, 1989.

Kasis, Hannah. *A New Concordance of the Qur'an.* University of California Press, 1983.

Murawiec, Laurent. *Princes of Darkness: The Saudi Assault on the West.* Rowman & Littlefield Publishers.1st Edition edition (September 7, 2005

Smith, Charles. *Palestine and the Arab-Israeli Problem.* Bedford.St. Martin's Press. 7th edition 2009.

Smith, Henry Preserved. *The Bible and Islam.* Charles Scribner's Sons, New York 1897.

Stoddard, Lothrop. *The New World of Islam*. Charles Scribner's Sons, New York, 1922.

Articles

Alexis de Tocqueville. "Travail sur Algerie." Vol. 1. La Pléiade rd. Paris: Gallimard. 1841.

Ansary, Abdullah F. "Combating Extremism: A Brief Overview of Saudi Arabia's Approach." Middle East Policy, vol. XV15, no. 2 (Summer 2008).

"AQAP Deputy Emir Said al-Shihri Alive." The Long War Journal, February 17, 2011.

Al-Arabiya News. "Twenty-Five Saudi Gitmo Prisoners Return to Militancy." http://world-countries.net/archives/45839. July 19, 2010. Accessed July 26, 2013.

Beam, Christopher. "Jihadis Anonymous: What happens in Terrorist rehab?" Slate, Jan. 23, 2009

Boucek, Christopher. "Jailing Jihadis: Saudi Arabia's Special Terrorist Prisons." Terrorism Monitor, Vol. 6, No. 2, Jan. 24, 2009.

Boucek, Christopher. "Counter-Terrorism from Within: Assessing Saudi Arabia's Relgious and Disengagement Programme." RI, December 19, 2008.

Cordesman, A. and Obaid, Nawaf. "Al-Qaeda in Saudi Arabia: Asymmetric Threats and Extremists."(Washington, DC: Center for Strategic and International Studies), January 26, 2005.

Durham, Nancy. "Where Saudis will send their most dangerous." December 18, 2007. CBC News-Analysis and Viewpoint.

Greenfield, Daniel. "A Special Relationship-Jews, America, and Israel." Doc's Talk (blogspot). July 13, 2010.

Goodenough Patrick. "Almost Ten years after 9/11, UN Still Grappling To Define Terrorism." CNS New.com. Thursday, April 21, 2011.

Habib, John S. "Wahhabi Origins of the Saudi State" in *Religion and Politics in Saudi Arabi*a. Ed. Ayoob, Muhammad and Kosebalaban, Hasan. Lynne Rienner, Boulder Edition, Boulder, Colorado, 2009.

Johnson, Charles. "Saudi Grand Mufti OKs Cyber Terrorism."11/28/03. Little Green Footballs.com.

Kampfner, John. "NS Interview - Jack Straw." November 2002.

Levitt, Matthew and Jacobson, Michael. "The Campaign to Squeeze Terrorists Financing." Journal of International Affairs, Columbia University, Vol. 62, no 1, Fall/Winter. 2008.

McEvers, Kelly. "A Test For Saudi Arabia's Terrorist-Rehab Program." NPR, February 15, 2010

McEvers, Kelley. "Changing the Ways Saudis Learn: Angry Teachers and Empty Libraries." Slate, September 9, 2009.

Miles, Donna. "Petraeus praises Saudi Fatwa Condemning Terror Financing." Washington, D.C. May 22, 2010. American Forces Press Service, United States Central Command.

Marisa Porges and Jessica Stern. "Getting Deradicalization Right." Foreign Affairs, May/June 2010.

Roggio, Bill. January 10, 2011, "Saudi Arabia's 47 most-wanted terrorists linked to al Qaeda." The Long War Journal from a list published at The Saudi Gazette.

Roggio, Bill, "AQAP Deputy Emir Said al-Shihri Alive." The Long War Journal, February 17, 2011, February 16, 2011

Shea, Nina "New Hope for Reform in Saudi Arabia." National Review, On Line, February 16, 2009.

Stern, Jessica. "Mind Over Martyr: How to Deradicalize Islamist Extremists." Foreign Affairs, January/February 2010.

Saudi Information Agency "Exclusive: Saudi Grand Mufti Ok's Cyber Terrorism." December 2, 2009.

Tristram, Pierre. "The 1979 Seizure of the Grand Mosque in Mecca: "The Attack and the Siege that Inspired Osama bin Laden." http://middleeast.about.com/od/terrorism/a/meo81120b.

Viorst, Milton. "The Kissinger Covenant and Other Reasons Israel is in Trouble." Washington Monthly, June 1, 1987.

Websites

http://awlaki.sethhettena.com. "The Anwar Aulaqi Timeline."

http://www.saudiembassy.net/files/PDF/Reports/Saudi—chronology-08.pdf.

http://www.bullfax.com -sell-fighter-jets to Saudis.

http: Wikipedia Naif bin Abdul-Aziz Al Saud, last accessed July 26, 2013.

http://Wikipedia.mobi. Ahmed bin Abdul Aziz Al Saud. Last accessed July 26, 2013.

http://www.cbc.ca/news/reportsfromabroad/durham/20071218.html.

http://www.saudiembassy.net/announcement/announcement 05071001.aspx

Made in the USA
Las Vegas, NV
19 December 2020